THE NEW BLUE MUSIC

THE NEW BLUE MUSIC

Changes in Rhythm & Blues, 1950–1999

RICHARD J. RIPANI

University Press of Mississippi / Jackson

www.upress.state.ms.us

The University Press of Mississippi is a member of the
Association of American University Presses.

Copyright © 2006 by University Press of Mississippi
All rights reserved
Manufactured in the United States of America

First edition 2006

∞

Library of Congress Cataloging-in-Publication Data

Ripani, Richard J.
  The new blue music : changes in rhythm & blues, 1950–1999 / Richard J. Ripani.— 1st ed.
    p. cm.
  Includes bibliographical references (p.), discography (p.), and index.
  ISBN 1-57806-861-4 (cloth : alk. paper) — ISBN 1-57806-862-2 (pbk. : alk. paper)
1. Rhythm and blues music—History and criticism. 2. Soul music—History and criticism.
3. Funk (Music)—History and criticism. 4. Rap (Music)—History and criticism. I. Title.
  ML3521.R58 2006
  781.643—dc22   2006002022

British Library Cataloging-in-Publication Data available

To the memory of my father,

whose love of American music was greater than

that of anyone I have ever met

CONTENTS

LIST OF EXAMPLES

LIST OF FIGURES

LIST OF TABLES

ACKNOWLEDGMENTS

This work would not have been possible without the support and assistance of a number of individuals: family, friends, colleagues, and mentors. It is my great fortune to have grown up in a family that cherishes music. My mother and father both strongly encouraged me to pursue music, first on drums, during which time they suffered countless hours of my pounding along with the music of the Miracles, the Temptations, Sam & Dave, and James Brown, among others. Later they were forced to bear my relentless trombone practice. I'm sure that my taking up piano in college was a relief for the entire family, although I never heard any words to that effect. I attribute any success I have had as a performer, and later as a researcher in American music, to the loving support of my mother and father, Millie and Joe Ripani, my three sisters, Mary Jo, Carolyn, and Barbara, and my stepfather, Bob Stephens.

This book began as a doctoral dissertation while I was a student at the University of Memphis. Dr. David Evans, editor, mentor, and friend, offered welcome guidance and encouragement as the research for this book was evolving. His considerable effort and time spent through the entire process, especially as chair of my doctoral committee, is deeply appreciated, and this work is far better due to his valuable suggestions and editorial comments along the way. The other members of my committee were also generous with their time, and each helped with the creation of this work in a significant way: Dr. Jack Cooper, Dr. Kenneth Kreitner, Mr. Jim Richens, and Dr. Richard Van Eck. Thanks also go to Dr. Gerhard Kubik, whose reading of my manuscript—and subsequent advice—helped greatly to increase my understanding of harmony and cycle in African music. Three days of discussions with Dr. Kubik also served to clarify in my mind his writings on the retention and reinterpretation of African musical elements in the United States.

My years as a performer in blues, jazz, rock 'n' roll, country, and rhythm & blues have resulted in a number of long-term musical friendships. Many

musicians have played an important role in the development of my understanding of American musical styles, perhaps more than they realize. The
following individuals are due gratitude not only for helping to further my
musical education, but also because of their moral support during my
research and writing of this book: Steve "Bubba" Anderson, Cole Burgess, Joe
Getsi, Lee Greenwood, Martin Kickliter, Ronnie McDowell, Gary McKinney,
Ronnie Milsap, Richard Lane, Greg Martin, Doug Phelps, Alan Stoker, and
Alan Suska. Thanks also go to James Brown, the "Godfather of Soul," for
graciously allowing me to interview him for this book. His insights into soul,
funk, and the rhythm of "the one" are, of course, invaluable.

I am grateful to the former president of Cumberland University,
Dr. Charlene Kozy, at whose prodding I continued graduate work and ultimately became a professor at that school. I would also like to express my
appreciation for the research assistance and expert advice offered me by
Bruce Nemerov at the Center for Popular Music at Middle Tennessee State
University and Dawn Oberg at the Country Music Hall of Fame and Museum
in Nashville, Tennessee.

Lastly, and most importantly, this work would never have come to frui-
tion without the unfailing support of my wife, Susan. She has endured countless hours of my ramblings about various topics in American music and has
been a constant source of strength throughout the process of writing this
book.

THE NEW BLUE MUSIC

CHAPTER ONE

THE NEW BLUE MUSIC AND RHYTHM & BLUES

In this work I suggest that a new musical system, the *new blue music*, became the dominant force in the creation of American music in the twentieth century. This organizational scheme is similar to many other more or less revolutionary changes of musical style throughout history in that it incorporates both traditional and newly created elements of musical form and substance. European musical innovations such as the *ars nova* of the early fourteenth century and the *stile moderno* of the early seventeenth were somewhat comparable departures from the musical status quo.[1]

I believe that future historians will mark the late nineteenth and early twentieth centuries as the beginning of a major directional change in American music. By that time, the cloth of the European "art" music tradition had begun to come unraveled.[2] The harmonic structure of the major-minor system, which had served European music well since the seventeenth century, was under constant attack, as composers such as Wagner, R. Strauss, Mahler, Stravinsky, Debussy, and Schoenberg explored various ways of creating new sound combinations. The rhythmic basis of this music was undergoing a similar transformation as composers experimented with the use of odd meters, mixed meters, and polyrhythms. Overall, the music began to take on a complexity and cultural distance that over time caused it to lose much of its universal appeal, and its audiences dwindled.

The new blue music had been a part of American culture since at least the mid-nineteenth century, where its origins can be found in African-American folk music. It was less complex than the art music being created at the time, and from those folk roots musicians drew elements to create the music of minstrelsy, spirituals, and, toward the end of the nineteenth century, ragtime. By the beginning of the twentieth century, it was poised to become *the* sound of American music, and its appeal grew throughout the twentieth century to a position of dominance. Historians might see the adoption of this musical system as the answer to the quest that Stravinsky, Debussy, and others had embarked upon to find new palettes of sound and rhythm.[3]

The new blue music is based on the use of various combinations of inherited elements, but the resulting blends are often wholly new and totally American. The theoretical foundation of this music is the *blues system*, a combination of factors of pitch, mode, rhythm, harmony, form, and other elements of style and content that are nearly universal in American popular music, including genres such as blues, jazz, country, rock 'n' roll, gospel, and rhythm & blues. Many of the characteristic musical traits of the blues system are markedly outside the sphere of European art music, and are derived to a large extent from specific African musical traditions. The concept of the blues system, including its identifying traits and theoretical underpinnings, is explored in detail in chapter 2 of this book.

Rhythm & blues is one of the descendents of a long-standing African-American musical tradition that includes spirituals, ragtime, blues, jazz, and gospel music. Each of these musical genres is a blend, more or less, of elements from both the African and European musical traditions. I envision rhythm & blues along a continuum with the African-American musical genres referred to above, and as the inheritor of many of their musical elements. The period of time from 1950 through 1999 witnessed a transformation in the melody, harmony, rhythm, and form of rhythm & blues. This book focuses on that change by examining the incidence of specific musical elements used in rhythm & blues and charting the degree of change that occurred in their use over time. These elements are components of the blues system, the overall musical scheme mentioned above. Also evident in rhythm & blues is the use of scales, harmony, formal elements, and stylistic features typical of European music. There is little doubt that rhythm & blues is neither strictly African nor European, but a blend of both musical traditions.

By investigating and analyzing the nature and function of musical elements in rhythm & blues, I seek to (1) display the blended nature of rhythm & blues and the musical spectrum that results from its incorporation of both African and European musical elements and aesthetics; (2) show how the use of specific musical elements in rhythm & blues changed over the course of the second half of the twentieth century, and thereby trace the development of recent musical styles and trends; (3) explain how rhythm & blues fits into the overall landscape of American music, specifically its relationship to blues, jazz, African-American religious music, country, and rock 'n' roll; and (4) describe the common musical elements used in rhythm & blues and related American musical genres—such as blues, jazz, gospel, country, and rock 'n' roll—and work toward defining a comprehensive musical system that includes these features.

WHAT IS RHYTHM & BLUES?

Since the phrase *rhythm & blues* (or *R&B*) is to be used many times in the upcoming pages, it seems sensible at this point to offer some sort of definition. A term like this can mean many things to many people, of course, and it is impossible to define any such label in a way that will satisfy all interested parties. However, I hope to establish at least a few points that most readers will find reasonable.

In 1923 the OKeh record company became the first to use the term "race records" specifically to identify its catalog of music created by and targeted to black Americans. Before long the term became standard in the record industry, and it remained so until after World War II.[4] By the late 1940s the word "race" began to have a negative connotation and was replaced with "rhythm & blues," a term first used by *Billboard* magazine in its June 25, 1949, issue when the company switched the name of the black record sales chart from "Best Selling Race Records" to "Best Selling Retail Rhythm & Blues Records."[5] However, according to Arnold Shaw, by the time the term rhythm & blues came into common usage it was "not a euphemism for something else . . . it was something else." He contends that rhythm & blues was, in contrast to country blues, "good-time dance music," "black ghetto music," and "group and joy music."[6]

Rhythm & blues is most clearly viewed as a broad range of popular music primarily created by and for black Americans. Like the even more general category of "popular music," rhythm & blues is a conglomerate of many different musical styles. Thus it is more a trade category than a genre. The earlier term "race" records was itself used to describe a collection of musical genres and other offerings such as blues, gospel, black vaudeville, recorded sermons, and some jazz that was marketed primarily to black Americans.[7]

Once one accepts the characterization of rhythm & blues as a trade category, it becomes easier to explain the periodic inclusion of songs that are decidedly not "good-time dance music," "black ghetto music," or "group and joy music" on the R&B charts. Two such releases, out of numerous possible examples, are David Seville's "Witch Doctor" (1958) and the Everly Brothers' "Cathy's Clown" (1960), both of which were recorded by white artists yet reached the number-one spot on *Billboard*'s rhythm & blues chart. The first of these songs is best characterized as a novelty song (this was Seville's precursor to the Chipmunks), the second a country vocal duet. According to *Billboard*, both of these singles sold in great numbers to African Americans and enjoyed significant airplay on black radio stations across the United States.[8]

But are songs such as "Cathy's Clown" and "Witch Doctor" truly "rhythm & blues" songs? If pressed for an answer to this question I suppose one would have to respond in the affirmative, if relying on the fact that these were hits in the black community, but in the negative if song style is considered. Perhaps one can simply say that songs such as those mentioned above are not part of the *core style* of rhythm & blues. Of course, asserting this point makes it necessary to describe exactly what the core style of rhythm & blues is. This cannot be done in a few words. In fact, much of the explanation lies in the research conducted for this book; an investigation into the changes in musical style, form, and content of rhythm & blues over the course of fifty years should help to identify the essential elements that make it distinct.

It *can* be said, however, that the core style of rhythm & blues inherits much of its identity from earlier African-American folk and popular music, such as work songs, string band and jug band music, fife and drum music, minstrelsy, black vaudeville, black religious music, blues, and boogie-woogie. Rhythm & blues style arose from, continued its development in, and still has its home in America's black community. It is more urban than rural, and cities such as Chicago, New York, Los Angeles, Memphis, New Orleans, Nashville, Houston, Oakland, Philadelphia, and Detroit were natural centers for rhythm & blues due to their large populations of African Americans. During the 1950s, rhythm & blues began to feature electric instruments, and this remains an important trait. As discussed later, much of the rhythm & blues music of the 1970s and later is highly dependent on the sounds of not only electric guitars and basses but also synthesizers.

One problem in defining rhythm & blues is that it overlaps a great deal with blues and jazz. On the other hand, it often has included songs from those two genres in its broad musical spectrum. Numerous examples exist of artists who have been successful in both rhythm & blues and jazz; Louis Jordan, Ray Charles, Grover Washington Jr., the Crusaders, and Herbie Hancock quickly come to mind. Some experts maintain that jazz incorporates more involved harmonic progressions and a higher level of improvisational complexity than does rhythm & blues. However, one could offer many examples—such as the music of Horace Silver and Miles Davis in the mid- to late 1950s, to name just two—that argue against these claims. The cut "Doodlin'" from the classic hard-bop album *Horace Silver and the Jazz Messengers* (1954) has an unadorned 12-bar blues progression as its harmonic underpinning, and much of the melodic material consists of blue notes. With the addition of a gospel music rhythmic feel, the overall effect is startlingly R&B-like. Miles Davis's "So What," from the album *Kind of Blue* (1959), is a composition made up of two modal scales that are built up from tonic notes one-half step apart. This, in effect, gives the piece two distinct tonal regions. While one would be hard-pressed to label this song rhythm & blues, the fact remains that it is a far cry from the complex harmonic compositions created by many jazz musicians. Later, especially in chapters 4 and 5, a similar technique is illustrated of using chords in a nonfunctional manner—in other words, each chord having its own pitch center and not necessarily relating to the others if viewed from a strict, European-harmony point of view—that became a hallmark of much R&B from the 1960s onward.

The black music charts of the 1940s reveal that songs by jazz and R&B artists were often listed together. It is not uncommon to find songs as diverse as Nat "King" Cole's "All for You," "Sentimental Lady" by Duke Ellington, and "See See Rider Blues" by Bea Booze reaching the number-one spot on the "Harlem Hit Parade" (the name of the singles sales chart at the time when these three records were released, 1943). The wide stylistic range represented by such songs is a feature that persisted in rhythm & blues throughout the time period 1950 through 1999, as we shall see.[9]

Rhythm & blues also overlaps to a great extent with the blues genre, so much so that the border between the two seems impossible to define exactly.

The *Billboard* charts referred to in this research include songs that became huge hits in the R&B market that many scholars would probably regard as straight-ahead blues. A good example is "I'm in the Mood," a 1951 release by John Lee Hooker that reached the number-one spot on the rhythm & blues charts. This song is arguably about as raw as blues gets. It features a declamatory vocal style, a very rough vocal delivery, no functional harmony in the European music sense, and seemingly few elements that would appeal to a mass market—yet, somehow it did. It is important to remember that since R&B is a broad category for black popular music in America, it naturally makes chart room for a big-selling blues hit like "I'm in the Mood" or, for that matter, any song that appeals to its audience at the time.

The wider popular music field has also had a strong influence on rhythm & blues. This can be witnessed in the number of R&B hits that came from Broadway or movie musicals (e.g., Roy Hamilton, "You'll Never Walk Alone," 1954, and Frankie Valli, "Grease," 1978); were covers of white popular songs (e.g., the Platters, "My Prayer," 1956, and Ike and Tina Turner, "Proud Mary," 1971); or were crossover hits performed by white popular artists (e.g., various releases by the Everly Brothers, 1957–1961, and Elvis Presley, 1956–1963).

Many songs that have appeared through the years on the R&B charts incorporate a European approach in their use of musical elements. Such songs often exhibit a reliance on equal-temperament diatonic scales, complex chord progressions with typical European dominant-to-tonic root movement, and performance practices that avoid pitch bends, slides, and blue notes. I would not presume to disqualify such songs from a hypothetical list of "authentic" rhythm & blues songs simply on the grounds that they incorporate elements of style, form, and content derived from Western art music. Indeed, the effort not only seems futile but also misses the point badly. In my view, every rhythm & blues song is a blend, more or less, of inherited African and European musical styles. It seems folly to try to determine which have a sufficient degree of a given musical characteristic to be considered "real."

Throughout the second half of the twentieth century rhythm & blues experienced periods of great acceptance by the American public at large. For example, during a period of time in the mid-1960s *Billboard* ceased publication of its rhythm & blues chart altogether, simply because it was apparently so similar to the general popular music chart ("Hot 100") as to be deemed unnecessary.[10] Rhythm & blues record labels such as Motown in Detroit, Stax in Memphis, King in Cincinnati, and Atlantic in New York produced a multitude of singles by black artists during the 1960s. These songs inundated the popular music charts with a new style that the youth of America apparently could not get enough of. The mass appeal of the music of African Americans increased so much over the time period studied that by the end of the century a large percentage of the top popular musical artists in America were black. By investigating rhythm & blues over the course of the second half of the twentieth century, I hope to shed some light on the development of this phenomenon, decade by decade.

THE TOP TWENTY-FIVE HITS OF EACH DECADE

I have selected for analysis the top twenty-five charted rhythm & blues records from each decade, 1950–1999, based on data compiled by Joel Whitburn from the *Billboard* magazine record charts.[11] The rationale for selecting these singles is that, being the biggest hits of each era, they were necessarily heard by the greatest number of listeners and likely had the most overall impact on the culture. These were the songs that often led the way to the development of new styles and served as creative starting points for up-and-coming artists.

The validity of the *Billboard* charts is something that should be discussed briefly at this point. I have used these charts for my research because I feel them to be the best way available to measure the pulse of the black record market during the 1950–1999 period. However, the methodology used by *Billboard* to compile their charts has changed many times over the years, and therefore inconsistencies inevitably occur. Beginning in the 1940s and throughout most of the 1950s, multiple R&B charts were maintained: (1) most-played on jukeboxes, (2) best-selling, and (3) most-played on radio. Beginning in 1958 the data were combined into one R&B chart. Since the sales and radio airplay data were collected by surveying sales outlets and radio stations selected by *Billboard*, the results do not always reflect the true success of a song. In fact, it is possible to argue that a given song does not deserve the high ranking it received because, for example, it was only a big radio hit in one region of the country, or because it sold in large numbers primarily in retail outlets many of whose customers were white. Other reasons a song's chart success might be skewed include the influence of payola and whether the record sold quickly in large numbers or more steadily over a longer period of time. I have accepted such inconsistencies as unavoidable, and proceeded with my research in the knowledge that the *Billboard* charts probably contain the best information available on the relative popularity of R&B songs, 1950–1999.[12]

On the other hand, it seems clear that mass popularity alone is not the only indicator of historical significance. Therefore, numerous musical examples taken from songs that have been deemed historically important and representative in their use of specific musical style traits are also examined in this study, regardless of whether or not they were chart-topping records. I have selected these songs primarily based on my personal experience as a performer in American music over a thirty-year time span, and my understanding of their importance in the overall development of popular musical styles and genres. Many of these song excerpts are from characteristic rhythm & blues songs, of course, but transcriptions from blues, jazz, gospel, country, rock 'n' roll, and other forms of American music that incorporate related musical elements are also presented. Since these songs are not included in the top twenty-five R&B songs of each decade, they are not counted in the statistical data this study offers. By presenting and analyzing these examples I hope to show a relationship between several genres of American music and thereby support my assertion of the existence of a larger continuum or "super-genre."

Specific details of the methodology used for record data collection are included in appendix A. However, a few words should be said about how this aspect of the research was conducted. In the song analyses I specifically examined the following musical features:

1. **Measures:** the total number of full and partial measures was tallied for each song studied. This number was calculated primarily to serve as a baseline for other measurements.
2. **Tempo:** approximate beginning and ending tempi were noted primarily to determine any change in tempo over the length of a given song, but also to ascertain whether tempo is correlated with other features of style, form, or content.
3. **Chord types:** the total number of different chord types—triads only—was counted in each song. The resulting numerical value is a measure of the amount of harmonic complexity found in each song.
4. **I, IV, V, "other," and "passing" chords:** the incidences of each of these chords were tallied as both a numerical value and as a percentage of the

total measures in each song. These data were collected for the purpose of showing historical change in the use of these chords in rhythm & blues.

5. *Blues form:* the incidences of the so-called "twelve-bar blues" form were counted in order to trace any change in its presence in rhythm & blues over the second half of the twentieth century.[13]

6. **Blues scale:** data were collected on pitches that are generally considered to be "blue notes," an integral part of rhythm & blues and many other American music genres and categories.

7. **Cyclic form:** this term is used to indicate a musical section that is characterized by the use of a repeating pattern, or "cycle," usually one to four measures in length. The cyclic form is often riff-based and sometimes features a solo performer with a group answer. The form includes a cessation of harmonic function or development and is thus outside the bounds of what has been generally accepted in European art music (although there has been some use of this feature in the minimalism movement in twentieth-century music). Investigating the increase or decrease in the presence of the cyclic form in rhythm & blues over the course of history was a key component of this study.[14]

8. **Triplet swing:** this element is sometimes associated with jazz, and can perhaps be most easily defined by saying that, in music with a triplet swing feel, each beat is theoretically (or actually) divided into triplets. Of course, this rhythmic trait is present to a large degree in many American music genres other than jazz, particularly blues, gospel, and hip hop.[15]

Achieving a greater understanding of the blues system is one natural outgrowth of this study because the process of examining recurring traits of rhythm & blues songs throughout history naturally helps to identify the most important and long-lasting features of the blues system. For example, the characteristics of rhythm & blues that *do not* change much over time are good candidates for inclusion in the list of fundamental elements of the blues system. This same concept holds true for elements of the blues system that are observed extensively across a wide spectrum of musical genres. If the evidence were to show, for example, that a certain group of notes existed consistently in several hypothetically related American popular musical genres, one might be able to conclude that such a scale should be included in the definition of the blues system. Conversely, musical traits that are present in only one musical genre, or remained in use for only a handful of years, would most likely prove to be less significant features of the blues system, or perhaps deemed not part of it at all.

NEW BLUE MUSIC SCHOLARSHIP

American music scholars often write about historical change in musical style. For example, Amiri Baraka promotes the idea that American society at large has historically co-opted the music of black Americans. This has often led it to become less African-American and caused the creators of the music periodically to seek new ways to express themselves.

> The continuous re-emergence of strong Negro influences to revitalize American popular music should by now be pretty well understood. What usually happened, as I pointed out, was that finally too much exposure to the debilitating qualities of popular expression tended to lessen the emotional validity of the Afro-American forms; then more or less violent reactions to this overexposure altered their overall shape. This was true as far back as the lateral and reciprocal influences Negro spirituals had on the white hymns they were superficially modeled upon. And these reactions almost always caused valid changes in the forms themselves.[16]

There appears to be some truth to Baraka's contentions, although he relies to a large degree on his personal impressions of the music in question. In this book I explore the validity of such suggestions by looking in depth at the actual music involved.

Another important work is Nelson George's *The Death of Rhythm & Blues*.[17] One might say that George's book lays the philosophical groundwork for the technical and analytic research presented here. His work guides the reader from the early days of rhythm & blues, when the music had a greater degree of "blackness," up to the late 1980s, by which time, he believes, that the potential for crossover success by black artists had sapped the music of its African-American cultural strength. In other words, in the act of becoming assimilated into white society the black musician lost some of what made his music distinctive. George's hypothesis is tested in these pages. Because the specific elements of the blues system are defined and then traced throughout history, we are able to observe any systematic changes in rhythm & blues music. If R&B has indeed become "whiter" over the course of the second half of the twentieth century, we should be able to see evidence of an increasing use of musical elements commonly associated with European art and folk music.

Much of the theoretical work presented in this book pertaining to pitch, scale, and stylistic traits in the blues system is based, at least in part, on work done by Gerhard Kubik. In *Africa and the Blues*, Kubik—who has conducted many years of fieldwork in Africa—presents a plausible theory about the origins of blues.[18] He postulates that the model for the blues tonal system in America is derived to a large degree from an integrated scale, primarily from the west-central Sudanic belt of Africa, reinterpreted by enslaved Africans. Kubik also suggests that the music, past and present, of Africans from that region features many other characteristics of blues in America, such as melisma, wavy intonation, and a declamatory vocal style. The author's research goes a long way toward explaining where the so-called "blues scale" originates. His model also seeks to explain—with the exacting detail of pitch measurement that is typical of Kubik's work—why certain notes are "worried" in the blues genre. In short, his findings help to explain the existence of the "blue notes" so often referred to in writings about American popular music.

Other researchers have explored global concepts that are similar, at least in part, to the new blue music and the blues system. To my knowledge, however, there is a certain level of uniqueness to the ideas presented in these pages. It is a given, nonetheless, that any insights presented in this work are dependent on original research done previously by various experts in the broad field of American music. Two such works that postulate a comprehensive system for the musical language of jazz are Winthrop Sargeant's *Jazz: Hot and Hybrid*[19] and Gunther Schuller's *Early Jazz: Its Roots and Musical Development*.[20] In the current work I am suggesting that the new blue music encompasses not only jazz, but also blues, rhythm & blues, and other American musical genres and categories.

In order to present a balanced look at rhythm & blues in the twentieth century, it is important first to gain an understanding of its African-American antecedents from the early 1800s onward. The reasons for such an investigation are somewhat obvious, the motivation primarily being that without establishing a basis from which the music began it would be difficult to evaluate the changes that occurred later. The blues system—and therefore the new blue music—did not appear out of thin air. To the contrary, elements of this musical language existed at a much earlier date, and were present in nineteenth- and early-twentieth-century black folk and popular music.

More than a few books about music in the nineteenth- and early twentieth-century United States have proven invaluable in the research I have conducted.[21] Such books provide scholarship that not only helps to trace the emergence and growth of the blues system in the U.S. but also offers proof of the influence of African music. In addition, several important articles published over the last century on the topic of African retentions and reinterpretations in the U.S. have led the way toward a greater understanding of the development of the blues system. For example, Richard A. Waterman's article, "African Influence on the Music of the Americas," deals with the blending of European and African music in the United States, and so is an essential point of departure for this study.[22] Several important later articles address related topics about African retentions and reinterpretations in the Americas and at times come to somewhat different conclusions from those of Waterman.[23]

Examining the blues genre in the period 1900 to 1950 has been particularly important to my research. Because of the close relationship between the two, one must follow the path that blues traveled in the first half of the twentieth century in order to have some sort of perspective on where rhythm & blues takes us in the second half.[24] I have also relied heavily upon writings of later experts in the field of blues research, particularly David Evans, Paul Oliver, and Jeff Todd Titon. Most important among the writings of these authors are Evans's *Big Road Blues*;[25] Oliver's *The Story of the Blues*[26] and *Savannah Syncopators*;[27] and Titon's *Early Downhome Blues*.[28]

One of the goals of this research is to shed light on the connection between rhythm & blues and other twentieth-century American popular musical genres and categories. Because much of the research conducted for this study involves an analysis of rhythm & blues recorded over a fifty-year span of time, significant works by other writers in the broad spectrum of recorded American popular music have also been of great use. These works contain important historical research as well as specific information about recordings of many types of American music such as African-American folk music, blues, jazz, gospel, country, rhythm & blues, and rock 'n' roll.[29]

Due to the nature of the research, a reliable source for R&B song and chart information was a necessity. The compilation of *Billboard* R&B chart data by Joel Whitburn, *Top R&B Singles: 1942–1999*, was selected as the main reference work for such information due to its thoroughness and usability. Whitburn's work is a valuable resource that should be in the library of any

R&B researcher, and the artist background information it contains would certainly interest the rhythm & blues aficionado as well. Unless otherwise noted, it should be assumed that *Billboard* chart and artist data included here are adapted from Whitburn's book.

It seems appropriate to proceed with a detailed look at the theoretical basis of the blues system. Chapter 2 includes many transcribed musical examples to help define each musical element being discussed and to offer insight into its role as a component of the system. To explain the blues system it is necessary to look, not only backward in time, but across a wide spectrum of American musical styles, genres, and categories.

CHAPTER TWO

THE BLUES SYSTEM

The blues system is a definable body of musical elements or traits, inherited from both African and European traditions, that forms the foundational language of much twentieth-century American musical style. It emerged from the nineteenth-century African-American musical tradition to become a driving force in American music, both secular and religious. In order to explain how the blues system is used in practice, I present in this chapter a detailed look at its characteristic elements. In the process, I demonstrate connections between several related American musical genres that help to establish the nature of the system.

The musical traits of the blues system are used in varying proportions from song to song and from genre to genre. Such variability in the use of elements of form, style, and content is a feature of any musical tradition. For example, one would not expect any two given pieces of European "classical" music to contain exactly the same proportion of elements simply because they were conceived using the same set of basic compositional rules. Likewise, no two American folk or popular music songs should be expected to contain all of the elements of the blues system in exactly the same proportions. However, part of the research for this book consists of measuring the degree to which a given piece of music conforms to the system. In order to make such judgments, we must first identify the important musical features of mode, melody, harmony, form, rhythm, and other components of the blues system.

Attempts have been made in the past to define such a musical system, specifically in regard to blues and jazz as genres. One of the most far reaching of these endeavors, in terms of formulating rules of form, tone quality, rhythmic organization, mode, blues song families, and text, was done by Jeff Todd Titon. In *Early Downhome Blues*, Titon fashions blues melodic templates using data derived from forty-four transcribed songs, and uses these plans to create a "typical" blues melody. Most impressive in Titon's work is his analysis of melodic tendencies (or "motional organization"), where he calculates the incidence not only of specific pitches but also of specific melodic fragments (e.g., the lowered third moving to the tonic) in his downhome blues sample group.[1]

Titon's method of collecting and analyzing data is not used in this book as the primary method of defining the blues system. Determining a valid statistical sample for the wide spectrum of music studied for this research would be problematic at best. For that reason, I rely more on description-based methods like those used by Evans and Peter van der Merwe. The former defines blues, broadly speaking, by offering a list of musical characteristics that are observable in the genre, with the idea that a song in that tradition contains some or all of those traits.[2] Van der Merwe offers a somewhat similar idea and presents many transcriptions of American and African music to back up his findings.[3] The work of Gerhard Kubik is relied upon heavily in this chapter as well, especially for the theoretical basis and origins of the scale used in the blues system. I do not suggest that this chapter is comprehensive in its attempt to define the parameters of the blues system; such an effort would likely require a dedicated study. The primary purpose of defining the blues system, it should be remembered, is to establish a basis for the study of musical elements in rhythm & blues in the 1950–1999 time period.

MODE

An important characteristic of the blues system is the use of a unique musical mode, the raw material of which seems to have been inherited from Africa and later developed in the African-American community.[4] This is, of course, not to imply that European modes are absent from African-American folk and popular music; it is simply to state that a key element of the blues system is its reliance on a non-Western pitch-set. A description of the mode used in the blues system is presented in the following pages, but first it seems impor-tant to define what the European system is, especially so that we can later recognize what it is not.

Musicologists and music theorists sometimes refer to the musical system used in Western art music from 1600 to 1900 as the *major-minor system*. This European musical scheme is based on the formation of twelve major and minor modes, each containing the same intervallic relationships between the various pitches and the foundational note, or tonic. This system ultimately became standardized in European music to such a degree that the three-hundred-year time span mentioned above came to be called the *common practice period*. To make the system consistent across a wide range of use, a manmade, homogeneous scale was formed using notes one-twelfth of an octave apart. This creation, called *equal temperament*, or sometimes *tempered tuning*, was highly controversial, and some of the greatest minds in Europe, such as Galileo, Newton, Rousseau, and Rameau, battled the pros and cons of it for much of the seventeenth and eighteenth centuries.[5]

The tempered system emerged and became the standard, to a large degree because of the great proliferation of keyboard instruments in Western culture during the sixteenth and seventeenth centuries, although the use of tempered tuning on fretted string instruments has also been noted at least as far back as the mid-sixteenth century. Vocalists and performers of string or wind instruments can make subtle corrections from key to key, and pitch to pitch, to account for the nonsymmetrical nature of the natural harmonic series. Any proficient violinist, for example, is well aware of the fact that even though the instrument is tuned in perfect fifths, pitch adjustments must be made in order to play with acceptable intonation. However, such instanta-neous pitch deviations are not possible on a harpsichord or piano. In order for these instruments to have any sort of reliability in different keys and on different chords, it was necessary to bend the rules of Pythagoras and divide the octave into twelve equal parts.

It should be understood that some of the pitches used in the major-minor system do not exist "naturally." To create the scheme, the pitches that resulted from the mathematical proportions described by Pythagoras—and later sup-ported by the discovery of the existence of the natural harmonic series—were altered to produce a system that is perfectly symmetrical in all keys. Of course, Western music did not suddenly change from the Pythagorean system to the modern equal-temperament system. The path toward equal temperament can be traced from simple plainchant melodies sung by European monks in the middle ages. At that point in the history of Western music, harmony in the modern sense did not exist, and the Pythagorean model functioned adequately. Such monophonic music eventually led to organum, which often added pitches a fourth or fifth above or below the melodic line.[6] By the late twelfth and early thirteenth centuries the English had incorporated intervals of thirds and sixths into their music, and this new technique eventually spread to the European mainland. As the use of keyboard instruments spread, and problems with creating chords on such fixed-pitch instruments became more and more evident, "just tuning" and later "mean-tone" tuning emerged. Both of these systems were attempts to "correct" the inherent difficulties in the Pythagorean system, and although they solved some of its problems, neither was totally successful. Both were subject to harmonic and melodic inconsistency due to the fact that theoretically identical intervals were sometimes unequal in size.

Figure 1 below illustrates the differences between the Western, equal-temperament scale and the one based on the natural overtone series. The number of "cents" of each pitch is indicated.[7] This system allows for a total of 1200 cents per octave, and is a useful tool for comparisons of pitch and scale. Pitches in the natural overtone series that are substantially different from those in the equal-temperament system are indicated by the use of diacritical marks (downward arrows). Numerical values that indicate the amount of

Western equal-temperament scale

| cents | 0 | 200 | 400 | 500 | 700 | 900 | 1100 | 0 (1200) |

Natural harmonic series, partials 4 to 11

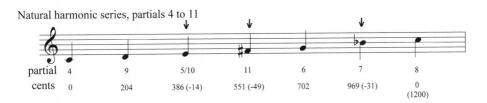

| partial | 4 | 9 | 5/10 | 11 | 6 | 7 | 8 |
| cents | 0 | 204 | 386 (-14) | 551 (-49) | 702 | 969 (-31) | 0 (1200) |

FIGURE 1. Comparison of pitches in the Western equal-temperament scale and those derived from the natural harmonic series. Adapted from Kubik, *Africa and the Blues*, 129.

deviation in cents are also shown. Note that some pitches in the harmonic series are so far removed from their tempered counterparts that accidentals are required in addition to the diacritical marks. It is important to recognize the fact that the seventh degree of the Western major scale, the leading tone, does not exist in the first eleven overtones of the natural harmonic series. In fact the nearest overtone is actually 131 cents lower than that of the leading tone B of the equal-temperament scale, and even thirty-one cents below the B♭ of the Western system. It is equally important to observe that the third and fourth notes of the equal-temperament scale also diverge considerably from those occurring in the scale based on natural harmonics. By creating the tempered scale, European musicians and theoreticians ultimately produced a homogenous, symmetrical, and very practical system, but in the process deviated considerably from the pitches found in the natural state. It can be observed that much American folk and popular music does, in fact, consist of major and minor modes that are derived from the Western equal-temperament system; *what is more significant for the purpose of our discussion is that much of it does not.*

To understand the mode used in the blues system we must first start with an understanding of the concept of the so-called "blues scale." This scale has been described numerous times by writers in the fields of blues, jazz, gospel, rock 'n' roll, rhythm & blues, and African-American folk music and is one of the key elements of the blues system that serves as a bridge across genres. The scale includes three steps that are variable in pitch: the third, fifth, and seventh. These scale degrees seem to be neutral—neither major nor minor—and impossible to show accurately in Western musical notation. They probably can be best perceived as pitch areas or "tonal areas."[8] This variability of pitch is certainly not the norm in the European system, where the sanctity of each note is maintained to a great degree. The second and sixth degrees of the scale, shown in parentheses in figure 2, represent notes that some writers do not consider part of the core blues scale, as is explained later.

FIGURE 2. The so-called "blues scale." The pitch-set in this illustration is not being promoted as the one and only "blues scale," but as a representation of how the scale is sometimes perceived.

It is essential that the blues scale be perceived not as simply an alteration of the Western system scale—*not* a major scale with a few notes changed, but as a very different configuration of pitches.[9] In practice, the blues scale does not exist exclusively in the form illustrated above. At best, we can think of the scale shown as a model that outlines the basic pitches of a more complex blues mode. To understand the blues mode, it is first necessary to grasp how the particular scale notes are used in context. The third note of the scale is particularly ambiguous, and the fact that this note is variable seems to have created a lot of confusion for some Western-trained musicians and writers over the years. This note, often called the "blue third," is sometimes so much lowered from the European major third as to approach the pitch level of E♭, or perhaps even lower (using the notes in fig. 2 as our reference). As suggested before, the third is neutral and probably more correctly understood as a *range* of pitch.

Example 1 below shows a melody from an African-American work song that uses the blues mode. This particular example has a tonic of B♭, and the D notes represent the variable third degree of the scale. Although not evident in the transcription (this is one of the frustrations in trying to explain the blues mode using a written musical system), the lowered D notes in the first measure are farther in pitch from their Western counterpart than the D in measure eight. To a Western ear it might sound as if measure one is in a minor key, and that the song changes to the major key on the last bar of the example. In truth, none of the scale third Ds in the example are precisely major or minor, but simply somewhere in an acceptable range of pitch. The very concept of major and minor is largely invalid in the analysis of a blues-mode melody such as this.

EXAMPLE 1. Allen Prothero, vocal, "Jumpin' Judy." CD track time 0:04–0:21. *Afro-American Spirituals, Work Songs, and Ballads*, Rounder CD 1510, 1998. Recorded in Nashville, Tennessee, 1933. See appendix B for an explanation of the diacritical marks used in this study.

I'll take her from that man____ gon - na bring 'er home____ if I can____ .

EXAMPLE 2. Lefty Frizzell, vocal, "Traveling Blues." CD track time 0:47–0:53. *Look What Thoughts Will Do*, Columbia CD C2K 64880, 1997. Recorded June 6, 1951.

Example 2, from a performance by country music singer Lefty Frizzell, illustrates a similar use of neutral thirds. Though it can be quite difficult to discern this effect when the track is played at regular speed, when the recording is slowed down it is revealed that the artist noticeably bends up to the first B note, and the pitch at which he eventually arrives is lower than the two Bs found later in the excerpt. All three notes are below the B natural of the equal-temperament scale. The use of the blues mode is extensive in country music and has been so throughout its recorded history. "Traveling Blues" was written and recorded earlier by Jimmie Rodgers (sometimes called "The Father of Country Music"), an artist whom Frizzell himself called "the biggest influence on my life."[10] Significantly, some of Rodgers's most important releases, such as "Blue Yodel No. 1," "The Brakeman's Blues," and "T.B. Blues," make extensive use of blue notes.

The use of neutral thirds is also a key element in the vocal style of blues singers, as shown in example 3 by New Orleans blues pianist Professor Longhair. To help visualize the particularly rich variety of pitch of the neutral thirds (Bs) in this example, two downward arrows have been used to designate a pitch sung particularly low (approaching B♭) compared to the Western scale equivalent, and single downward arrows for notes that are not quite so low. Measuring these pitches exactly is beyond the scope of this study, and furthermore, deemed unnecessary; the key point is to grasp that these notes are included in a *range* of pitch that is available to the performer. There are

Hey lit - tle girl, gee you sure looks fine____

EXAMPLE 3. Professor Longhair, vocal, "Hey Little Girl." CD track time 0:33–0:43. *Professor Longhair's New Orleans Piano*, Atlantic CD 7225-2, 1989. Recorded in New Orleans, Louisiana, 1949.

countless possible examples of the use of neutral thirds in blues-system songs such as those shown here.

The seventh step of the blues scale is typically so much lower than the seventh degree of the Western scale as to warrant the inclusion of a flat sign in the notation. Note that this pitch is close to the seventh partial of the natural harmonic scale. For reasons of clarity I call this pitch the "flatted seventh," even though use of the term indicates a certain Western bias. Of course, this note is not necessarily considered to be "flatted" by an individual who performs music using the blues mode; it simply is the *correct* note to use. Although this flatted seventh exists in practice as a range of pitch, it is not nearly as variable as the third step. There are many examples of lowered flatted sevenths in the blues mode, and they sometimes even approach the sixth scale degree.

The previous example provides a case in point (ex. 3). In measures one and three the artist sings a noticeably lowered, flatted seventh (F natural). Perhaps he does so because the chord being played at that point in the song is C7, and the lowered seventh of the parent scale would clash with the third of that chord (E). So, to follow that logic, the singer reacts by lowering the flatted seventh in order to more closely match the chord being played. Later in the same verse the singer slightly *raises* the pitch of the flatted-seventh scale degree over the D7 chord, therefore approaching the F♯ of that chord. Although such applications do indeed exist, exceptions abound to the idea of any sort of standardized use of lowered or raised flatted sevenths.

Professor Longhair (the performer of the above excerpt) often played on piano a V chord with a *minor* third, thereby eliminating the theoretical need for the raised flatted seventh as described above. One of his disciples, Mac "Dr. John" Rebennack, recalls this tendency in the music of Longhair (or "Fess," as he was nicknamed): "One of my favorite things that he used to do was a lick he played on a Paul Gayten song, 'Hey Little Girl.' He'd get to the five chord of that song, and in the bass line he'd play a minor note in his left hand against a major chord in his right, which totally reversed what everybody else would be doing."[11] Note that the idea of pitch ambiguity is central to Rebennack's perception of Longhair's use of the flatted seventh. He plainly understands that Longhair was intentionally "blurring" the pitches by simultaneously playing two different versions of the seventh degree of the scale.

Perhaps the most thought-provoking explanation of the neutral-third and flatted-seventh pitch areas in the blues scale comes from Gerhard Kubik.

His many years of field experience in Africa give weight to Kubik's observations about the music of that continent. He suggests that the blue notes at the third and flatted-seventh degrees of the scale originate with a mental template—inherited from the west-central Sudan area of Africa—that consists of overlapping female and male vocal ranges, which he illustrates as scales. When these two scales are combined into one larger scale, the outcome is the integrated model shown in figure 3. Kubik says that "the surprising result is a combined model that encompasses the melodic repertoire of the blues."[12] The mental template of this scale was retained by Africans enslaved in the United States, who found that it conflicted with the European scale in two important places, the third and the seventh. The example below reveals the difference, shown in parentheses, between the cents values of pitches in Kubik's integrated scale with the corresponding cents values of notes in the Western system. In order to construct a workable system, African Americans incorporated the use of pitch areas to replace multiple discrete pitches.[13]

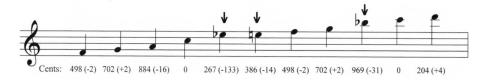

Cents: 498 (-2) 702 (+2) 884 (-16)   0   267 (-133) 386 (-14) 498 (-2) 702 (+2) 969 (-31)   0   204 (+4)

FIGURE 3. Integrated model: melodic repertoire of the blues, according to Kubik. Adapted from Kubik, *Africa and the Blues*, 139.

The other variable pitch used in the blues system, sometimes called the "flatted fifth," "blue fifth," "sharp fourth," or "sharp eleventh," is more problematic than the neutral third and flatted seventh. There seems to be little agreement about how this pitch is used, and its origin seems somewhat clouded as compared to the third and seventh. A look at the scale built on the natural harmonic series (fig. 1) reveals that the fourth degree is almost exactly halfway between F and F♯. Kubik discusses the existence of the flatted fifth, but does not include it in his integrated scale model (fig. 3).

Example 4 illustrates how John Lee Hooker uses the flatted fifth in one four-bar excerpt. For clarity's sake, the key signature in this example, and others from this point onward, is written per Western music conventions. In other words, this song is analyzed as having a tonic of A, so the key signature of A major is used. Although the validity of using this method is open to dispute,

EXAMPLE 4. John Lee Hooker, vocal, "Hobo Blues." CD track time 2:06–2:16. *John Lee Hooker: The Ultimate Collection*, 1948–1990. Rhino R2 70572, 1991. Original release: Modern single 835, 1949. Note: The transcribed vocal part is sung in an extremely rubato manner (rhythmically elastic), and exact rhythmic representation is impossible using Western notation. The excerpt is transcribed in 12/8 time because the guitar accompaniment (not shown) strongly implies such a configuration.

it at least allows the reader to quickly visualize the ways in which the notes "diverge" from the equal-temperament scale. It should be pointed out that the third (C♯) and the fifth (E) in the example are sung markedly below the notated Western pitches. In fact, at times they both approach the note one-half step lower than indicated. Of course, it is much better to listen to such an excerpt than to view it on paper, because the many variants of pitch then become evident. Hooker sings the lowered fifths on strong beats; thus they are greatly emphasized. It should be noted that the flatted fifths in this example all eventually resolve downward to the fourth, and then to the tonic.

In the next illustration we can see that Jimmy Smith uses the flatted fifth to bend *up* to the fifth of the scale (D♭–D) (ex. 5). This usage is very common in keyboard blues, rhythm & blues, jazz, and rock 'n' roll (this technique can also be seen in example 6B, in which Horace Silver uses the flatted fifth to bend up to the fifth and also down to the fourth). Based on personal experience, I feel that the flatted-fifth degree's function is fundamentally different from those of the neutral third and flatted seventh in many blues system genres and categories, such as gospel, country, blues, and rhythm & blues. When the flatted fifth is sung or played on a strong beat, it is often part of a bend that "resolves" upward to the fifth, or downward to the fourth. Landing on this note on an emphasized beat, *and remaining there*, is not as common in the blues mode as similar usages of the neutral third or flatted seventh.

EXAMPLE 5. Jimmy Smith, organ, "Bucket." CD track time 1:55–2:00. *Bucket!* Blue Note CD 7243 5 24550 2 7, 2000. Recorded February 1, 1963.

However, and this is a significant exception, the flatted fifth (or "sharp eleventh") played or sung on a strong beat *is* somewhat common in jazz.

So many opinions exist about the use of the flatted fifth that examples can be offered to prove almost any hypothesis. David Evans once suggested that the flatted fifth might function as the "blue note of the blue note" in some instances, such as in "Hobo Blues." But the existence of the flatted fifth has never been fully explained.[14] For the purpose of defining the blues mode, and thus the blues system in general, I assert that the flatted fifth should be included in the list of identifying characteristics, with the understanding that the use of this element is somewhat less common than that of the neutral third or flatted seventh.

We have seen some of the ways a vocalist might create neutral pitch areas or bend notes in compliance with the blues mode concept. Many instrumentalists use similar methods to effect gradations of pitch. Such techniques are plentiful in guitar playing and include use of metal or glass sliding devices; finger-bending of strings (pulling the string across the neck); finger vibrato (moving the finger on the string parallel to the neck); use of tunings that contain non-Western pitches; and vibrato bars (on electric guitars). Guitar is a particularly versatile instrument when it comes to changing pitch during performance, and this is probably one of the reasons why it has become a favored solo instrument in blues, jazz, rock 'n' roll, country, and rhythm & blues.

Harmonica (or "harp") players often use techniques that mimic the human voice. To play a blues mode–based song on harmonica it is usual to select an instrument that is a fourth in pitch above (or a fifth below) the key of the song being performed. This is a technique often called "cross-harping." When using a harmonica a fourth above the key of the song, the player gains a lowered-seventh scale degree. For example, a harp in F has a B♭ in its scale, and if such an instrument is used on a song in C, the player has available the flatted seventh necessary to play in the blues mode. The basic harmonica is laid out in such a way that some notes are blown and some are drawn (inhaled), and these are arranged, for the most part, in an alternating fashion on the instrument. Harp players long ago discovered that it is possible to bend the pitch on drawn notes by pulling air hard against the reeds and also changing the shape of the mouth cavity by repositioning the tongue. Notes are laid out in such a way as to allow the player to create a scale with a neutral third and fifth (and the flatted seventh is already available, as stated above). Depending on how hard the notes are drawn, and how much the mouth cavity is changed, the harp player has a great deal of control over the amount of pitch change when using this technique.

These pitch variations cannot be duplicated exactly on a fixed-pitch keyboard instrument such as piano or organ, of course. For that reason, piano and organ players have created a pool of stylistic effects in order to approximate the neutral pitch areas of the blues mode. The existence of this body of techniques reveals that there is an overriding musical language at play; otherwise, it is difficult to see the reason for the widespread use of such effects. The two examples below show typical keyboard right-hand "bends" that are used in the blues mode (ex. 6A-B). In example 6A, Ray Charles bends up to the scale fifth (B) beginning on the last sixteenth note of the first measure, and down to the fourth of the scale (A) on the second eighth note of beat two in the second measure. This example gives weight to the argument expressed before that the flatted fifth of the scale can be used as part of either an ascending or descending bend.

The transcription of Horace Silver's piano in example 6B is particularly enlightening as an approach to piano playing in the blues-system mode. In this excerpt Silver plays the flatted third (F♭) to the exclusion of the major third (F natural), although in the song as a whole he plays both. This technique imparts a particularly "bluesy" sound. Playing the major third would give the passage a much "sweeter" sound and, although it can also be used, it would not likely be the first choice for a performer with experience in music of this style. Silver's extreme use of the bends up to the fifth and down to the fourth in this example makes it obvious that the artist is attempting to create a blurred effect, or pitch *areas*. Silver gives the impression that he is mimicking a blues-mode vocal or wind instrument performance. This effect

EXAMPLE 6. Blues mode "bends" as performed on keyboard instruments. (A) Ray Charles, piano, "What'd I Say." CD track time 0:27–0:30. *Atlantic Rhythm and Blues: 1947–1974*, 1991. Atlantic CD 82305-2. Recorded on Feb. 18, 1959. (B) Horace Silver, piano, "Doodlin'." CD track time 2:12–2:19. *Horace Silver and the Jazz Messengers*. Blue Note CD CDP 7 46140 2, 1987. Recorded on Dec. 13, 1954.

is reinforced by the pianist's extreme rubato playing of the passage, which is also reminiscent of the vocal styles of many blues and R&B performers.[15] The overall rhythmic effect could be described as an example of a melody that "floats" over the underlying beat, and it imparts an ambiguity to the rhythmic structure. This technique is typical of many forms of African-American music, and I suggest that it is directly related to the use of offbeat phrasing and swing, both discussed later.

"Tipitina," one of the classics of New Orleans blues/boogie/barrelhouse piano, exemplifies Professor Longhair's use of characteristic blues-mode piano "note-bending" techniques. Measure two in example 7 contains "bent notes" similar to a type already discussed. This example, however, shows that the blues mode sometimes goes far beyond the simple seven-note scale presented earlier. Note that the artist slides up from the flatted-sixth to the major-sixth scale degree in measure two (D♭-D). Later in the same verse (not shown), the artist bends up to the major seventh of the scale (E♭-E) on the C7 chord. In both cases the pianist slides up to the third of the chord being played, or implied, in the left-hand piano part. It must be pointed out that the lowered sixth and the major seventh are not normally included in the basic blues scale model. However, these notes do in fact exist in practice, especially when the IV and V chords are played, and many examples could be offered as proof.

EXAMPLE 7. Professor Longhair, piano, "Tipitina." CD track time 0:01–0:12. *Professor Longhair's New Orleans Piano*, Atlantic CD 7225-2, 1989. Recorded in New Orleans, Nov. 1953. Note: Track is the second version of the song included on this CD.

In measure four of this example, Longhair dramatically blurs the pitch F by using a multiple-grace-note run. Note that this run does not serve to create a bent note on the third of the chord (or even the sixth, or major seventh), but on the fifth, which in this case is the root of the key.[16] To explain the use of this variable chord fifth and also the variable chord thirds mentioned above, one may posit the theory that Longhair perceives each of the chords as defining a separate tonic "level" on which to build a blues scale. According to this suggestion, the pianist has at his disposal the following musical pitches for the song, and he uses all but one in the verse from which the excerpt is taken:

1. The blues scale based on the tonic: F, G, A♭-A, B♭, C♭-C, D, E♭, F.
2. The blues scale based on the scale fourth: B♭, C, D♭-D, E♭, F♭-F, G, A♭, B♭, to be used over the IV chord.
3. The blues scale based on the scale fifth: C, D, E♭-E, F, G♭-G, A, B♭, C, to be used over the V chord.

Combining all of these pitches into one scale results in the following pitch-set: F, G♭-G, A♭-A, B♭, C♭-C, D♭-D, E♭-E, F, in other words, the entire Western equal-temperament, chromatic scale. Thus, it *could* be said that the blues-mode scale consists of every note in the Western chromatic scale plus a range of pitch variants up or down from them. Such a characterization would not be particularly enlightening since it would do nothing to help identify the most important notes of the system. Analyses of songs like "Tipitina" make it evident, however, that one of the essential features of the blues mode is pitch ambiguity, and in practice it is acceptable to bend up to or down from any note.

In addition to the techniques discussed above, piano and organ players have devised other ways to create pitch ambiguity when playing in the blues mode. A few examples of such practices are playing both the flatted third and major third in the right or left hand simultaneously, glissando, and tremolo. Some researchers have even suggested that bent-note techniques of this type can be observed in ragtime piano music.[17] In any case, without the blues-mode elements discussed above, a keyboardist would most likely be considered a lesser player; *to play an authentic "bluesy" piano style, pitch blurring is an absolute necessity.*

Our blues scale model (fig. 2) includes two notes that some scholars and theoreticians do not consider essential parts of the blues scale, the second and sixth degrees. Part of the reason for this is that these two pitches supposedly occur less frequently than the root, third, fifth, and flatted seventh. Since the scale second and sixth are not part of the basic seventh chord structure, they are often thought of as "added" notes that do not change the basic harmony. Thomas Brothers, for example, has called these scale degrees "dangling intervals," because they are "perceived as distinct from the fundamental triadic structure, but not directly opposed to it."[18]

In *Early Downhome Blues* Titon presents forty-four blues songs as performed by a variety of artists. He then calculates the total number of times that each pitch appears in one stanza of the vocal part of the songs transcribed. Titon's reckoning is based on the identification of forty-one discrete pitches within a two-octave range, an ambitious project. After presenting the data in its raw state, he groups some of the pitches into general pitch regions, which he calls "complexes." This results in the identification of scalar regions at the third, fifth, and seventh in which considerable variation upward or downward in pitch occurs. Figure 4 is an adaptation of Titon's data and figure 5 a similar presentation of data collected by John Fahey on the blues and blues-ballads of Charley Patton. Fahey contends that the flatted third and natural third often exist as two distinct pitches in the vocal parts of the blues recordings he studied. He therefore presents them as separate scale tones.[19] However, in figure 5 I have combined all scale thirds (and, similarly, scale fifths and sevenths) into regions in order to compare Fahey's data with that collected by Titon.

The results of the work of these two researchers are surprisingly similar. Based on their findings, one can conclude that the second degree of the scale is relatively uncommon in some early blues. Conversely, one can see that

1	2	♭3→3	4	♭5→5	6	♭7→7
31%	3%	26%	4%	23%	7%	5%

FIGURE 4. Incidence of scale pitches in Titon's sample group. Titon, 153–54.

1	2	♭3→3	4	♭5→5	6	♭7→7
29%	2%	33%	4%	17%	8%	8%

FIGURE 5. Incidence of scale pitches in Fahey's transcriptions of Charley Patton songs. Adapted from "unadjusted" data on blues and blues-ballads, Fahey, 38–42.

the sixth of the scale occurs at least as much as the combined scale sevenths in the songs studied. Interestingly, the data of both researchers indicate that the use of the fourth of the scale is somewhat rare in their sample groups. However, Fahey includes the scale fourth in his scale of "stressed pitches" that Patton uses: 1 2 ♭3 3 4 5 6 ♭7 8.[20] Despite any implications to the contrary in the findings of these two researchers, the scale fourth *is* commonly used across a variety of styles and genres in the blues system, a fact that can be observed in numerous examples throughout this study.[21]

In rhythm & blues and jazz the second scale degree appears to be used with greater regularity than in the blues genre. Some theoreticians of American popular music refer to this pitch as an "extension," "upper extension," or "added note" because it can be perceived as the ninth of a chord. In other words, the note can be thought of as part of a chord stacked up in thirds from the root, in accordance with rules of Western music harmony. In R&B and jazz the second note of the scale is typically called the ninth when the seventh is also present in a chord; where the seventh is not present the note is typically perceived as the second degree.

Example 8 illustrates the first four measures—after a short introduction—of "Now's the Time," recorded by jazz saxophonist Charlie Parker. One of the originators of the bebop style of the late 1940s, Parker commonly performed songs like "Now's the Time" based on the twelve-bar blues form but with added chords that jazz musicians sometimes call "substitutions." The use of the second degree of the scale in this song is somewhat typical of much post-1940 jazz. Significantly, the note is featured on downbeats and stands on its own as a pitch level, not simply as a passing note.

Tonic: F

EXAMPLE 8. Charlie Parker, alto saxophone on "Now's the Time." CD track time 0:05–0:11. *The Essential Charlie Parker*, Polygram 314517 173-2, 1992. Recorded in New York, July 30, 1953.

MELODY

The blues mode described above tells only part of the story of how pitches are used in the blues system. My experience as an educator in jazz, blues, and

R&B has brought me to the realization that it is very difficult to teach anyone how to use these notes in an authentic blues-system manner. The reason for this may be quite simple: there is an infinite number of possible note combinations, and making a value judgment on each one is out of the question. In order to play blues-mode melodies, especially those that are improvised, a musician must establish a vocabulary of note combinations—licks, if you will—that are appropriate. This may take a number of years, and requires much listening to other musicians who are experienced in the style.

A similar point could be argued for melodic tendencies in any musical tradition. It is fair to say, for instance, that in European art music, certain pitches have a predilection to fall, or resolve, one way or another: the leading-tone seventh normally resolves to the octave, and the fourth of the scale—when it is part of the dominant-seventh chord built upon the fifth step of the scale—usually resolves downward to the scale third. However, these illustrate *tendencies* only. If Western art music followed such prescribed rules (and others) exactly, it might have run out of melodic ideas in the early eighteenth century. Explaining exactly how a melody is, or should be, constructed is virtually impossible, and the best one can do is describe typical cases or show statistical likelihoods. With that caveat in mind, a discussion of the functional tendencies of notes in the blues mode is presented below. Fortunately, we are able to rely on the work of other researchers who have previously made attempts to codify the melodic tendencies in the blues system, particularly in the blues and jazz genres.

One of the earliest attempts at defining the melodic tendencies of notes in the blues mode was made in 1946 by Winthrop Sargeant in *Jazz: Hot and Hybrid*. In that work the author discusses "melodic behavior" of individual tones in jazz. He asks the important questions: "Are certain tones used more often or held longer than others? Are certain tones likely to be followed or preceded by certain other tones, forming characteristic melodic patterns? Are some tones used incidentally and passed over quickly as mere embellishments?"[22] To illustrate his understanding of the relational tendencies of pitches, Sargeant includes the graphical presentation shown in figure 6. He groups the notes into arrangements that highlight their perceived functions. The arrows show the inclination of a given note to lead to another. Any such presentation must not be taken too literally; it should be remembered that Sargeant is simply attempting to show tendencies, not steadfast rules. My personal experience as a performer in R&B, jazz, blues, and country music

FIGURE 6. Melodic tendencies in "hot jazz," according to Sargeant, 167.

and my activities in music research lead me largely to support Sargeant's findings about melodic inclination.

The above discussion of Sargeant's work leads us into Peter van der Merwe's "ladder of thirds" concept. His hypothesis seeks to explain the melodic tendencies of the blues mode by perceiving its notes as thirds that are stacked above and below the tonic note of the key. For example, from C the thirds moving upward are E♭-E, G, and B♭, and the third below is A.[23] This concept does seem to describe the way note combinations occur in many blues-system melodies, where the notes may be thought of as "swinging" up or down a third in many cases. One can see that this idea is also inherent in Sargeant's illustration of melodic tendencies, above (fig. 6). Some of the song transcriptions presented earlier in examples 3 and 4 may also be interpreted to support the ladder of thirds concept. Following van der Merwe's logic, one can further hypothesize that the extensively used scale ninth in jazz and R&B is yet another third in the ladder, in this case stacked above the seventh.

Both Sargeant and van der Merwe point to the affinity of the lowered or flatted third to resolve downward and the sixth scale degree to move upward to the tonic. One major difference between the two writers, however, is their understanding of the universality of the blue fifth. While van der Merwe finds evidence of the blue fifth across the American music spectrum,[24] Sargeant finds its existence unproven.[25] Perhaps the difference between the two conclusions lies in the fact that Sargeant was studying early jazz and did not delve as deeply into the blues genre or African-American folk music. Sargeant could have found the flatted fifth if he had listened to the same late-1920s recordings that Jeff Titon studied, though the incidence of that pitch is relatively rare even there.[26] During my research for this book, I investigated numerous examples of the flatted fifth across a variety of American music genres, several transcriptions of which are included in these pages.

Titon's work represents one of the most thorough investigations of melodic tendencies in the blues mode. Using his sample group of forty-four songs as a basis, the author creates a graphic presentation—similar to Sargeant's (fig. 6), albeit more complex—which shows the affinity of each note to move to another. While this is somewhat helpful to the researcher, it can also give the wrong impression; knowing where a note *might* resolve is not the same as knowing where it likely *will* resolve. Therefore, in order to further explain melodic tendencies in the early blues songs, Titon also presents information about *phrase contour*. He concludes, and I simplify greatly here, that most of the phrases, lines, and stanzas have either a strictly descending (falling) contour or a rise to melodic highpoint followed by a descending contour (sometimes called an "arched" contour).

The conclusions reached by Sargeant, van der Merwe, and Titon might seem obvious to students of blues and related African-American music but are significant because they are based on observation of actual musical elements in songs, not opinion alone. For that reason they have been particularly important to my research for this book, because I also examine specific musical traits in order to follow the development of R&B as part of a larger music continuum. I shall not retrace the steps of these three scholars and perform a detailed study of the ways notes function in blues-mode melodies. For my purposes, the descriptions of general melodic tendencies as presented by Sargeant, van der Merwe, and Titon are more than sufficient for describing melody in the blues system.

HARMONY

In Western music, *harmony* generally pertains to the creation and function of chords. Chords are built from intervals, and the way they function is related to melodic tendencies within the scale. Although it is possible to study the connection between chords and melody, in this section I am primarily addressing the function of chords as harmonic units that progress one to another in Western music and the degree to which this type of harmonic movement is used in the blues system.

One of the fundamental features of the Western music system of harmony is its use of "dominant-to-tonic" or "circle-of-fifths harmony." A Western music circle-of-fifths chord progression, such as iii-vi-ii-V-I, can be thought of as basically a series of dominant-to-tonic harmonic cadences. Even though these chords are not all major triads, the root movement is a fifth in each case.

Often this same root/chord movement exists with major chords being substituted for the minor ones: III-VI-II-V-I. To go a step further, these chords can each have a flatted seventh added: III⁷-VI⁷-II⁷-V⁷-I (in the key of C the first chord would be an E7, and spelled as follows: E, G♯, B, D). This way of using chords developed over centuries in Europe. The period of time 1600 to 1900 was its heyday in Western art music. By the late 1800s musicians and composers of such music had grown tired of using these same combinations of chords and began to experiment with other methods of composition.

Harmony in the blues system is not necessarily "functional" in the Western art music sense—that is, it does not always rely on the dominant-to-tonic chord relationship. However, to say that such harmonic progressions are entirely absent from blues system–based music would be far from the truth. All types of American popular music use the Western chord system to a greater or lesser degree, and this fact highlights the blended nature of the music. The point here is that the blues system often uses chords in ways *not* typical of the Western system. It is important to discuss some of the more significant features of harmony in the blues system, especially since the subsequent investigation of musical elements of rhythm & blues music, 1950–1999, specifically targets ways in which the use of harmony has changed.

Songs that are steeped in the traditions of the blues system can and do use the type of Western chord progressions discussed above. But they also use harmony in a very static manner, in which the chords do not "progress" from one to another in the Western music sense. This harmonic notion goes back at least to the 1800s in the Americas, and the current thought is that it derives from various African musical styles. The music of much of Africa is based on cycles or clusters of cycles and a rhythmic relationship to body movement. The chords in such music seem to be perceived as tonal-harmonic steps progressing one to another. There are many examples of such static harmony in jazz (as in the aforementioned "So What" from Miles Davis's album *Kind of Blue*), gospel, Pentecostal, blues, and rhythm & blues, and in other types of American folk and popular music.

"Say It Loud, I'm Black and I'm Proud, Part 1," a number-one R&B hit by James Brown, is an interesting study in the use of static harmony, as opposed to functional chords. The song, released in 1968, has three basic sections—verse, chorus, and bridge—each of varying lengths throughout the song. Shown in example 9 is the formal structure of the song. All sections of the piece, except the twenty-four measures of bridge sections, are played over a B♭7 chord, often with added notes such as the ninth or raised ninth (B♭9 and B♭7 ♯9).[27] The bridge harmony is an E♭7 chord, and even though this is built on the fourth step of the parent key, it does not function here as it would in a typical Western art music composition. Following rules of Western art music harmony, the IV chord with an added flatted seventh would likely resolve to the chord built on the *flatted seventh of the parent key*. In other words, in this case, the E♭7 chord would be expected to resolve to an A♭ chord. This understanding of function is not at all in the minds of James Brown and his band, of course. The E♭7 in this song simply represents another tonic level, and when we eventually arrive at the B♭7 again, we do not get a feeling of harmonic resolution as much as a realization that we are back at that "other tonic level." In the blues system it is not quite accurate to say that a song is in, for example, B♭ major. The reason is perhaps obvious; songs with a tonic of B♭ in the blues system would normally have an A♭ in the scale, and this note is not part of the Western key of B♭ major. This topic is looked at in more detail during the discussion of the function of the dominant-seventh chord in the blues system, later in this chapter.

SECTION	NUMBER OF MEASURES	TONIC LEVEL
Intro	2	B♭7
Chorus 1	4	B♭7
Verse 1	12	B♭7
Chorus 2	6	B♭7
Verse 2	8	B♭7
Chorus 3	8	B♭7
Bridge	10	E♭7
Chorus 4	4	B♭7
Verse 3	10	B♭7
Chorus 5	8	B♭7
Bridge (fade out)	14	E♭7

EXAMPLE 9. Formal/harmonic structure of "Say it Loud, I'm Black and I'm Proud, Part 1." James Brown, *James Brown: Star Time*, Polydor CD 849 110-2, 1991. Recorded in Los Angeles, Aug. 7, 1968.

The above discussion of "Say It Loud, I'm Black and I'm Proud, Part 1" illustrates the harmony typical of much R&B music in the 1960s and beyond, especially the genres of funk and, later, rap and hip hop. However, this type of harmonic sense abounds in the blues genre as well. "Hobo Blues," by John

Lee Hooker (ex. 4), is a good example of a blues song with static harmony. Hooker is well known for his "boogie" songs that do not adhere to the rules of Western functional harmony, such as two of his other hits, "Boogie Chillen'" and "Crawlin' Kingsnake," both released in 1949. Earlier blues artists employed similar techniques. The following is a just a small sampling from the multitude of such early blues songs: Blind Lemon Jefferson, "Black Snake Moan" (1926); Henry Thomas, "Old Country Stomp" (1928); Charley Patton, "Mississippi Boweavil Blues" (1929); Skip James, "Hard Time Killin' Floor Blues" (1931); and King Solomon Hill, "Down on My Bended Knee" (1932). Most of these songs use one chord primarily, but when another is used, such as the chord built on the scale sixth that Jefferson uses in "Black Snake Moan," it does not function in a typical Western manner. In fact, Jefferson often uses this chord in place of the V chord, which he avoids in a number of his songs.[28]

Our investigation leads us to look at the three primary chords used in the twelve-bar blues. Though we have not yet discussed this form, it consists of, roughly speaking, the following chords (shown in the key of C):

C_7	C_7	C_7	C_7
F_7	F_7	C_7	C_7
G_7	F_7	C_7	C_7

All of the chords are indicated as seventh chords even though they might just as well appear as triads, simple intervals of a third or a fifth, or even single notes. In other words, these chords are often implied and not played as a whole. Based on the melodic content that is typically present in both the vocal and instrumental parts, the potential for adding a flatted seventh to each chord usually exists. Because the chords have a flatted seventh, Western music theoreticians might expect them to resolve to a chord based on a root a fifth below. This is not what happens in the twelve-bar blues, however. Even though the C_7 does "resolve" to the "correct" note (F), that pitch itself stands as the root of a chord with a flatted seventh. The twelve-bar blues chord progression breaks all rules when in the seventh measure it returns to the C_7 chord, and thereby firmly establishes that chord as the tonic.

A very important point is perhaps obvious but rarely stated: *a chord such as C, E, G, B♭, known as a "C7," cannot function as a tonic chord in Western art music.* Such a structure is often called a dominant-seventh chord because it normally occurs in the Western system when thirds are stacked up from the fifth degree of the scale. However, in the example above such a structure is built upon the tonic (as well as upon the subdominant and dominant), and this is, in a word, "impossible" in Western music theory. As a graduate student I once had a Western music theory instructor—who was wise and knowing in such matters—tell me that such a chord "does not exist." I remember thinking at the time that he was dead wrong. I had been using that chord as the tonic for years in blues, jazz, rock 'n' roll, country, R&B, and a lot of other music. But I have re-evaluated my position on this topic and now believe he is absolutely correct *as far as Western art music is concerned*. After years of searching I have not been able to find a single piece of European art music from the period 1700 to 1900 that makes use of this type of formation as a tonic seventh chord. Such a harmonic structure would be given the label of "V7 of IV," which in effect establishes its function as being the dominant-seventh chord of the note that is a fourth up (or a fifth below). Some Western music scholar might be able to offer proof that this chord has in fact been used in this "impossible" way in *some* piece of Western art music, but I am relatively certain that any instances of the sort are rare and that no large body of such music exists. The simple reason is: chords in Western music are built according to principles of the major-minor system discussed earlier. The seventh note of any major key in that system is *not* a flatted seventh, but a major seventh. This is a significant difference between the Western art music system and much of the music steeped in the blues system tradition.

The use of parallel harmony can also be found in some blues system music. This way of using chords is nonfunctional in the European way of thinking because the chords do not "resolve" to one another based on the circle-of-fifths progression discussed above. What is important to grasp is that these parallel harmonic structures are not meant to resolve in the Western sense, because they are based more on the African musical tradition than the European.[29]

Vocal parts in songs using such "parallelism" are often not exactly parallel. In such songs the intervallic relationship between any two given parts might change, for example, from a major third to minor third within the phrase in order to stay consistent with the scale being used. Over the course of many years the creation of harmony in African music of this type has come to be much better understood. A phenomenon described in 1930 by Percival Kirby, when comparing harmony in African-American spirituals to that in some South African vocal music,[30] eventually coalesced into the concept explained by Kubik as a melodic "span process" or "skipping process."[31]

In Kubik's words the "skipping process" is "a structural principle implying that usually one note of a given scale is skipped by a second singer to obtain harmonic simultaneous sounds in relation to the melodic line of a first vocalist."[32] In pentatonic scales this can sometimes result in some "parallel" intervals being thirds and others fourths.[33]

Harmonic parallelism is evident in a great deal of American popular music. This is true even in some of the "sophisticated" styles such as big band jazz, where the parts for the wind sections of the group—saxophone, trumpet, and trombone—are often scored in parallel motion similar to that described by a number of researchers in African music. It would be most difficult to write compositions or arrangements for such jazz ensembles if one relied solely on rules of Western music harmony and voice leading. For example, the movement of parts in parallel fifths, generally a forbidden practice in European music, is commonplace in the big-band jazz music of Duke Ellington, Count Basie, Benny Goodman, and countless others.

Example 10 shows parallelism in the vocal parts of the 1984 release by Prince, "When Doves Cry." Note that all four vocal lines move in the same direction; one can also observe in this passage that the vocal parts do not move in *exact* parallel, but remain in the A minor scale ("natural minor") throughout. Compare this parallel harmony with that in the Luvale song in example 11. Although parallel harmony is widespread across much of the spectrum of American popular music, it is relatively rare in blues—probably due to the fact that solo vocals predominate in that genre. However, some

EXAMPLE 10. Harmonic parallelism in vocal parts of "When Doves Cry." CD track time 2:19–2:26. Prince, *The Very Best of Prince*, Warner CD R2 72472, 2001. Originally released in 1984.

EXAMPLE 11. Harmonic parallelism in vocal parts of Luvale song. "Kangongue ('A Small Mouse')." Adapted from Kenichi Tsukada, 733.

blues feature duet singing with parallel vocal parts, as in some of the music of Brownie McGhee and Sonny Terry.

There is often an ambiguous quality to chords used in the blues system. For example, rock 'n' roll guitarists, especially those who perform in the "heavy metal" or "speed metal" sub-genres, often make use of what are known as "power-chords." In reality these are not chords in the traditional Western music sense, but simply open fifths (e.g., the two notes E and B played together comprise a typical power-chord). These power-chords are used for two reasons. The first is that they can often be played with open strings making them louder and richer in harmonics. The second reason—and more important to our discussion—is that these open fifths allow the use in the melody line of a wide variety of thirds: major, minor, and in between. In other words, they allow for harmonic ambiguity. Interestingly, country music performers, and keyboard players in particular, often adopt a similar harmonic structure for the very same purposes. The reasons for such usage are clear; if one plays a major third, the sound is sometimes too "sweet," while the minor is too "dark." Problems may arise if either of these thirds is used on a fixed-pitch instrument like piano, especially if the vocalist or instrumental soloist employs neutral or flatted notes. The simple solution that has emerged is to leave the thirds out of the chords entirely, and allow the tonality to be defined by the lead vocal or instrument.

Contrary to Western music rules, the melody and harmony of music in the blues system often do not match. By this I mean to say that blues-mode melodies often stand in contrast to their chord accompaniment if analyzed according to the rules of European harmony. An illustration of such disagreement appears in example 12, in which Mahalia Jackson's vocal melody at times does not match the harmony. For clarity, the example includes chord symbols based on a reduction of the piano part. Several pitches are so much lowered by the vocalist that it seems most accurate to notate them as

EXAMPLE 12. Mahalia Jackson, vocal on "Just Over the Hill." CD track time 2:25–2:33. *The Great Gospel Women: 31 Classic Performances by the Greatest Gospel Women.* Shanachie CD 600492, 1993. Recorded in 1950.

flatted notes with an upward arrow above them. There are instances in this segment where a lowered scale third ($C\flat$) is sung above a chord with which it does not belong according to Western music theory (e.g., in measures 1, 2, and 3). Other "wrong notes" might include the $G\flat$ (the flatted seventh) in measures two and three. Western music theory might be able to account for these pitches as passing notes were they being used in that manner, but such an analysis is questionable in these instances. Their function in this piece—and in an incalculable number of other gospel songs and blue music in general—is primarily as part of a blues-mode melody, and their relationship to harmony is secondary.

In blues-system songs the major V chord is sometimes avoided entirely, perhaps due to the fact that in Western music the chord contains the major-seventh scale step, which is not part of the blues mode. Van der Merwe states that over the twentieth century in American popular music there has been a "weakening of the opposition between the tonic and dominant," and also that there has been a "supplanting in importance of the dominant by the subdominant."[34] The reliability of these important points is tested later in this study of changes in R&B over the second half of the twentieth century. Van der Merwe speaks correctly at least as regards the blues genre's avoidance of the V chord. This topic was touched upon earlier in the discussion of "Tipitina," by Professor Longhair (ex. 7). However, classic examples of the avoidance of the V chord can be heard in much earlier songs by artists such as Skip James, who, like other early blues performers, sometimes played single notes in place of the V chord. Songs such as "Cypress Grove Blues," "Four O'clock Blues," and "Cherry Ball Blues" typify his hesitancy to play a major V chord. In addition, James uses another device that is somewhat typical in the blues system when he employs the *minor* V chord on "Devil Got My Woman."[35]

A few words should be said here about the so-called "gospel blues." This form has little relationship to the twelve-bar blues in the structural sense, and therefore the term itself is misleading. What is important to our current discussion is the harmonic structure and function of such twentieth-century African-American gospel songs. The harmonic structure in a typical gospel song, "Lord I've Tried," composed by William Herbert Brewster, is shown below in example 13. This type of harmony became a staple of gospel music in the second half of the twentieth century and was incorporated into rhythm & blues in the 1950s and 1960s. Note that at the end of the eighth measure there exists what is sometimes called a "half-cadence" where the phrase

Tonic: E♭

4/4	E♭ C7	F7 B♭sus7	E♭ A♭	E♭
	E♭ C7	F7	B♭ F	B♭
	E♭	E♭7	A♭	F7 Fm7
	E♭	F7 B♭sus7	E♭ A♭	E♭

EXAMPLE 13. Harmonic structure of "Lord I've Tried." William Herbert Brewster, 1945. Boyer, 215. In this example chords appearing in a single measure are underlined together.

ends on the chord built on the scale fifth (B♭). At the end of the sixteenth measure the full cadence appears, and so the piece has closure according to Western musical ideals.

An important point should be made concerning the use of harmony in black gospel music of this type: *for the most part, the chords in this progression function as a circle-of-fifths harmony typical of much Western art music.* Harmonic movement of this kind in American popular music has sometimes been called "barbershop" or "parlor" style.[36] In a watershed article, "'Play That Barbershop Chord': A Case for the African-American Origin of Barbershop Harmony," Lynn Abbott traces the history of this type of harmony in American popular music, particularly as it relates to barbershop quartet harmony. Abbott's work counters the prevailing assumption that whites of the late nineteenth century were the originators of the barbershop quartet and its characteristic harmonies. His work points out likely African-American origins not only for the so-called "barbershop chord" but for male barbershop quartet singing in general.[37]

FORM

Discussion of harmony in the blues system leads us to the topic of form. No attempt is made here to identify all of the song forms used in the blues system; such a task is far beyond the scope of this study. However, a few important forms should be discussed, especially those that have been in use for a number of years and/or across a wide spectrum of American folk and popular music.

In the discussion about "Lord I've Tried" (ex. 13) we encountered a typical sixteen-bar gospel song form with a more or less standardized harmonic structure. Adaptations of this form, and the barbershop harmony it employs, are present in both jazz and rhythm & blues of the 1950s and 1960s. The music of Horace Silver and the Jazz Messengers, especially tunes such as "The Preacher" (1955), typifies this effect in jazz.[38]

The music of Ray Charles and others brought gospel elements to rhythm & blues in the mid- to late 1950s. The use of variants of the gospel song form (and harmonic structure) is particularly evident in many songs by Charles during that period including hits like "Drown in My Own Tears" (1955) and "Hallelujah, I Love Her So" (1955).[39]

One of the most widely discussed musical forms used in American popular music is the so-called twelve-bar blues. Despite its name, this strophic form is not always twelve measures in length. The musical structure is often divided into three lines (of four measures, more or less), each of which often consists of a vocal part and an instrumental response. This "call-and-response" occurs in one line of music where the vocal part, which typically lasts a little over two measures, is answered by an instrumental part (often guitar or piano) that fills out the remainder of the phrase. The exact lengths of the vocal part and instrumental response are flexible, which accounts for the variable length of both the phrase and the overall form. For our purposes, it should suffice to say that the twelve-bar blues, especially in the folk idiom, is a flexible three-phrase structure that *often* consists of 12 measures, but can also have 11, 12½, 13½, or just about any number of measures.[40]

The twelve-bar blues has been used across a very wide range of American folk and popular music. Some question remains as to exactly how and when this form first came into use, though we know for certain that it existed by 1912, when songs like H. Franklin "Baby" Seals's "Baby Seals Blues" and W. C. Handy's "Memphis Blues" were first published. Edward A. Berlin notes, however, that the 1904 ragtime piano piece, "One of Them Things?" by James Chapman and Leroy Smith, includes both the familiar twelve-bar blues pattern and blue notes, and it is possible that the form existed earlier in black folk music.[41] The twelve-bar blues eventually became one of the most important structures in jazz, country, rhythm & blues, and rock 'n' roll.

An important formal structure in African-American folk and popular music is sometimes called the "vamp" or "drive." Defining this form presents some difficulty, not only because it is used across a range of genres and styles and for a variety of purposes, but also because the terminology itself is not standardized. For example, in gospel music the terms "drive," "hang-up," "riff," "working section," and "repeat" are sometimes used to describe the same musical phenomenon. During the initial stages of this study I considered using the term "vamp" to describe the form that is, generally speaking, an extended, repeating section of music with a cessation of harmonic movement. However, the word "vamp" itself is used to describe other musical phenomena, and I eventually came to see its use as more confusing than helpful. I prefer the term "cyclic form" to the other names listed above.

For the purpose of investigating changes in the use of the cyclic form structure in R&B from 1950 to 1999, I have defined the important characteristics of the form as follows:

- The term "cyclic form" is used to describe a section of music that generally features the use of a repeating musical phrase, or "cycle."
- The cycle is defined as the smallest unit of music that is repeated within the form, usually one to four measures in length.
- Cycles are generally composed of riffs, which are short, repeated musical figures. The nature of a riff is melodic and rhythmic, sometimes with a harmonic element as well.
- Often involves a cessation of harmonic movement.
- Sometimes involves a short, repeated, harmonic progression (e.g., I, vi, ii, V).
- Often features a solo performer.
- Often includes a call-and-response element.
- Often begins at a low emotional level and builds to a high point.

Many commentators on African and African-American music have discussed the topic of cyclic musical forms. For example, in "Nguni Vocal Polyphony," David Rycroft explains how such repeating patterns are one of the key features of that music. Rycroft also describes the "double-ended overlap," in which "solo [part] phrases begin in about the middle of one chorus [part] phrase, and end and restart midway through the next one, so that the phrases are completely interlinked."[42] The cyclic form often includes the organizational scheme referred to as "call-and-response" or "leader-and-chorus" (similar in structure to Rycroft's double-ended overlap). This element, which is evident in the ring shouts and spirituals of nineteenth-century African Americans, features a musical statement by a leader that is answered by a group or congregation.[43]

Black gospel music in the United States, and African-American spirituals before that, relied heavily on the cyclic music form. In his book *Fire in My Bones*, Glenn Hinson explains how the cyclic form—"drive," in his terminology—is used in gospel music.[44] Often a vehicle for building religious fervor during the service, the repeating cycle commonly supports a soloist of some sort—for example, the preacher or a lead singer—and a responsorial element provided by the choir or congregation. The emotional level of the soloist gradually builds, and over time the process moves the entire congregation to a higher level of religious excitement.

In much blues-system music, such as jazz, R&B, and rock 'n' roll, cyclic form sections often underlie extended improvised instrumental solos, and some of the musicians might say it gives them an opportunity for "stretching out." In the blues genre one finds fewer incidences of such extended sections of cyclic form. However, the use of static harmony and the call-and-response feature, two important elements of the cyclic form, are both common in blues. Some blues artists—John Lee Hooker and Muddy Waters quickly come to mind—include in their repertoire a number of riff-oriented "boogie songs" with limited harmonic variety that seem related to the cyclic-form aesthetic.

The cyclic form most noticeably became an important element in rhythm & blues during the development of funk music in the 1960s and 1970s with the music of James Brown, Sly & the Family Stone, and others. In R&B music of that period the cyclic form is often used as a vehicle for an extended instrumental solo. However, it also can function as the structure for an entire song or for a majority of the song length, such as in "Shotgun" by Junior Walker (1965) and "Thank You (Falettinme Be Mice Elf Agin)" by Sly & the Family Stone (1970).

RHYTHM

The intention of the following discussion about rhythm in the blues system is not simply to review the scholarship on the topic, but to describe the elements and how they are used. However, a few pertinent topics investigated by other researchers should be touched on in order to present a clear picture of how the elements of rhythm are used in practice. It seems particularly important to discuss some of the work done on the music of West Africa, especially since many claims have been made over the years about the influence of the rhythms of that region on African-American music.

The early writings of Richard A. Waterman helped define "hot" rhythms in African music and the retention in the Americas of related musical elements. Waterman describes two very important rhythmic traits present in African music: (1) percussion polyrhythms or "mixed metres" and (2) temporal displacement of the melodic phrase or "offbeat phrasing" of melodies.[45] Waterman also puts forth the theory that Africans enslaved in the United States were often not allowed to keep percussion instruments, so their use of African multi-metered polyrhythms eventually disappeared.[46] It can in fact be observed that there is generally less use of polyrhythms in the music of North America than in that of Central America, South America, or the Caribbean. Perhaps this caused the African-American music of the United States to be more "European than African," as Waterman states.[47] However, it may be, as Oliver and others have suggested, that the black music of North America was more influenced by African music from another part of that continent—the savanna region of West Africa—than that of the rain forests of the Guinea coast where such polyrhythms were widespread.[48]

In any case, the polyrhythmic drumming of the West African coast seems to have gotten much of the early researchers' attention. Similarities exist between the complex West African polyrhythms and those present in much Latin American music. Particular rhythms found in Latin America, such as the rhythmic patterns of the habanera, samba, and other dances, have been identified in African music as well. Since at least the mid-nineteenth century these beats have periodically been the vehicles for the reinvigoration of North American popular music.[49]

Writers often use the term *syncopation* in discussing many types of American music, including ragtime, jazz, and rhythm & blues. The problem with using the term in our current discourse is one of accuracy. The *Harvard Dictionary of Music* defines syncopation as follows: "A momentary contradiction of the prevailing meter or pulse."[50] While this might be a good way to describe the occasional use of offbeat accents in the music of Beethoven, for example, it does not adequately account for music that *regularly* uses offbeat patterns. To describe such rhythmic phenomena in the African-American music we are investigating, I instead use the terms suggested by Richard A. Waterman to describe this musical feature, "offbeat phrasing" or "offbeat phrasing of melodic accents."[51] However, since "syncopation" has been used extensively by earlier writers in the description of American musical styles and genres, avoidance entirely of the term in our discussion is difficult.[52]

Some writers have claimed that American music inherits the vast majority of its offbeat phrasing from Africa, and that Western art music has manifested no significant incidence of the feature.[53] But syncopation *does* exist in European music, as any student of Beethoven symphonies knows. One might rather ask the question: *What are the specific differences in the use of offbeat phrasing in the blues system from that of syncopation in the European system?* Whereas offbeat phrasing in jazz and much other blues system–based music occurs as a regular part of the musical scheme, a composer of European music typically incorporates offbeat phrasing in an effort to introduce something out of the ordinary, a change from the regular beat. One might think of the latter as a musical special effect. However, blues-system music often uses offbeat phrasing as the foundation for its rhythmic structure. Such phrasing is decidedly *not* a "momentary contradiction of the prevailing meter or pulse"; *it is the fundamental beat upon which the music is built.*

Perhaps the earliest use of extensive offbeat phrasing in American popular music occurs in ragtime. Piano rags composed by musicians from the 1890s through the early 1910s display offbeat rhythmic patterns of many varieties. Some common rhythmic figures, taken from various ragtime pieces of Scott Joplin, are shown in figure 7A-D. Of course, ragtime music inherited many of its characteristics of form and style from previous types of music such as marches, minstrel songs, "coon songs," and black folk dances such as the cakewalk and wing dance.[54] The book *Slave Songs of the United States*, published in 1867, contains proof that such a rhythmic sensibility was an ingredient in African-American music at least as far back as the mid-1800s. Songs in that collection, such as no. 25, "Gwine Follow," no. 39, "I Wish I Been Dere," and no. 87, " 'Round the Corn, Sally," display considerable use of offbeat phrasing. In fact, as shown in figure 7, "I Wish I Been Dere" uses the same basic rhythm associated with the habanera (discussed later in this section).[55] Another source for evidence of such rhythms in early African-American

FIGURE 7. Typical offbeat phrasing of rhythms in ragtime piano music.

music is Lydia Parrish's *Slave Songs of the Georgia Sea Islands*, first published in 1947 but a result of fieldwork begun in 1909. Because of the isolation of the black residents of those islands, there is reason to believe that there was a great deal of retention of African characteristics in their music, and in fact some of the song texts are in African languages.[56]

The rhythmic influences described above came to bear not only on ragtime but also jazz, blues, rhythm & blues, and other types of American music. Many later forms of American popular music incorporate a greater variety of offbeat figures than ragtime, which relied heavily on typical sixteenth- and eighth-note patterns such as those illustrated in the previous example. Jazz incorporates a wide range of offbeat rhythms and has over the years been willing to borrow heavily from Latin American music.

Use of offbeat phrasing in the blues genre, on the other hand, is somewhat different from that found in jazz or ragtime. The evenly spaced offbeat accents that are prevalent in ragtime are less common in blues, especially in the melody. In fact, the rhythm of the "typical" melodic phrase in blues is probably best described as "floating" above the basic beat (such as that shown in example 4). However, there are many examples of blues in which the common eighth and sixteenth note offbeat pattern is apparent, as seen earlier in examples 3 and 7. In Professor Longhair's "Hey Little Girl" (ex. 3), the vocal part is made up of figures such as one might see in ragtime. In "Tipitina" (ex. 3), the left hand of the piano part not only accents the offbeats but also shows the influence of Caribbean music such as the rumba. Perhaps these two seemingly different concepts of rhythm, the floating melody versus the offbeat, but more rhythmically rigid, melody, can be explained by Kubik's theory about the source of the blues, in which he claims that blues drew from two different African traditions, the Arabic-Islamic and the ancient west-central Sudanic. He states that the first of these is characterized by melisma, wavy intonation, pitch instabilities, and a somewhat bardic nature, while the second contains "simple work rhythms in a regular meter, but with notable offbeat accents."[57]

Offbeat phrasing has remained an important ingredient in rhythm & blues as well. This should not come as much of a surprise since many of the early R&B hits were either jazz songs or blues songs with a dance-oriented beat. The funk era in rhythm & blues, from the late 1960s through the 1970s, saw an increase in the use of complex offbeat rhythms, as illustrated below (ex. 14). In addition to the obvious emphasis on the offbeats in the bass part,

EXAMPLE 14. Offbeat rhythmic phrasing in "Low Rider." CD track time 0:13–0:20. *The Very Best of War*, Avenue/Rhino CD R2 73895, 2003. Originally released in 1975.

there is a certain Latin American rhythmic feel to the song that is perhaps partly due to the rhythm of the cowbell part.

In rhythm & blues of the late 1960s and 1970s there was also an increase in the use of complex interlocking rhythms, especially in the style of music commonly called "funk." The music of James Brown and Sly & the Family Stone was typical of this increased rhythmic complexity, which often occurred at the expense of harmonic movement and development. This feature is evident in the James Brown song "Say It Loud, I'm Black and I'm Proud, Part 1" (ex. 15). An essential mind-set in this type of music is that *a musician is expected to play the exact same part throughout a song section, or perhaps even the entire song.*

The above point may seem obvious to some readers, but it bears emphasis because the concept of repetition to this degree is not typical of Western music. The bass and drum parts shown in "Say It Loud"—each basically a one-bar pattern—remain essentially the same for much of the A sections of the track, which constitute the majority of the song's duration. The horns and guitar are working with a different phrase scheme; although the example doesn't indicate it, these musicians are repeatedly performing a five-bar phrase. On the other hand, the lead vocal (semi-improvised) and the background vocal phrases are performed in sections of four, six, eight, and twelve measures. The result is that the rhythms of the different parts—consisting of one, four, or five bars—do not coincide throughout the track as one might expect in a piece of Western music. In a performance such as that shown in the illustration, the rhythmic parts rely on one another, and *together* they make a whole.

Much West African music uses what writers sometimes call "additive rhythms," and this tradition has been retained to some degree in blues-system

EXAMPLE 15. Rhythmic complexity in "Say It Loud, I'm Black and I'm Proud, Part 1." CD track time 0:38–0:43. James Brown, *James Brown: Star Time*, Polydor CD 849 110-2. Recorded in Los Angeles, August 7, 1968.

music. For our purposes the most important concept related to additive rhythms is that of the "timeline," which basically refers to a short rhythmic pattern that serves as a reference rhythm for an entire ensemble. In Western music the beat is often based on the quarter note or eighth note, in other words, a simple pulse. In some music of Africa, however, a longer asymmetrical pattern is used for the same purposes. A typical one-measure timeline—often described as a "3 + 3 + 2" rhythm—is shown in figure 8A-B.[58] The accents of the rhythm do not always coincide with the regular pulses, 1 . . . 2 . . . 3 . . . 4 . . . , but create, in effect, a simple cross-rhythm. This rhythm has been used extensively in American folk and popular music as the rhythmic basis for many blues, jazz, rhythm & blues, and rock 'n' roll songs, and also as the basis for African-American shout songs.[59]

A rhythm closely related to that shown above is the habanera, which has been a part of American popular music since the mid-1800s. This rhythm can be found extensively in ragtime, blues, boogie-woogie, R&B, and rock 'n' roll.

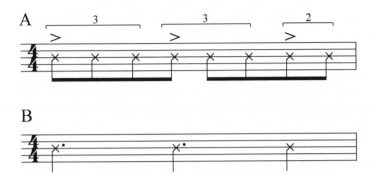

FIGURE 8. One-measure timeline. (A) 3 + 3 + 2 rhythm; (B) resulting beat.

Typical use of the rhythm is seen in example 16, a piano solo by blues/boogie-woogie musician Jimmy Yancey. The left-hand part in measures two and three makes use of the basic habanera beat, which is used in a slightly modified manner elsewhere in the segment. This rhythm has been the basis for not only the habanera but also the tango, samba, and other popular dances. The name apparently comes from *Havanese contradanza* and its basic style from an Africanization of a European dance.[60] Later we shall see that the habanera had a particularly strong effect on the rhythm & blues of the 1950s and early 1960s and is manifested in some of the biggest hits of that time period.

EXAMPLE 16. Habanera rhythm in "Death Letter Blues." CD track time 0:00–0:09. Jimmy Yancey, piano, *Barrelhouse Boogie*, Bluebird/RCA CD 8334-2-RB, 1989. Recorded in Chicago, Sept. 1940. Note: wavy lines above right-hand part indicate that the chords are rolled from the low note up.

The use of additive rhythms, such as 3 + 3 + 2, sometimes results in the superimposing of duple and triple rhythms in both African and African-American music. In many styles of blues-system music in the United States the time signatures 6/8, 9/8, and 12/8 have been used extensively, probably because they easily can be divided into either groups of two or three per beat.

In addition, the use of such time signatures allows the incorporation of the "triplet-swing" feel discussed below. The use of compound time is readily apparent in the so-called "gospel waltz" feel. This rhythmic structure—popularized by gospel composer and pianist Lucie E. Campbell and continued by W. Herbert Brewster, among others—is not a waltz in the Western music sense of the word, but a rhythmic overlay of triplets on each of the basic pulses, transforming 2/4 into 6/8, 3/4 into 9/8, and 4/4 into 12/8.[61] The soul music movements of the late 1950s and 1960s in both jazz and R&B relied heavily on these time signatures, as did much American popular music in general.

The concept of *swing* is exceedingly complex. One of the stumbling blocks in the explanation of the phenomenon is that there is no way to accurately write swing using the Western system of music notation. It often exists between the beats on the printed page and is constantly changing, measure to measure, and beat to beat. In this study I use the term "swing" in the broadest possible sense: *a rhythm that has swing creates a level of ambiguity because of its intentional at-oddness with the basic beat.* One way to think of swing in music is to equate it with a swing of the playground variety. Such a swing moves back and forth across a fixed point, ever-changing but always staying within the confines of its domain. Similarly, music with swing can be ahead or behind the basic pulse, but somehow never moves completely outside of the overall rhythmic structure of the music. Almost all blues system–based American popular music incorporates the swing element at times; it is one of the most universal of all characteristics of the system.

It is important to stress that I am not referring to "swing" in the limited sense that some jazz musicians use the term, where two eighth notes are perceived as the first and third of a group of eighth-note triplets. For that subset of swing I use the more specific term "triplet swing." For years triplet swing has been taught to aspiring jazz musicians as the one and only way to perceive swing.[62] This is understandable to a degree, because the entire truth of the matter is perhaps too complex for a beginner. But, an important fact is that *triplet swing is tempo-dependent.* Swing jazz played at a slow tempo usually features a very "wide" swing, in which the eighth notes approach the triplet division described above. Generally speaking, however, the faster the tempo the more evenly spaced (or "straight") the eighth notes become.

The famous recording of "April in Paris" by the Count Basie band illustrates the difficulty in defining swing exactly.[63] The saxophone section is featured on the track, and together these musicians play a harmonized version of the melody. What does not show up on the written music, but is plain when hearing the recording, is that the saxophonists are playing far behind the beat, especially on the half-note triplets in the first measure of the melody. This section, in the parlance of jazz musicians, "swings hard." As discussed earlier, blues system–based songs often incorporate the compound time signatures 6/8, 9/8, and 12/8. These divisions of the measure create a sort of structured version of triplet swing to the music because they allow each beat to be divided into three parts. In the 1950s, rhythm & blues songs relied heavily on the triplet-swing feel that 12/8 time brings to the music.

The more encompassing term "swing" includes not only triplet swing and its entire range of variation from straight-eighth to triplet feel, but also passages sung or played in a rubato manner specifically for the rhythmically ambiguous effect. "Hobo Blues" (ex. 4) features a John Lee Hooker vocal performed in a manner that incorporates rubato-swing to a great degree. Listening to the vocal melody as sung by Hooker—accompanied by a relatively even 12/8 rhythm—gives one the impression that the melody is floating above the accompaniment. There is a definite at-oddness between the two parts. The same sort of swing occurs in instrumental blues-system music as well, especially in improvised solos or embellished melodies. Numerous examples of this element can be found in blues, jazz, R&B, country, rock 'n' roll, and other American popular music genres.

In an interview with James Brown, I was able to gain an insight into that artist's concept of swing. It was obvious to me, based on our conversation, that Brown was aware of a "feel" that some musicians call "half-swing."[64] This concept is often used to designate swing that is somewhere between the straight-eighth feel and triplet swing. Example 17A-B shows two versions of the basic rhythm of "Think," originally recorded by Brown in 1960. Example A

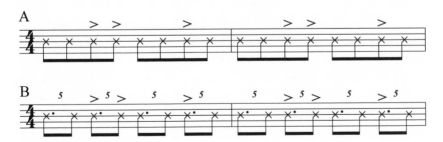

EXAMPLE 17. Two versions of the rhythm of "Think." *James Brown: Star Time.* Recorded in Hollywood, CA, Feb. 20, 1960.

shows how I clapped the rhythm, and example B shows the corrected, half-swing version subsequently tapped by Brown. The transcription of Brown's version is as accurate as the Western system of notation allows. What Brown actually tapped was somewhere between a triplet feel and straight-eighth-note rhythm. Although the example illustrates the rhythm in groups of five sixteenth notes per beat (the artist taps on the first and fourth of each group), it is not being suggested that Brown was thinking in those terms. I include such a representation solely as an attempt to approximate the rhythm he performed.

Some styles of American folk and popular music exhibit a noticeable acceleration of tempo. The downhome blues songs in Jeff Todd Titon's study group, for example, averaged an acceleration of tempo of about twenty-five beats per minute between the first stanza and the last. Titon states, on the other hand, that vaudeville blues songs generally retain a more constant tempo.[65] Significant acceleration of tempo is an element of the blues system perhaps more common in solo or duo styles, or in early group styles such as jug band music. In my experience musicians in the jazz, country, and rock 'n' roll genres do not typically strive to make the tempo faster as the song goes along. In order to determine whether the biggest R&B hits of the second half of the twentieth century show significant acceleration, my song analyses included both the beginning and ending tempi of each song studied.

IMPROVISATION

Improvisation is one of the essential ingredients of the blues system. Its use is widespread across a broad range of styles and genres of American popular music. Improvisation is sometimes defined as the real-time creation of melody during performance. But improvisation is not a simple matter of playing or singing anything that comes into one's head, as if it were solely a product of divine inspiration. Talent, of course, does come into play when a performer extemporaneously creates a melody, but such melodic inventions adhere to a set of musical rules of mode, melodic contour, and other factors of style and content learned by the musician. In addition, to create a coherent improvised solo that is stylistically "authentic" the performer must have some knowledge of the overall musical culture of which the music is a part. In other words, a keyboard improvisation by Mozart, no matter how technically advanced, would not be stylistically appropriate for use in "Pinetop's

Boogie-Woogie" (unless a comedic musical effect were the desired outcome, of course).

In theory, the particular combination of pitches and rhythms used is unique to each improvised performance. But in practice, there occurs a certain amount of recombination by the performer of previously learned musical figures and patterns. Blues system musicians often learn to improvise by listening to other, more accomplished, performers either in person or on recordings and then emulating not only elements of their style, but also particular melodic and rhythmic phrases. After accumulating a large body of such phrases the performer is able to incorporate them into his songs, combining them in various ways along with original melodic ideas.

Several of the songs presented above (exs. 2, 3, 4, 6A-B, and 12) demonstrate improvisation in the blues system, some because of the presence of vocal "trimmings" and others because they feature instrumental solos constructed at the time of the performance. The fact that improvisation is part of the overall aesthetic of blues-system music is related to a sensibility in African-American culture in general to strive for individualism. Skill in improvisation is an important part of the blues system overall because it allows the performer to demonstrate his cultural connection to the audience, while at the same time allowing him the opportunity to demonstrate personal innovation.

The art of improvisation was also once a highly regarded skill in the European classical music tradition, but in the late eighteenth and early nineteenth century composers began to feel that their music should be performed exactly as written. This led such musicians largely to abandon improvisation during the nineteenth and twentieth century.

In the blues system, improvisation is often manifested in the vocal part of a song, which is likely to be sung differently each time it is performed. The vocalist has many techniques at hand to create a spontaneous and unique performance, such as alteration of the pitches, phrasing, timbre, or lyrics; "scat" singing; and swing. Example 18A-C illustrates three versions of the same musical phrase. Each of these segments consists of the final line of a verse section of the song "Papa's Got a Brand New Bag, Part 1," by James Brown. Note the differences of pitch, rhythm, and text in each example. Such techniques of changing the way a given line is performed are part and parcel of the blues-system vocal style.

Improvisation in instrumental music in the blues system is one of its most visible elements, and examples are not difficult to find. One need only

EXAMPLE 18. Three versions of title line of "Papa's Got a Brand New Bag, Part 1." A) CD track time 0:19–0:23; B) CD track time 0:41–0:45; C) CD track time 1:19–1:23. James Brown, vocal, *Foundations of Funk: A Brand New Bag, 1964–1969*, Polydor CD 31453 1165-2, 1996. Recorded in 1965.

recall that many of the most influential performers across a wide range of American musical genres and categories, such as blues, jazz, country, rhythm & blues, and rock 'n' roll, have been famous for their improvisational skills.[66] It seems important to point out that instrumental improvisers often seek to emulate their vocal counterparts by reinterpreting a melody in a manner similar to that illustrated in the above examples of "Papa's Got a Brand New Bag, Part 1." In other cases, such as John Coltrane's saxophone solo on "Giant Steps," instrumentalists often express themselves in improvisations that are less related to vocal styles.[67]

OTHER STYLISTIC TRAITS

Many other stylistic traits of the blues system can be found across a broad spectrum of American musical genres and categories. A list of such features must be considered to be open-ended and, ultimately, incomplete; however, some of the more widespread of these elements are briefly discussed below. I do not wish to imply that these stylistic traits are secondary or less important than others described earlier, simply because they are presented without a detailed explanation and transcribed musical examples for each. On the contrary, these traits are essential to the blues system, and in fact the absence of all or most of them would indicate that a given song is probably not under the blues-system umbrella. Some of the characteristic features listed here have been mentioned earlier in connection with other elements of the blues system: (1) melisma, (2) rubato, (3) vibrato, (4) glissando, (5) gravelly timbre or "dirty" tone, (6) falsetto vocal, (7) declamatory and/or highly emotional vocal style, (8) spoken song text, and (9) dance orientation.

A common trait of blues-system music is the technique of singing many notes on one syllable, often called "melisma." The use of a high degree of melisma imparts a sense of individualism that is related to ambiguity of both pitch and rhythm. Of course, melisma can also be perceived as a form of improvisation since highly melismatic passages are typically performed differently each time. "Just Over the Hill," as sung by Mahalia Jackson (ex. 12), presents a good illustration of the use of melisma in a blues-system performance. Idiomatic use of melisma in the gospel vocal style is evident in measure three of that example, on the word "storm," but it is actually much more prominent earlier in the recording where there is no strict tempo and the singer is able to stretch out the syllables to any length desired.[68] As we shall see in chapter 7, the extreme use of vocal melisma became a prominent feature in R&B in the 1990s, especially with the music of artists such as Mariah Carey.

Evidence of rubato in blues system music has already been presented in this chapter, for example in our discussion about the vocal part in "Hobo Blues" by John Lee Hooker (ex. 4), the piano solo in "Doodlin'" by Horace Silver (ex. 6B), and the gospel vocal style of "Just Over the Hill" by Mahalia Jackson (ex. 12). Although specific data for this trait were not collected in my study of R&B 1950–1999, it is a feature whose presence was evident throughout the research. As I indicated earlier in this chapter, I consider rubato—performing with an intentionally elastic rhythm—to be a feature related to the larger concept of "swing."

Several ways of modifying the timbre and pitch of a voice or instrument are commonly used in the blues system. Vibrato, a variance of pitch, is used extensively in blues-system vocals, a good example of which can be heard in Howlin' Wolf's "Moanin' at Midnight."[69] At the beginning of the song the artist uses a pronounced vibrato on a vocable (*umm*), and the overall effect is reminiscent of a slide guitar. Another typical example is heard in the guitar style of B.B. King. His use of fingered vibrato, in which he moves the finger touching the string in a manner that is parallel to the neck of the guitar, is part and parcel of his guitar sound.[70] Glissando, the bending upward or downward to or from a pitch, is a topic that has already been explored at considerable length in our discussion about pitch bending, blurred notes, and slides. The transcriptions of Lefty Frizzell's "Traveling Blues" (ex. 2) and Professor Longhair's "Hey Little Girl" (ex. 3) both clearly exhibit this feature.

The use of gravelly or "dirty" tone is important in that its use in blues-system music represents a significant departure from Western music norms. Unless a musical special effect was the goal, one would not normally expect to use an intentionally rough-hewn, gravelly tone in European-style music. However, such a tone—whether performed vocally, on a saxophone, or on a fuzz guitar—is often the preferred sound in blues-system music. It imparts to the listener, who is a member of the overall cultural setting of which the new blue music is a component, a particularly soulful, often gut-wrenching sound that indicates that the performance is "coming from the heart." Examples of this feature abound in blues-system music, but one that quickly comes to mind is Junior Walker's hard-edged saxophone sound on "Shotgun."[71] In early blues music one might listen to the vocal sound of Charley Patton, for example his song "Pony Blues," as evidence of a gravelly vocal tone in that genre.[72] I have many times discussed this musical trait with friends and colleagues schooled in Western music, who wonder why any performer would accept such a "poor" tone as is evidenced in the above examples. Since these individuals (the Western-trained musicians) were taught to pursue a perfectly clear and unadorned tone, it is no wonder that they view a gravelly sound with bends, scoops, and pitch variances to be the product of bad training (or none). However, a musician who performs blues system–based music realizes that such timbre, along with other stylistic traits, helps to communicate with his audience in an essential way, and learning to effectively use these features is important in mastering the style.

Another element of much blues-system music is the use of falsetto vocal, another trait for which European music norms do not apply. Falsetto can be used in a variety of ways, ranging from a short yodel or high-pitched scream to an entire melody that is sung in a falsetto register. An example of the former can be heard in Little Richard's "Lucille" (or just about any of his hits, for that matter), where the artist uses his falsetto voice to jump into a higher range on the song's title.[73] The use of falsetto singing to perform large portions of the melody of a song has been widespread, and many early to mid-1970s R&B groups made it a featured sound. Philip Bailey's soaring vocal part on the Earth, Wind & Fire song "Fantasy" is a prime example.[74]

Spoken song text is another widespread feature of the blues system. Examples can be found in such varied music as Louis Jordan's "Caldonia" (1945),[75] one of a number of humorous songs by this artist that feature this trait; "Strollin'"[76] by Jack Dupree (1958), a blues song the entire lyrics of which are spoken; and the aforementioned "Say It Loud, I'm Black and I'm Proud, Part 1" by James Brown (1968).[77] Rap music can be viewed as a reinterpretation of this element in a modern setting.

In the blues system vocal parts are often performed in a declamatory and/or highly emotional style, which in many instances goes hand in hand with other traits described above, particularly gravelly timbre. Emphatic vocal deliveries are not unique to the genres of music we have been describing; they also exist in music as diverse as European opera and American Indian music, to give but two examples. Still, this trait dominates much blues-system music, especially the blues and gospel genres. For raw emotionalism one could point to any number of impassioned gospel performances, such as "Just Over the Hill" by Mahalia Jackson (ex. 12). The music of the soul era relies heavily on highly emotional, pleading vocals. Otis Redding epitomized this style, as can be heard on songs such as "These Arms of Mine" (a segment of which is shown in ex. 29, chapter 4).[78] Evidence of a declamatory vocal approach is found in abundance in blues-system music. The song "Sixty-Minute Man," by Billy Ward and the Dominoes (1951), features a booming bass vocal that is a very lightly-veiled sexual boast.[79] In another vein of R&B, funk, a declamatory delivery that exudes self-confidence can be heard in "Super Bad, Part 1" by James Brown (1971). In that song the singer emphatically states phrases—often more yelled than sung—such as "Watch me! I've got it!," "I'm super bad!," and "Jump back! I wanna kiss myself."[80]

Lastly, blues-system music has a long history of being related to dance and body movement in general. In fact, this danceable nature can be said to be a hallmark feature of the music. The religion-based ring shouts of the early and mid-nineteenth century; the cakewalks danced to ragtime music later in that century; the Charleston and the Black Bottom in the early twentieth century; and the Madison, the Twist, and the Mashed Potato in the 1950s and 1960s can all be held up as typical examples of the countless dances related to blues-system music. The dance orientation being discussed here is, of course, related to the fact that blues-system music often has a definite beat that one can feel, a trait found in much African music. This is opposed to the majority of European art music which—although there is often a set tempo—is typically much less beat oriented unless the music is specifically written for performance dancing, such as ballet.

SUMMARY

The blues system is a pool of musical elements of form, style, and content that are used across a wide range of American folk and popular musical styles, genres, and categories. Any of these elements might be more prevalent in one musical type or song than in another. The blending of these ingredients in varying amounts accounts, in part, for the distinctiveness of each genre and style. Of course, outside factors also affect each of these types of music, such as song function, size of the performance group, performance environment, notions of "standard" instrumentation, influence of other musical traditions, and many others.

One of the most important overall qualities of the blues system is its ambiguous nature. We have seen that there is much ambiguity of pitch, as in the neutral or blue notes, pitch bends, glissando, and the avoidance of chord thirds. There is also an ambiguous nature to the way harmony is used in the blues system, at least from the viewpoint of a musician schooled in the European tradition. Chords in blues-system songs often do not resolve where they are "supposed" to. For example, the major V chord is avoided and the dominant-seventh chord is often used as a tonic chord. Offbeat phrasing and swing both impart an at-oddness with the basic pulse and so bring rhythmic ambiguity to the blues system. Improvisation is, of course, by its very nature ambiguous and ever-changing. Though I have not discussed it at length here, there is also great ambiguity of lyric content—such as double-entendre and slurred speech—in much blues-system music.

The universal nature of the blues system in American folk and popular music becomes evident if one considers that accomplished musicians in jazz, blues, country, gospel, rhythm & blues, and rock 'n' roll, among others, all share a common musical language. For example, a skilled performer in any of these genres would be expected to know and be able to use the blues scale, along with characteristic bends, slides, and vibrato. Such a musician would also be well-versed in the musical elements of offbeat phrasing and swing, two primary ingredients of the blues system that are used extensively in American popular music. Therefore, it is theoretically possible for musicians from all of these genres to perform together an authentic twelve-bar swing-blues in 12/8 time, including the use of a variety of characteristic traits. A very close relationship between many types of American music often goes unmentioned, or perhaps unnoticed. The common denominator between them all, which constitutes the essence and foundational core of much American folk and popular music, is the blues system.

CHAPTER THREE

BLUES WITH A BEAT: 1950–1959

After World War II African Americans made great gains in their struggle to become part of mainstream American society and to achieve equal treatment under the law. The G.I. Bill of Rights (1944) provided for education, home loans, and a promise of economic prosperity for American veterans, including the unprecedented number of blacks who had fought for their country during the war. In 1948, in the face of some opposition, President Truman signed an executive order that integrated the U.S. armed services. Representative of the great gains made toward inclusion in society during the late 1940s and 1950s are legal victories such as the Supreme Court decision on *Brown v. Board of Education* that outlawed school segregation (1954) and the triumphs of athletes such as Jackie Robinson and politicians such as Adam Clayton Powell Jr.

These social successes naturally caused more people, some grudgingly, to begin to take a closer look at black culture in America. Black popular music was one field that had for years held the interest and attention of the wider population of the country. Black musicians since Louis Armstrong and Duke Ellington had significant success in the broader record market, and this trend continued in the 1940s with artists such as the Mills Brothers, the Ink Spots, Louis Jordan, Billy Eckstine, Ella Fitzgerald, and Nat "King" Cole.

In a dramatic shift in the 1950s, a multitude of black R&B artists—although often copied, and sometimes outsold by white artists—became nationally known and hugely successful in the broader music market. Ray Charles, Fats Domino, Sam Cooke, the Drifters, the Platters, the Coasters, Johnny Ace, and others, were the idols not only of black Americans, but of many whites as well. The idea that a black person could be thought of in this way was, of course, a relatively new and controversial concept in America of the 1950s.

The years 1945 through 1947 in rhythm & blues can reasonably be described as "Louis Jordan and others," such was the level of that artist's dominance in the field. Fully half of all the number-one R&B songs in that three-year period—eleven out of twenty-two chart-toppers—were by Jordan, a feat that surely will never be matched. Jordan's brand of "jump swing" typically featured a twelve-bar blues progression, an emphasis on beats two and four, a highly-energized dance rhythm, jazz inflection, and a good dose of showmanship. Some of that artist's biggest hits during the late 1940s were: "G.I. Jive" (1944), "Caldonia" (1945), "Choo Choo Ch'Boogie" (1946), "Ain't Nobody Here But Us Chickens" (1947), "Run Joe" (1948), and "Saturday Night Fish Fry, Parts 1 & 2" (1949). Jordan proved that the black record-buying audience wanted music that was not as complex as the bebop jazz then being created by musicians such as Charlie Parker and Dizzy Gillespie, but a more down-to-earth dance style.[1] Jordan, along with his combo the Tympany Five (a group that typically had more than five members), revolutionized rhythm & blues.

It should be noted that Jordan's label during his big string of hits was Decca Records, one of the few majors having significant success in the R&B market at the time. In addition to their great success with Jordan, Decca also produced several hit records for the Mills Brothers, the Ink Spots, and Ella Fitzgerald, three of the biggest acts (other than Jordan, of course) in rhythm & blues during the 1940s. However, by the early 1950s major changes were taking place in R&B. By 1950 Louis Jordan's popularity had begun to slip noticeably, and in that year he enjoyed just a single number-one record. An even clearer signal that new artists and styles had begun to get a grip on the R&B marketplace is that Jordan, who so dominated the field in the late 1940s, never charted another R&B record after August 1951.[2]

MAJOR STYLES AND ARTISTS

Toward the end of the 1940s and into the 1950s, popular black music in America began to experience significant change. During this period new styles of music began to compete for popularity with the older blues and jazz genres and eventually almost entirely replaced them on the charts. At first, the change was gradual and mostly a matter of degree, not a sudden stylistic transformation. For example, the song "I Wonder" (1944), recorded by Pvt. Cecil Gant and later covered by Roosevelt Sykes, is somewhat less sophisticated than hits earlier that year by the King Cole Trio ("Straighten Up and Fly Right") and the Mills Brothers ("Till Then"), but in essence it is not all that different in style. The smooth, jazzy-ballad vocal delivery caused Gant, and later singers such as Ivory Joe Hunter, Charles Brown, Jimmy Witherspoon, and Johnny Ace to be referred to as "Sepia Sinatras," in obvious reference to their crooning style.[3] The ballad style popularized by these and other artists remained an important vein of rhythm & blues into the 1990s.

In the pivotal year 1948, a number of rhythm & blues artists emerged with styles that would dominate the field for years to come. Ivory Joe Hunter's "Pretty Mama Blues" and Dinah Washington's "Am I Asking Too Much" were the first number-one hits for two artists who would become huge stars in R&B. Both of these performers are more polished than many R&B artists, often incorporating jazz and gospel vocal styles along with more complex harmony, slick arrangements, and bigger backup bands. However, it would not be completely accurate to label these performers "jazz singers." Even though their style is generally more sophisticated than that of most other rhythm & blues singers, it often exudes a more blues-influenced, rough-edged attitude and a greater degree of emotion than is typically found in jazz-vocal recordings of the period. Although the R&B charts during the late 1940s did sometimes include songs by "bona fide" jazz artists, as mentioned earlier, by the early 1950s these became the exception rather than the rule.

The influence of jazz singers of the 1940s on R&B is significant, with Nat "King" Cole, Ella Fitzgerald, and Billie Holiday being some of the most emulated. Vocalists such as Ivory Joe Hunter had a style very much like Cole's in the sense that he sang in a clear, generally soft tone, and with precise diction. Many of Hunter's singles exude an air of sophistication, as if one were listening to him in an upscale urban nightclub. Example 19 shows a short segment of one of Hunter's biggest hits, "I Almost Lost My Mind" (1950). Note that in

EXAMPLE 19. Ivory Joe Hunter, vocal on "I Almost Lost My Mind." CD track time 0:33–0:45. *I Almost Lost My Mind 1945/1950*, EPM CD 159992, 2001. Originally released in 1950.

the last line of verse one, the singer makes conspicuous use of neutral thirds of the V7 (D♭'s) and I (lowered G) chords. Earlier in the same verse, however, he uses scale thirds that are not significantly lowered, but very close to the Western scale norm. Since the song is basically a twelve-bar blues, one might expect the singer to make consistent use of neutral thirds in order to achieve a typical bluesy effect. In the earlier measures Hunter apparently is going for a somewhat more precise sound, one that perhaps implies a level of formal musical training. It is likely that this recording, even though it is performed in the crooning style Hunter was famous for, probably still sounded somewhat unpolished to the even more sophisticated jazz audience of the early 1950s, which was used to hearing the refined sounds of singers like Fitzgerald and Cole.[4]

As discussed earlier, the 1950s witnessed many R&B chart hits that reasonably can be labeled "blues" songs. Roy Brown's "Hard Luck Blues" (1950), Jimmie Nelson's " 'T' 99 Blues" (1951), John Lee Hooker's "I'm in the Mood" (1951), B.B. King's "3 O'clock Blues" (1952), and Willie Mabon's "I'm Mad" (1953) are representative of blues songs that reached number one on the R&B charts during this period. Most of these songs are more or less in the twelve-bar blues form; all utilize the blues scale to a large degree. It should be noted that as the decade of the 1950s wore on, songs in the slower twelve-bar blues style appeared less often at the top of the charts. This style appears to have been largely replaced on the charts by either jazz- or gospel-influenced slow songs that generally used more chord types. Music in this more sophisticated vein of rhythm & blues persisted throughout the 1960s and beyond, and its continued existence can be clearly traced in the data collected for this study.

The twelve-bar blues form did not disappear from the R&B charts in the mid-1950s. On the contrary, it emerged as one of the most important song forms of the decade. A style of R&B that emerged in the late 1940s and continued its popularity into the 1950s was that of the hard-hitting blues song with a medium or fast dance beat. Key artists in this style include Amos Milburn, Eddie Vinson, Roy Brown, and Wynonie Harris.[5] Many of the singles released by these artists have a style noticeably more raw than earlier R&B hits by Louis Jordan and others. By this I mean to say that the vocal parts often have a rough, gravelly texture, along with an emotional and declamatory style of delivery. The vocal approach popularized by these and other singers caused them to be called "shouters," for obvious reasons. Such recordings typically featured a small combo of musicians (no orchestra) and often a recording quality somewhat less technically advanced than might be heard, for example, in the recordings of Nat "King" Cole.[6]

Another important element often found in this style is a strong emphasis on beats two and four, making it possible for some scholars to suggest that these artists were the true creators of rock 'n' roll. There is at least a kernel of truth in such a suggestion, especially when one considers, for example, that songs such as "Good Rockin' Tonight," one of Wynonie Harris's biggest hits (1948), and "Hound Dog," by "Big Mama" Thornton (1953), were later covered by and became hits for Elvis Presley in 1954 and 1956, respectively. The shouter style led the way for the emergence in the mid-1950s of performers such as Chuck Berry and Little Richard, who were hailed as two of the creators of rock 'n' roll.[7] The raw and aggressive, backbeat-driven twelve-bar blues song designed for dancing was one of the most important stylistic innovations of the late 1940s and early 1950s; hence the inclusion of the phrase "blues with a beat" in the title of this chapter.

The instrumental equivalents of the vocal shouters of the period were the "honkers," saxophonists who played in a similar raw and aggressive style, generally with a very dirty tone. This style probably originated to a large degree with hard-driving swing saxophonists such as Illinois Jacquet, Earl Bostic, and also Louis Jordan (whose saxophone tone was, however, noticeably less dirty than that of some players). Two early songs in the style that had a big influence on its development were Hal Singer's "Corn Bread" (1948) and Cecil J. ("Big Jay") McNeely's "The Deacon's Hop" (1949). Eventually, the hard driving and harsh tenor saxophone became a staple in the R&B sound. The 1949 instrumental hit "The Hucklebuck," by Paul Williams, was hugely popular and influential as well, and featured a slightly less aggressive saxophone style. According to Shaw: "This song was significant as an R&B song and dance because it cut across color lines. It may well be the earliest instance of the crossover that became a pop phenomenon in the 1954–56 period and that spelled the end of R&B as a segregated music."[8]

By the 1950s the saxophone had become one of the key instruments in R&B, and a biting solo on the instrument almost seemed to be a prerequisite for any medium- or up-tempo dance song. Example 20 illustrates a segment of the tenor saxophone solo from Lloyd Price's 1952 hit "Lawdy Miss Clawdy." This was one of the biggest hits of the era—it was awarded *Billboard* R&B "record of the year"—and is representative of a lot of the music that was being created in New Orleans at the time. Note the blues system elements used by the saxophonist: blues scale (lowered third C♭ and lowered seventh G♭), triplet swing (12/8 time), and glissando.

Tonic: A♭

EXAMPLE 20. Saxophone solo on "Lawdy Miss Clawdy." CD track time 1:35–1:43. From *Lloyd Price Greatest Hits*, Curb CD D2-77305, 1990. Originally released in 1952.

Probably the biggest instrumental R&B hit of the 1950 s was "Honky-Tonk" (1956), a danceable blues song that featured the tenor saxophone of Clifford Scott, although the recording is credited to Bill Doggett, bandleader and keyboard player of the group.[9]

Music of Latin America also had a big impact on the rhythm & blues of the 1950s. A significant part of that influence came from New Orleans and was exemplified by the music of Antoine "Fats" Domino, the top R&B artist of the 1950s as calculated by Whitburn based on chart action.[10] Much of Domino's style was acquired from New Orleans pianist Henry Byrd, otherwise known as Professor Longhair. Although he was never much of a success on the record charts, Longhair took the elements of blues, boogie, and barrelhouse and united them in a new way with rhythmic elements of New Orleans and Caribbean music. His unique musical blends had a significant, long-term effect on the music of New Orleans, and therefore rhythm & blues and American popular music in general.[11] Of course, Longhair was not the first to create such blends. Latin rhythms had been used extensively in black popular music since at least the early twentieth century. However, his particular creations were probably the immediate inspiration for much of the R&B that came out of New Orleans in the 1950s.

Longhair's rendition of "Hey Little Girl" (1949) makes significant use of Latin rhythms (ex. 21). Note not only the habanera bass part, but also the rhythmic figure played by the drummer, which is often associated with a number of Latin American dances, particularly the beguine and rumba.[12] This last point highlights the fact that significant Latin elements had long been part of the musical currents of New Orleans, as is evidenced by the music of the Mardi Gras Indians.

EXAMPLE 21. Basic rhythm section groove as performed by Professor Longhair and band on "Hey Little Girl." CD track time 0:04–0:10. *Professor Longhair's New Orleans Piano*, Atlantic 7225-2, 1989. Recorded in New Orleans, Nov. 1949.

Latin American music also began to appear in R&B from other directions, notably from the music being created by artists on Atlantic Records, perhaps partly because of the large Latin population in New York City where the company was based. Some of these artists, and their hits are: Ruth Brown, "Mambo Baby" (1954); the Drifters with Clyde McPhatter as lead vocalist, "Honey Love" (1954), and also later Ben E. King with "There Goes My Baby" (1959); and Ray Charles with "What'd I Say, Part 1" (1959). The trend toward the production of Latin-inflected R&B continued well into the 1960s at Atlantic and elsewhere, during which time the Drifters in particular released many additional hits based more or less on the song formulas they used in the 1950s.[13] Example 22 shows the Latin-based musical style of "Honey Love," a number-one R&B hit for the Drifters in 1954, and one of the top twenty-five songs of the decade. It is evident in this segment of music that the drums and bass are playing patterns similar to those shown in the previous example, Professor Longhair's "Hey Little Girl" (ex. 21).

The musical style often called "doo-wop" was a highly visible segment of the rhythm & blues category in the 1950s, although the term "doo-wop" was not actually used to define that type of music until much later. Based to

EXAMPLE 22. Latin influence in 1950s R&B. The Drifters, "Honey Love." CD track time 0:19–0:25. *Atlantic Rhythm and Blues: 1947–1974*, Atlantic CD 82305-2, 1991. Originally released in 1954.

a large degree on the styles of earlier jazz-influenced vocal groups such as the Ink Spots and the Mills Brothers, doo-wop recording artists often began as neighborhood-based *a capella* vocal groups. To make the records more sellable, instruments were usually added to the songs in the recording studio. Some of the identifying features of the classic doo-wop style are: (1) group vocal harmony, with parts often ranging from a high tenor to a low bass, (2) use of vocables (nonsense syllables), such as the term "doo-wop" itself, (3) simple rhythms, melodies, and chords, (4) lyrics dealing with teenager love, (5) featured bass vocals parts, which often provided the most memorable part of a song (such as can be heard in "Don't You Know I Love You" by the Clovers, 1951), and (6) falsetto lead vocals.[14]

A powerful influence on the doo-wop groups was the black gospel vocal quartets of the 1940s and 1950s. Some of the most important of such gospel groups were the Soul Stirrers, the Dixie Hummingbirds, the Swan Silvertones, the Famous Blue Jay Singers, the Trumpeteers, the Golden Gate Quartet, the Five Blind Boys, the Fairfield Four, the Spirit of Memphis, and the Pilgrim Travelers.[15] The doo-wop groups borrowed various elements of style from such gospel groups, including three- or four-part harmony accompanying a vocal lead, featured bass parts and nonsense syllables, and a highly emotional style of presentation.

Significantly, doo-wop was often produced for a young audience, especially from the mid-1950s on. This is in contrast to many other rhythm & blues songs created during the 1950s, which often dealt with adult themes and sometimes included transparent double-entendre lyrics. A good example of such "adult" lyrics can be found in the song "Sixty-Minute Man" (1951) by the Dominoes (ex. 23), the second charted single by the group. It not only reached the top position on the *Billboard* R&B chart, but also rose to number seventeen on the popular music chart. The Dominoes eventually became a very influential and popular doo-wop group, singing primarily love songs, but their early success with "Sixty-Minute Man" was due, at least in part, to song lyrics with a very adult theme.[16]

Bridge:
There'll be fifteen minutes of kissin'.
Then you'll holler "Please don't stop."
There'll be fifteen minutes of teasin', and fifteen minutes of squeezin',
And fifteen minutes of blowin' my top.

EXAMPLE 23. "Double-entendre" lyrics in "Sixty-Minute Man." *Sixty Minute Men: Billy Ward and His Dominoes*, Rhino CD R2 71509, 1993. Originally released in 1951.

More typical of the general doo-wop style is "Don't You Know I Love You," the first charted single by the Clovers in 1951 (ex. 24). This was a very influential early release that contained most of the elements that defined the classical period of doo-wop a few years later. Note the use of nonsense lyrics and a featured bass part (measures 3 and 4), two hallmarks of music of this style. Also present are a saxophone part that answers the vocals (notated on the staff with the lower vocal parts) and a habanera- type bass part. The song is performed with a triplet-swing feel, a trait that eventually lost favor to a large degree in later doo-wop style periods.

A list of some of the most successful and influential doo-wop groups of the late 1940s and 1950s—along with important releases—includes: the

EXAMPLE 24. The Clovers, doo-wop style traits in "Don't You Know I Love You." CD track time 0:18–0:26. *Atlantic Rhythm and Blues: 1947–1974*, Atlantic CD 82305-2, 1991. Originally released in 1951.

Ravens, "Ol' Man River" (1948); the Orioles, "It's Too Soon to Know" (1948) and "Cryin' in the Chapel" (1953); the Dominoes, "Have Mercy Baby" (1952); the Clovers, "Don't You Know I Love You" (1951) and "Ting-A-Ling" (1952); the Five Royales, "Baby Don't Do It" (1953); the Drifters, "Money Honey" (1953), "Honey Love" (1954), "There Goes My Baby" (1959), and "Save the Last Dance for Me" (1960); the Charms, "Hearts of Stone" (1954); the Penguins, "Earth Angel" (1954); the Platters, "Only You" (1955), "The Great Pretender" (1955), and "Twilight Time" (1958); the Coasters, "Searchin'" (1957) and "Yakety Yak" (1958); the Silhouettes, "Get a Job" (1957–58); and the Flamingoes, "I Only Have Eyes for You" (1959).

A trend not often discussed, but significant nonetheless, is the dramatic rise in the number of songs by white artists on the R&B charts in the mid-1950s. No less than 37 percent of the number-one hits on the *Billboard* R&B charts in the years 1957 and 1958 were performed by white artists. Many of these songs were performed in a black musical style, such as Elvis Presley's

"All Shook Up" (1957) and the Elegants' "Little Star" (1958). Others, however, were performed by white artists with a decidedly country music bent, such as Jimmie Rodgers's "Honeycomb" (1957) and the Everly Brothers' "All I Have to Do Is Dream" (1958). Of course, one might argue that the placement of these songs atop the R&B charts simply indicates inconsistencies in data collection methodology by *Billboard* (a topic that was discussed in chapter 1). However, the fact remains that each of these songs was ranked number one, not only in sales, but also in R&B airplay during its run on the *Billboard* chart. One would therefore have to assume that they enjoyed significant airplay on black radio stations.

After 1958 the incidence of white artists at the top of the R&B charts declined dramatically, although there have been some exceptions.[17] On the strength of his R&B chart successes in the 1950s Elvis Presley is calculated by Whitburn to be the second biggest R&B artist of the decade, behind only Fats Domino. Perhaps one should not read too much into this particular chart information—especially because of the mass appeal of Presley during that time period—but it does suggest that there was, for a period of time in the 1950s, a shared acceptance of a body of musical styles by both white and black consumers. Not only were some white performers having success on the R&B charts, but also songs by black performers were showing up more and more on the popular music charts. In the book *Race, Rock, and Elvis*, Michael Bertrand looks at sociological issues that are related to the crossover of music discussed above.[18] He contends that rock 'n' roll (and therefore rhythm & blues) was a contributing factor in the success of the civil rights movement in the United States. I believe that Bertrand's suggestions have a lot of credibility, and the late 1950s integration of the music charts themselves may serve as partial proof.

One of the most important and long-lasting trends that emerged in 1950s R&B was the influence of gospel music. This phenomenon was mentioned above in the discussion of doo-wop, but the gospel musical style was influential in other, perhaps longer-lasting ways. In the mid- to late 1950s a direct link was formed between gospel and rhythm & blues, and the fusion had a profound impact on black music for much of the next twenty years. Of course, the influence of black church music on secular music goes back at least to the late nineteenth century, so I am not suggesting that any such connection is new to the 1950s. Many secular black performers, perhaps it is safe to say most, have in the past professed musical roots in the black church. The two most important figures in 1950s rhythm & blues who made significant use of the gospel music style were Ray Charles and Sam Cooke, and these artists led the way to what in the 1960s would be termed "soul" music.

Although there are earlier examples of gospel style in R&B songs by solo singers—particularly in the music of women performers such as Dinah Washington and Big Maybelle—the movement in that direction began in earnest with the recordings of Ray Charles. By 1955 Charles had already charted five top-ten R&B records, but his release in that year of "I Got a Woman" led the entire R&B field toward a style far more openly based on gospel music than previously heard. Following that single Charles, who recorded for Atlantic Records at the time, released several other gospel-tinged singles including "This Little Girl of Mine" (1955), "Hallelujah I Love Her So" (1956), and "What'd I Say" (1959).

Taking the gospel train into secular music was not necessarily a safe route, however. There had always been a philosophical separation of secular and church music in the black community. The co-opting of religious music for the popular market was usually considered wrong, even profane, by many people, including the secular artists themselves. As blues singer and guitarist Big Bill Broonzy once said about Ray Charles: "He's mixin' the blues with spirituals. That's wrong. . . . He's got a good voice, but it's a church voice. He should be singin' in the church."[19]

The gospel vocal style itself, as typified by Ray Charles, consists of a variety of features of the blues system, such as use of blues-scale notes, pitch bends, glissando, melisma, gravelly vocal style, and extreme vocal range (falsetto and full voice). Charles's rendition of "I Got a Woman" is in his "gospel-shouter" style (ex. 25): an extreme emotion exists in the performance (which cannot

* this pitch sung with exceptionally gravelly tone

EXAMPLE 25. Gospel-style vocal performance by Ray Charles in "I Got a Woman." CD track time 0:21–0:31. *Atlantic Rhythm and Blues: 1947–1974,* Atlantic CD 82305-2, 1991. Originally released in 1955.

be transcribed all that well to paper, it must be admitted). Additionally, the song is built on the sixteen-bar gospel song form discussed in chapter 2.

Sam Cooke also brought the gospel style to secular music, as even a brief comparison of his early gospel lead vocals with the Soul Stirrers to his later singing as a solo R&B artist bears out. Cooke's vocal style is less blues-influenced than Charles's, for the most part. He nevertheless exudes a definite gospel sound, complete with the melismatic turns and emotional delivery he was famous for as a gospel singer prior to his crossover into the secular music world. Cooke was a major force in the popularization of the gospel sound that grew into soul music.[20]

Example 26A–B shows a signature vocal riff that Cooke made famous. Example A is taken from the R&B hit "You Send Me" (1957), and example B is taken from a song titled "I Gave Up Everything to Follow Him," which was released as a gospel single (1953). This sort of melismatic passage was referred to by some singers as a "yodel." As R. H. Harris, leader of the Soul Stirrers, says about Cooke's yodel: "He made a change about '53 or '54. He made a change in the yodel. See the yodel is originally mine, but he perfected another sound and that's the thing that really made a difference between him and myself."[21]

EXAMPLE 26. Vocal riffs in Sam Cooke songs. (A) "You Send Me." CD track time 1:37–1:40. *Sam Cooke: Greatest Hits*, RCA CD 07863 67605-2, 1998. Originally released in 1957; (B) "I Gave Up Everything to Follow Him." CD track time 0:29–0:32. *The Soul Stirrers Featuring Sam Cooke, Paul Foster, and Julius Cheeks: Jesus Gave Me Water*, Specialty SPCD-7031-2, 1992. Recorded in 1953.

It is perhaps significant that in both of these examples Cooke uses the major seventh (F♯) of the scale, as opposed to the flatted seventh (F natural) that is a trait of the blues system. By using this pitch—and also because he *does not* use neutral thirds or fifths—Cooke's style begins to deviate from the well-established black vocal style of the period. In recording "You Send Me" Cooke also toned down his typical emotionalism significantly. Peter Guralnick calls Cooke "a great singer holding himself in check."[22] Cooke apparently found just the right formula; "You Send Me" reached number one on both the R&B and popular music charts in 1957.

TOP TWENTY-FIVE R&B SONGS OF THE 1950s

Tables 1 and 2 contain information about the top twenty-five R&B hits of the 1950s. Similar tables are later presented for each succeeding decade of music studied. Table 1 includes (1) song title, (2) date that the song first reached the number-one chart position, (3) artist, and (4) record label information. The information in this table is primarily for reference purposes and is included because it is sometimes necessary in the course of our discussion to refer to the artist, record label, and the date of the peak chart position of the songs.

Table 2 includes information collected from song transcriptions done for this study in a specific attempt to trace possible changes in the use of particular elements in R&B over the 1950–1999 time period. This table includes (1) song title, (2) tempo (in beats per minute, or b.p.m.), (3) chords (the number of different chord types used in the song), (4) incidence of the I chord as a percentage of the total measures of the song, (5) incidence of the IV chord, (6) incidence of the V chord, (7) incidence of other chords, (8) use of the twelve-bar blues progression ("yes," "no," or "partial"), (9) incidence of the cyclic form, (10) number of blues-scale notes used, and (11) use of triplet swing (listed as "3-swing" in the table). Specific methodology on how this data was collected is described in Appendix A.

Since this study largely investigates change over a course of years, the findings presented in table 2 serve largely as benchmarks by which to compare the data collected from later decades. However, some important tendencies are implied by even such a limited list of songs. For example, it is evident that the tempo remained fairly consistent for most songs in the group.[23] Only two of the songs listed showed a marked tendency to speed up: "Juke," a Chicago blues instrumental featuring Little Walter on harmonica, and "Honey Hush," a rollicking twelve-bar blues by shouter Joe Turner. Note that both songs are up-tempo to begin with. Based on my own performance experience, I would suggest that acceleration in songs of this sort is often done, consciously or unconsciously, to increase excitement as the song progresses.

TITLE	DATE	ARTIST	LABEL & NO.
Double Crossing Blues	3/4/50	Johnny Otis Quintette	Savoy 45-735
Pink Champagne	5/27/50	Joe Liggins and His Honeydrippers	Specialty 355
Teardrops from My Eyes	12/9/50	Ruth Brown	Atlantic 919
Black Night	3/3/51	Charles Brown and His Band	Aladdin 45-3076
Sixty-Minute Man	6/30/51	The Dominoes	Federal 45-12022
Have Mercy Baby	6/14/52	The Dominoes	Federal 45-12068
Juke	9/27/52	Little Walter and His Night Cats	Checker 758
My Song	9/27/52	Johnny Ace with the Beale Streeters	Duke 102
I Don't Know	12/27/52	Willie Mabon and His Combo	Chess 1531
Shake a Hand	9/19/53	Faye Adams	Herald 416
Money Honey	11/21/53	Clyde McPhatter and The Drifters	Atlantic 45-1006
Honey Hush	12/5/53	Joe Turner and His Band	Atlantic 1001
The Things That I Used to Do	1/30/54	Guitar Slim and His Band	Specialty 482-45
You'll Never Walk Alone	3/27/54	Roy Hamilton	Epic 9015
Honey Love	7/10/54	The Drifters Featuring Clyde McPhatter	Atlantic 1029
Hearts of Stone	11/27/54	The Charms	Deluxe 6062
Pledging My Love	2/12/55	Johnny Ace	Duke 136
Ain't It a Shame	6/11/55	Fats Domino	Imperial 5348
Maybelline	8/20/55	Chuck Berry and His Combo	Chess 1604
The Great Pretender	1/7/56	The Platters	Mercury 70753
I'm in Love Again	5/19/56	Fats Domino	Imperial 5386
Honky Tonk (Parts 1 & 2)	8/25/56	Bill Doggett	King 4950
Blueberry Hill	11/3/56	Fats Domino	Imperial 5407
Searchin'	6/10/57	The Coasters	Atco 6087
It's Just a Matter of Time	3/9/59	Brook Benton	Mercury 71394

TABLE 1. Top 25 rhythm & blues singles of the 1950s: artist and label information.

—Adapted from Joel Whitburn, *Top R&B Singles: 1942–1999* (Menomonee Falls, WI: Record Research Inc., 2000).

TITLE	TEMPO	CHORDS	I	IV	V	OTHER	12-BAR	CYCLE	SCALE	3-SWING
Double Crossing Blues	72	8	57%	16%	10%	16%	Y	0%	3	Y
Pink Champagne	98	4	57%	27%	12%	3%	Y	0%	3	Y
Teardrops from My Eyes	138	5	61%	17%	10%	13%	N	0%	3	Y
Black Night	65	8	50%	26%	18%	5%	Y	0%	3	Y
Sixty-Minute Man	130	8	29%	13%	25%	33%	N	15%	3	Y
Have Mercy Baby	143	3	67%	18%	15%	0%	Y	0%	3	Y
Juke	136-149	3	63%	24%	13%	0%	Y	0%	3	Y
My Song	66	6	31%	19%	18%	32%	N	52%	1	Y
I Don't Know	108	3	77%	17%	6%	0%	Y	0%	3	Y
Shake a Hand	66-76	3	45%	25%	30%	0%	N	0%	2	Y
Money Honey	126	3	72%	16%	12%	1%	Y	0%	3	Y
Honey Hush	162-174	3	66%	25%	8%	0%	Y	0%	3	Y
The Things That I Used to Do	64-67	3	55%	33%	10%	0%	Y	0%	3	Y
You'll Never Walk Alone	65-68	13	29%	17%	20%	34%	N	0%	1	N
Honey Love	157	4	44%	13%	36%	6%	N	0%	1	N
Hearts of Stone	153-148	3	52%	24%	24%	0%	N	0%	2	Y
Pledging My Love	54	6	46%	11%	20%	23%	N	0%	1	Y
Ain't It a Shame	120-123	3	53%	33%	14%	0%	P	0%	3	Y
Maybelline	118	3	79%	11%	11%	0%	Y	0%	3	Y
The Great Pretender	77	4	47%	31%	17%	4%	N	0%	1	Y
I'm in Love Again	120	3	61%	19%	19%	0%	P	15%	3	Y
Honky Tonk (Parts 1 & 2)	106-102	3	56%	33%	11%	0%	Y	0%	3	Y
Blueberry Hill	92-96	7	41%	21%	24%	15%	N	0%	2	Y
Searchin'	145-148	3	75%	13%	13%	0%	P	33%	3	Y
It's Just a Matter of Time	67	5	44%	38%	10%	8%	Y	0%	2	Y
Average	106	4.68	54%	22%	16%	8%	60%	5%	2.4	92%

TABLE 2. Top 25 rhythm & blues singles of the 1950s: song transcription data.

The average number of different chord types used in the top twenty-five rhythm & blues songs of the 1950s is 4.68. When one cross-references the number of chords used with the tempo of the song, an important conclusion can be made: *in general, the faster songs use far fewer different chord types than do the slow songs.* In fact, of the eleven songs in the table with tempos of 120 b.p.m. or greater, eight have only three different chords. Conversely, the nine songs that have a beginning tempo of less than 80 b.p.m. incorporate an average of over six different chords. One might be initially tempted to come to the conclusion that this information is patently obvious; fast songs use fewer chords because the tempo itself restricts the use of harmonic movement. Perhaps this hypothesis is true to a degree, but I see no reason that tempo alone should limit the amount of chords used in any piece of music. In bebop jazz, for example, use of a wide variety of complex harmonic structures at breakneck speed is not at all unusual. It seems much more likely that fewer chords are used in the faster R&B songs studied because complex harmony is not an essential element in the music, but rhythmic drive and a good dance feel are.

The song with by far the most chord types (thirteen) in the 1950s sample group is "You'll Never Walk Alone," and it is probably the least connected to the new blue music. The song is a Rodgers and Hammerstein composition from the musical *Carousel* (1945), and does not use any of the important elements of the blues system traced in this study: the twelve-bar blues form, the blues scale, the cyclic form, or triplet swing. The great success of the song is probably due in large part to the message contained in the lyrics, which could easily serve as an inspiration to American blacks struggling to gain civil rights in American society:

When you walk through a storm hold your head up high,
And don't be afraid of the dark . . .
Walk on, through the wind. Walk on, through the rain.
Though your dreams be tossed and blown, walk on.

EXAMPLE 27. Excerpt from "You'll Never Walk Alone." Roy Hamilton, lyrics by Oscar Hammerstein II. Epic 9015, 1954.

Incidence of the I, IV, V, and other chords is related to the number of chord types used. The emphasis on the I chord—the songs spend an average of 54 percent of their duration on the tonic—probably comes as little surprise. The fact that the IV chord is more prevalent than the V, on average, is more interesting and illuminating. To understand this phenomenon, the first thing one should realize is that in a twelve-bar blues form the IV chord typically (but not always, of course) occurs more than the V chord. Obviously this affects the chord ratios because 56 percent of the songs listed in table 2 use the twelve-bar blues form at least part of the time. The ratio of I to IV to V chords in the most common twelve-bar blues chord progression is roughly 8 to 3 to 1, and the percentages for those chords are 54, 22, and 16 percent, respectively. Additionally there is an inclination to avoid the V chord entirely in much blues-system music, as discussed in chapter 2. The data show that the top twenty-five R&B songs of the 1950s exhibit an overall tendency to use the I, IV, and V chords in amounts similar to those of the twelve-bar blues progression.

Table 2 shows little incidence of the cyclic form in the top twenty-five R&B hits of the 1950s, an important point for later comparison. The form *was* in use during the time period in question, but most songs incorporating this structural element simply did not rank in the top twenty-five of the decade. Perhaps the most well-known of all the hit songs of 1950s R&B built on a cyclic form with nonfunctional harmony is Bo Diddley's first charted single, "Bo Diddley" (1955). Significantly, the song remains on the I chord for 88 percent of the track time. The other 12 percent of the record's duration is primarily spent on the major chord built on the flatted seventh of the scale (there are also a few passing chords thrown in here and there). Bo Diddley avoids entirely the use of the V chord and, therefore, the major seventh of the scale. This important feature needs to be kept in mind as we investigate the music of the 1960s and 1970s in the next two chapters.

The use of blue notes in the group of songs discussed here averages about 2.4 on our scale.[24] This measurement is somewhat subjective but accurate enough for our purposes, and tells us that in the songs presented here the use of blue notes averages about midway between "moderate" and "marked." Cross-referencing the use of blue notes against song tempo is even more revealing: of the five songs with little or no incidence of blue notes, all but one are less than 80 b.p.m., and the nine songs on the list with a beginning tempo of less than 80 b.p.m. averaged 1.9 on the 1 to 3 scale of blue-note use, a figure that is somewhat lower than the overall average of 2.4. In other words, the slower songs in our 1950s sample group make noticeably less use of blue notes than do the faster songs.

The trait that appears most consistently is the triplet-swing feel, which is present in 92 percent of the songs studied. The only two songs that do not exhibit a pronounced triple-swing feel are "Honey Hush," a song built on Latin-derived rhythms, and "You'll Never Walk Alone," a slow song from a Broadway musical. Thus, one could conclude that the triplet-swing feel was an expected part of the musical style of much rhythm & blues in the 1950s. As we proceed chronologically through the music of each decade, we can determine whether or not triplet swing remains a significant factor in rhythm & blues in the 1960s and beyond.

CHAPTER FOUR

THE SOUL ERA: 1960–1969

The 1960s saw great acceptance of rhythm & blues by the American public in general. Although R&B in the 1950s had made substantial inroads into the mass market, it was its offspring rock 'n' roll that enjoyed much of the financial reward. However, in the 1960s rhythm & blues, often appearing under the name "soul" music, took the popular market by storm. The music had such mass appeal that in late 1963 *Billboard* discontinued its rhythm & blues chart for over one year, apparently because it was similar enough to the more general Hot 100 music chart as to be redundant (very likely reacting to the song rankings of the late 1950s and early 1960s).

However, beginning in early 1964 the British Invasion had a major effect on the Hot 100 music charts. In that year, for example, nine of the twenty-three number-one singles were by British artists such as the Beatles, Peter and Gordon, and the Animals.[1] The black record-buying public was not drawn to this music, however, and none of these records was able to earn a position on the R&B charts. Much of the early music of the British Invasion was derived from R&B and rockabilly styles of the mid-1950s, and by 1964 the musical tastes of black Americans had moved on.

Some rhythm & blues artists of the 1960s figured out how to create a brand of music that appealed to a wide range of buyers, both black and white. To turn such a trick, these black artists and their record labels had to straddle a musical fence or risk losing their black audience entirely. A few independent record labels were so dominant in R&B in the 1960s that they came to be thought of almost as majors. The Motown, Atlantic, and King record labels were all hugely successful during this period; they and their affiliates were responsible for an amazing 76 percent of the top twenty-five R&B singles of the decade. Of these three labels it has sometimes been suggested that Motown created the "whitest" sound, and that Atlantic, with its affiliation with Memphis' Stax Records, and King, with its mega-star James Brown, kept much closer to the core style of rhythm & blues.

There is little doubt that Motown had the greatest success of the three in the general market. The label's stars—including the Supremes, the Four Tops, the Temptations, Marvin Gaye, Stevie Wonder, and the Miracles—were consistently on the Hot 100 chart during the 1960s. However, some writers do not even consider the songs of Motown to be soul music but simply popular music performed by blacks that was aimed largely toward the white audience.[2] Such generalizations do not tell the whole story of the music produced at Motown, however. Although the songs produced by Atlantic and Stax often exude a highly emotional, southern-gospel-based sound, a number of soulful records were also created by Motown, including gospel-tinged hits such as the Marvelettes, "Please Mr. Postman" (1961); Martha and the Vandellas, "Heat Wave" (1963); Little Stevie Wonder, "Fingertips, Part 2" (1963) and "Uptight (Everything's Alright)" (1966); Marvin Gaye, "Pride and Joy" (1963); Junior Walker, "Shotgun" (1965); and Gladys Knight and the Pips, "I Heard It Through the Grapevine" (1967). The Motown label was not just a watered-down, crossover pop music phenomenon. It enjoyed tremendous success on the R&B charts as well. Of the top twenty-five rhythm & blues singles of the 1960s, twelve of them, or 48 percent, were produced by Motown Records. Such data clearly show that the music of Motown was accepted by the black record-buying audience and should not be dismissed out of hand as less than "soulful."

Some of the definitive hits of the era were produced in Memphis, at Stax. A few such releases are Sam and Dave, "Hold On, I'm Comin'" (1966) and "Soul Man" (1967); Eddie Floyd, "Knock on Wood" (1966); the Bar-Kays, "Soul Finger" (1967); and Otis Redding, "(Sittin' On) The Dock of the Bay" (1968). The Stax rhythm section during the height of the label's success in the 1960s included Booker T. Jones (keyboards), Steve Cropper (guitar), Donald "Duck" Dunn (bass), and Al Jackson, Jr. (drums), collectively known as Booker T. and the MG's. In addition to a string of instrumental hits on their own, such as

"Green Onions" (1962), "Hip Hug-Her" (1967), and "Time Is Tight" (1969), the four musicians created the basic soul groove for many of the hits on Stax in the 1960s.

MAJOR STYLES AND ARTISTS

Many of the important styles of R&B that were discussed in the previous chapter on the 1950s continued into the early 1960s. But a stylistic transformation began to occur during the 1964–1967 period. Doo-wop vocal groups of the 1960s enjoyed significant airplay and sales, especially from 1960 through 1964. The Marcels, a group whose career included only two charted rhythm & blues singles, were responsible for one of the most memorable doo-wop songs of any era in 1961 when they had a number-one hit with "Blue Moon." The Drifters garnered eight top-ten R&B singles during the early years of the decade, including some of their most memorable songs: "This Magic Moment" (1960), "Save the Last Dance for Me" (1960), "Up on the Roof" (1962), "On Broadway" (1963), and "Under the Boardwalk" (1964). The Drifters' success during these years is due in part to the group's continued use of the Latin-tinged style that had brought them major success in the 1950s. However, the Latin influence in R&B began to fade by the mid-1960s as the soul music movement gained strength.

As the decade wore on the older doo-wop styles began to wane in popularity, and by the mid-1960s a different type of vocal group emerged. The bass vocal part in doo-wop, as well as in many black gospel quartets, became less and less prominent due to the increased use of the electric bass guitar. This instrument had the advantages of volume and sustain over the acoustic bass, and soon took over the chord roots. This led to a fundamental change of roles in the vocal group. Even though a bass voice was typically still included in the group, that part usually did not have a unique solo-type character. In other words, the bass voice gradually began to act primarily as the lowest harmony voice of a more homogenized background vocal group that accompanied the lead vocalist.

Groups that incorporated this more modern vocal-group style became some of the most successful R&B acts of the 1960s and beyond: the Miracles, "Shop Around" (1960), "You've Really Got a Hold on Me" (1962), and "I Second That Emotion" (1967); the Impressions, "It's All Right" (1963), "People Get

Ready" (1965), "We're a Winner" (1968), and "Choice of Colors" (1969); the Temptations, "My Girl" (1965), "Get Ready" (1966), "Ain't Too Proud to Beg" (1966), "Beauty Is Only Skin Deep" (1966), and "(I Know) I'm Losing You" (1966); and the Four Tops, "I Can't Help Myself" (1965) and "Reach Out I'll Be There" (1966). White vocal groups also had success on the rhythm & blues charts, especially in the early part of the decade: the Four Seasons, "Sherry" and "Big Girls Don't Cry" (both no. 1 in 1962); and the Beach Boys, "Surfin' U.S.A." (no. 20 in 1963) and "Surfer Girl" (no. 18 in 1963).

Another significant trend in vocal music was the emergence of a large number of highly successful female groups of various sizes and configurations. In fact, it is possible to assert that these so-called "girl groups" were the leaders of the 1960s vocal group movement, because much of their success predates that of the male vocal groups mentioned above: the Shirelles, "Will You Love Me Tomorrow" (1960) and "Soldier Boy" (1962); the Marvelettes, "Please Mr. Postman" (1961) and "Don't Mess with Bill" (1966); the Crystals, "He's a Rebel" (1962) and "Da Doo Ron Ron (When He Walked Me Home)" (1963); the Chiffons, "He's So Fine" (1963) and "One Fine Day" (1963); the Ronettes, "Be My Baby" (1963); the Shangri-Las, "Leader of the Pack" (1964); and the Supremes, "Where Did Our Love Go" (1964), "Baby Love" (1964), "Stop! In the Name of Love" (1965), "Back in My Arms Again" (1965), "You Can't Hurry Love" (1966), "You Keep Me Hangin' On" (1966), "Love Is Here and Now You're Gone" (1967), and "Love Child" (1968). Another group that deserves mention is Gladys Knight and the Pips, whose lineup included a lead female vocalist (Gladys Knight) along with three male background vocalists. Their 1960s hits include: "Every Beat of My Heart" (1961), "I Heard It Through the Grapevine" (1967), "The Nitty Gritty" (1969), and "Friendship Train" (1969).

Of course, the 1960s also had their share of talented solo vocalists. However, the polished vocal style that was the hallmark of 1950s singers such as Nat "King" Cole, Charles Brown, and Ivory Joe Hunter lost considerable ground in the 1960s to the emotion-filled gospel styles which had been championed by Sam Cooke and Ray Charles in the 1950s (both of whom had continued success in the 1960s). Although there are many exceptions, it can be reasonably stated that the preferred vocal style for slower songs in 1960s R&B is basically that which had come to be known as "soul." Example 28A–B illustrates the differences between a segment of Ray Charles's version of "I Can't Stop Loving You" and an earlier version recorded by country music artist

* this pitch sung with exceptionally gravelly tone

EXAMPLE 28. Comparison of vocal styles in two versions of "I Can't Stop Loving You." (A) CD track time 1:24–1:37. Ray Charles, *Modern Sounds in Country and Western Music*, Rhino CD R2 70099, 1988. Originally released in 1962; (B) CD track time 1:32–1:43. Don Gibson, *Don Gibson: RCA Country Legends*, Buddah/RCA CD 74465 99791 2, 2001. Originally released in 1958.

Don Gibson, the writer of the song. Several observable features in the Ray Charles rendition give the recording its gospel-soul tinge: (1) use of melisma; (2) use of blues-scale neutral thirds (lowered A); (3) high tessitura (both examples are shown in original key); and (4) extremely gravelly vocal style (indicated in the example by the use of an asterisk). The vocal yodel (or cry) in Charles's version on the word "has" is a characteristic musical effect that the artist uses often in this and many other songs.

The vocal style of Otis Redding epitomizes the power of gut-wrenching emotion in soul music. In fact, Redding's vocal performances are sometimes so emotion-filled that it is possible to surmise that this trait caused him to have less success in the general market than would have otherwise been the case. The lone number-one song of his career, "(Sittin' On) The Dock of the Bay" (1968), was recorded three days before his death and reached the top spot on both the R&B and Hot 100 charts. That song was at the time considered more "pop" than many of Redding's other releases to date.[3] Until the time of "Dock of the Bay," only five songs, out of twenty-one releases on Volt and Stax by Redding, had become top-ten R&B hits. Example 29 shows Redding's vocal style in his first single release, "These Arms of Mine" (1963). Note the variety of effects the artist uses in even this short passage: (1) melisma, (2) use of blues-scale neutral thirds (lowered D), (3) exceptionally gravelly tone, and (4) ambiguity of rhythm.

This single rose only to number twenty on the R&B chart and eighty-five on the Hot 100. In the record industry such results do not constitute

* this pitch sung with exceptionally gravelly tone

EXAMPLE 29. Vocal style of Otis Redding on "These Arms of Mine." CD track time 1:42–1:52. *The Complete Stax/Volt Singles 1959–1968*, vol. 2. Atlantic CD 82218-2, 1991. Originally released in 1963.

an extremely successful outing. Perhaps the record buyers were not quite prepared for Redding in 1963, but in 1965 he earned a number-two rhythm & blues single with "I've Been Loving You Too Long (To Stop Now)," a song stylistically similar to "These Arms of Mine." Regardless of chart success, Otis Redding was a very influential performer and in many ways the heart and soul of the Stax record label. In the words of Jim Stewart, co-owner of Stax, "The day Otis Redding died that took a lot out of me. I was never the same person. The company was never the same to me after that. Something was taken out and never replaced. The man was a walking inspiration. He had that effect on everyone around him."[4]

The list of 1960s solo R&B vocalists who performed in the soul music style is seemingly endless. No attempt will be made to discuss all of them here, but a few of the most significant should be mentioned. Any such listing has to begin with the "Godfather of Soul," James Brown. This artist's musical accomplishments are so great that a separate discussion is presented later about him. Besides James Brown, Ray Charles, Otis Redding, and Sam Cooke, the most successful and influential solo soul music artists of the decade (and some of their hits) are as follows: Marvin Gaye, "Pride and Joy" (1963), "I'll Be Doggone" (1965), "Ain't That Peculiar" (1965), "Ain't Nothing Like the Real Thing" (1968), and "I Heard It Through the Grapevine" (1968); Aretha Franklin, "I Never Loved a Man (The Way I Love You)" (1967), "Respect" (1967), "Baby I Love You" (1967), and "Think" (1968); Bobby Bland, "That's the Way Love Is" (1963); Jackie Wilson, "Baby Workout" (1963) and "(Your Love Keeps Lifting Me) Higher And Higher" (1967); Wilson Pickett, "In the Midnight Hour" (1965), "634-5789" (1966), and "Land of 1000 Dances" (1966); and Stevie Wonder, "Fingertips, Part 2" (1963), "Uptight (Everything's Alright)" (1966), and "I Was Made to Love Her" (1967).

There are also examples of R&B songs during the 1960s that borrow more heavily from the sophisticated crooning style of the 1950s. A few such releases are Ruby and the Romantics, "Our Day Will Come" (1963); Barbara Lewis, "Hello Stranger" (1963); Lou Rawls, "Love Is a Hurtin' Thing" (1966); and Aaron Neville, "Tell It Like It Is" (1967). It could be argued that such songs from the 1960s are somewhat more impassioned than many of those by the 1950s crooners. Some even more sophisticated releases were produced by Scepter Records of their artist, Dionne Warwick, who was very successful in the broader record market despite the fact that she never had a song rise above the number-five position on the R&B charts during the 1960s. Songs of a romantic nature and with a polished style of delivery were also a part of the repertoire of the male vocal groups of the 1960s. Releases like the Miracles, "Ooo Baby Baby" (1965) and "Tracks of My Tears" (1965); and the Temptations, "My Girl" (1965), are representative of a large body of such hits.

An R&B phenomenon that must be mentioned in any discussion of the early 1960s is the dance craze spawned by the song "The Twist." During the first few years of the decade this dance came to be accepted by Americans young or old, black or white, and rich or poor, and its most visible performer, Chubby Checker, became a household name. One of reasons the Twist became such a huge success was the TV exposure it gained, especially on the teenage dance show *American Bandstand*. The song titled "The Twist," which was written and originally recorded in 1959 by Hank Ballard and the Midnighters, became a number-two R&B hit for Chubby Checker in 1960. In late 1961 the song was re-released, and by early 1962 it had risen to number four on the *Billboard* rhythm & blues chart.[5] There were numerous other songs that capitalized on the popularity of the dance craze, such as: Chubby Checker, "Let's Twist Again" (1961); Joey Dee and the Starlighters, "Peppermint Twist, Part 1" (1961); Sam Cooke, "Twistin' the Night Away" (1962); and the Isley Brothers, "Twist and Shout" (1962).

Of course, the Twist was just another in a long line of African-American dances to enter the consciousness of the American public at large. Earlier examples, some dating back to at least the late nineteenth century, include Snake Hips, Cakewalk, Black Bottom, Shimmy, Camel Walk, Skate, Horse, Madison, Charleston, and others.[6] Based in part on early African-American slave dances, the Twist included body movements that a person of high moral character or upbringing supposedly would consider suggestive and lewd.[7] However, by 1962 the rich and famous were twisting along with (though not necessarily side-by-side) the poorest black ghetto-dweller.

No artist in rhythm & blues was more successful or influential in the 1960s than James Brown. According to Whitburn's calculations based on chart data, Brown far outdistanced his nearest competitor, Ray Charles, in the 1960s R&B market.[8] But it was not sheer commercial acceptance that caused Brown to become known by such epithets as "The Godfather of Soul," "Soul Brother Number One," "The Hardest Working Man in Show Business," and "Mr. Superbad." James Brown was a hero to the black community in that he embodied the move upward that black America in general was trying to make. Brown had pulled himself up from as poor and disenfranchised an upbringing as one could imagine, to the point of becoming rich, successful, and powerful enough to advise the vice-president of the United States.[9] Most importantly, Brown never compromised his music for the white audience. His music eventually gained great popularity in the general popular music audience, but this success was strictly on Brown's own terms.

In the 1950s James Brown had been what some writers have called a "cry singer." Such a moniker was reserved for those artists who incorporated an extremely emotional, crying style into their vocal performances, and who often specialized in slow tearjerker types of songs. One of the best-known examples of this style is the Johnnie Ray song "Cry," which soared to number one on both the R&B and pop charts in 1952. Brown's first big hit, "Please, Please, Please" (1956), was in this style, as was his second, "Try Me" (1958). He continued to use this technique on slow songs over the years and had some success with "Bewildered" (number eight in 1961), "Lost Someone" (number two in 1962), and "It's a Man's Man's Man's World" (number one in 1966).

In the early 1960s James Brown hit his stride when he began to create medium-to-fast, dance-oriented songs such as: "Think" (1960), "Night Train" (1962), "Shout and Shimmy" (1962), and "Out of Sight" (1964). He was also responsible for the hit "(Do the) Mashed Potatoes, Part 1" (1960), which is credited to his drummer at the time, Nat Kendrick. The song was recorded by the James Brown backup band with Brown himself playing piano.[10] All of the songs mentioned above were important in the development of Brown's rhythmic and harmonic style. However, the very bedrock of rhythm & blues, and American popular music in general, began to shake when in 1965 James Brown released his seminal hit, "Papa's Got a Brand New Bag, Part 1." Probably no other song in 1960s rhythm & blues had such a great influence on musicians and popular music in general.

"Papa's Got a Brand New Bag, Part 1," and also the flip side of the record, "Papa's Got a Brand New Bag, Part 2," quickly emerged as the philosophical cornerstone for an entirely new style of music. In Brown's own words:

> The song started out as a vamp we did during the stage show. There was a little instrumental riff and I hollered: "Papa's got a bag of his own!" . . .
>
> It's hard to describe what I was going for; the song has gospel feel, but it's put together out of jazz licks . . .
>
> . . . I had discovered that my strength was not in the horns, it was in the rhythm. I was hearing everything, even the guitars, like they were drums. I had found out how to make it happen . . . Later on they said it was the beginning of funk. I just thought of it as where my music was going. The title told it all: I had a new bag.[11]

Brown's new bag was a mixture of blues and interlocking rhythmic figures that basically showed the way to a whole generation of R&B artists who wanted to interpret blues in a more modern way. Example 30 highlights the rhythmic nature of the song. Note that the rhythms played by the horns, guitar, bass, and drums are all different, yet complementary. The idea that each

EXAMPLE 30. Interlocking rhythmic parts in James Brown's "Papa's Got a Brand New Bag, Part 1." CD track time 0:01–0:09. *James Brown: Star Time*, Polydor CD 849 110-2. Originally released in 1965.

of these instruments could play a separate, often very simple part, yet collectively create a rhythmically complex sound, was somewhat new in R&B.

After the success of "Papa," Brown and other artists who were trying to adopt this new style began to think more and more in terms of creating a unified rhythmic structure comprised of several simpler individual parts. While the rhythms of James Brown's music do not match those of regions of West Africa and the Caribbean for sheer rhythmic complexity, he does seem to be following some of the same basic rules of that music, including the use of dense, overlapping and interlocking rhythms in a setting of limited harmonic functionality in the Western music sense. It should also be pointed out that overlaid above the rhythmic soup described above (and exemplified by ex. 30) was one of the grittiest blues-and-gospel-laced vocals in R&B, and it is the combination of all of these elements that was responsible for the new funk style.

The form of "Papa" is very important to an understanding of the great influence the song had not only on rhythm & blues but on popular music in general. The verses of the song are in a twelve-bar blues form, which Brown had used to good effect in earlier songs such as "Night Train" and "Out of Sight." Significantly, however, the song also includes an eight-bar bridge section that remains on the I chord throughout its duration. Along with this cessation of harmonic movement are one-bar riffs in the horns, bass, and guitar parts, making the whole section a textbook example of the cyclic form. "Papa's Got a Brand New Bag, Part 2," the flip side of the single release, uses the cyclic form for its entire duration. The "jam" on "Papa, Part 2," featuring Maceo Parker's funky tenor sax, would naturally have been heard on the air when disc jockeys flipped the disc over. Example 31 illustrates a portion of Parker's saxophone improvisation on the song. The transcription reveals that the note selection is entirely within the blues scale discussed previously, along with the added "extension notes." The question is: *Why would the blues scale be the preferred vehicle for solos of this sort, played over extended cyclic sections of R&B grooves?* The answer seems to be that when musicians performing in this style want to communicate a certain "deep-soul feeling," the blues scale is usually the language used to express it. Parker's "dirty" tone, like Brown's vocal timbre, is also part of the style and transmission of a desired feeling. The sax solo would have been something else entirely if Parker had used a "pretty" tone along with Western diatonic scales. It seems significant that "Papa's Got a Brand New Bag, Parts 1 & 2," as described here, presents together

EXAMPLE 31. Excerpt from Maceo Parker's saxophone solo on James Brown's "Papa's Got a Brand New Bag, Part 2." CD track time 2:08–2:38. *Foundations of Funk: A Brand New Bag, 1964–1969*, Polydor CD 31453 1165-2, 1996. Originally released in 1965.

on one record both the older twelve-bar blues model and the newer cyclic form–based groove-oriented jam.

It should be stated that as innovative as the music of James Brown and his band was, it did not spring forth out of nowhere. As was discussed in chapter 2, the blues system provides a large pool of musical style traits, or elements, and it is likely that antecedents can be identified for almost any American popular music song, style, or genre. "Papa's Got a Brand New Bag" provides a case in point. While there is general agreement among scholars that the song is one of the cornerstones of R&B from 1965 onward, it can be shown to rely heavily on earlier songs, for example, "Shotgun" (1965), a number-one single for Motown tenor sax screamer Junior Walker. As example 32 shows, "Shotgun" exhibits a style very similar to that of "Papa's Got a Brand New Bag"—but "Shotgun" was released more than five months earlier. The song uses the cyclic form for 99 percent of the track's duration, and it alternates between sections that feature a hard-edged, honking sax solo, and one with an equally rough-hewn, shouting vocal.

As important as "Papa's Got a Brand New Bag" was, a 1967 single by James Brown, "Cold Sweat, Part 1" (ex. 33), probably did more to clearly define the new funk style. The song incorporates many of the same blues-system elements that were evident in "Papa" but has an even more complex and dense rhythmic texture. Typical of much of Brown's music from the mid-1960s onward, "Cold Sweat" includes two guitar parts, one of which consists of a melodic riff, and the other which is simply a rhythmic pattern that is "scratched" across the strings (both riffs are two measures long). One

EXAMPLE 32. Four-bar excerpt from Junior Walker and the All Stars' "Shotgun." CD track time 0:04–0:12. *Hitsville U.S.A.: The Motown Singles Collection*, Motown CD 374636312-2, 1992. Originally released in 1965.

EXAMPLE 33. Early funk style in James Brown's "Cold Sweat, Part 1." CD track time 0:07–0:15. *Foundations of Funk: A Brand New Bag: 1964–1969*, Polydor CD 31453 1165-2, 1996. Originally released in 1967.

significant difference between "Papa" and "Cold Sweat" is the much more complex bass pattern in the latter. The trend toward ever more complex bass lines continued for several years in this and related styles. The offbeat phrasing of the bass part in this example makes for an especially intricate rhythmic pattern overall.

Another important feature of this song, and others created in this style, is the emphasis on beat one. Until this time period much popular blues-system music, notably jazz and 1950s R&B, emphasized beats two and four. James Brown related to me in a personal interview that he listened to earlier artists such as Louis Jordan and Nat "King" Cole, but, "I looked at these people, and I admired them and gave them a lot of respect, and I sang their songs. But, I knew I wasn't going nowhere . . . with two and four. So I changed it . . . and that's all I had to do."[12] Brown's idea to emphasize beat one (and to a lesser degree, beat three) does not seem to be particularly earth-shattering until one hears the results. To a modern ear it seems very normal to hear popular songs that accent the first beat of a measure, but in the context of the mid-1960s such a concept was much more radical.

Even Brown's band seems to have had some trouble understanding where the artist was going with "the one," as can be heard on the first take (a false start) of "Cold Sweat" on the CD set *Foundations of Funk*. At the end of track fourteen Brown sings the drum part to Clyde Stubblefield and specifically shows him that a "pop" goes on beat one.[13] James Brown explains how he shared his philosophy of "the one" with bassist Bootsy Collins, who joined the band in 1970: "I think Bootsy learned a lot from me. When I met him he was playing a lot of bass—the ifs, the ands, and the buts. But I got him to see the importance of the *one* in funk—the downbeat at the beginning of every bar. I got him to key in on the dynamic parts of the one instead of playing all around it. Then he could do all his other stuff in the right places—*after* the one."[14]

The rhythms of New Orleans street beats may have also fed the James Brown funk style.[15] One possible way that Brown was influenced by the New Orleans rhythms was from his drummer in the early 1960s, Clayton Fillyau, who had learned the New Orleans street beats from Huey "Piano" Smith's drummer and then added to them his own marching band experience. Fillyau brought this syncopated rhythmic mixture to Brown's band and was the drummer on the important recording *Live at the Apollo* (1962). Although he stayed with Brown only a few years, he shared his grooves with others, and some of Brown's later drummers followed in his style.[16] In fact, Clyde Stubblefield—one of Brown's most influential drummers—himself states that Fillyau "taught me the show," referring to James Brown's live act.[17]

Alfred "Pee Wee" Ellis, a key member of Brown's band during the mid-1960s, feels that there is more to the development of the James Brown funk style than can be explained solely by the influence of New Orleans beats. Ellis says that the "New Orleans beat" was already known to musicians by the mid-1960s, and that Clyde Stubblefield, one of Brown's drummers at the time, was a master at it. But Ellis also claims that the presence of the funk style in Brown's earlier song "I Got Money" (1962) proves that for Brown "the thing was always there."[18] In other words, one factor in the creation of Brown's music was personal innovation by the artist (a drummer himself), who had begun to develop a funky rhythmic style very early on.

In this new style Brown knew he had found something special, and he continued to pump out funk jam after funk jam for the rest of the decade and into the next. Many of the songs use similar techniques of form, being basically made up of one or two different sections of music that are in essence repeating cycles featuring interlocking riffs and little functional harmony in the Western sense. Some of the most successful of Brown's 1960s hits in this style are: "There Was a Time" (1968), "I Got the Feelin'" (1968), "Lickin' Stick" (1968), "Give It Up Or Turnit a Loose" (1969), "Mother Popcorn (You've Got to Have a Mother for Me)" (1969), and "Ain't It Funky Now, Part 1" (1969).

By the late 1960s the funk created by James Brown had become one of the most influential styles in R&B, and it inspired a number of other artists to create songs with such rhythmic complexity. Perhaps the most important of these artists is Sly & the Family Stone, a California-based band led by Sylvester "Sly Stone" Stewart. From 1968 until 1971 the brand of funky pop created by this group was one of the most popular and influential in all of R&B. Although the band borrowed from James Brown, it must be said that it also had a sound of its own, and it appealed to a huge audience. The first two hits by the group, "Dance to the Music" (number nine in 1968) and "Everyday People" (number one in 1969, R&B and Hot 100), both rely heavily on the cyclic form, and there is no Western functional harmony in either song. Their 1969 song, "I Want to Take You Higher," became an anthem at the Woodstock music festival, although the song was the flip side of a single that had "Stand" as the A side. This song also relies on the cyclic form for 100 percent of the track and makes use of both blues riffs and rhythmic emphasis on beat one. As we see in the next chapter, Sly & the Family Stone were one of the most important groups of the early 1970s, and perhaps as much as James Brown helped to bring great commercial acceptance to the funk-style cyclic-form jam.

Another important trend that emerged in the mid- to late 1960s—and would continue to have great impact in the 1970s and beyond—was the blurring of the distinction between major and minor modes. Although on the surface one might be tempted to explain such a technique as being similar to that used in European music—when one "borrows" a chord from the minor mode to use in a song in a major key—it is in reality an entirely different effect. The blurring of major and minor modes in blues-system music is related to the melodic ambiguity discussed previously in this book in the discussion about the blues mode. Specifically, the use of neutral thirds, flatted fifths, and flatted sevenths in blues-system music creates a situation in which a musician often plays a major triad, while the vocalist or instrumental soloist sings the lowered or fully flatted pitch. In the 1960s it seems that musicians began to make greater use of the minor mode (and minor chords), which in practice caused the melodic line and chords to match each other more closely.

I am not suggesting that this was necessarily a conscious decision, for there is little data to support such an assertion. However, there are many examples in the 1960s of a gradual tendency to blur the lines dividing the two modes. The two excerpts below, both of which are from number-one hit versions of the song "I Heard It Through the Grapevine," help to illustrate this effect (exs. 34 and 35). The first, by Gladys Knight and the Pips (1967), uses blues-system elements identified earlier in this book. The piano part incorporates the use of "bent" notes (see chapter 2) on the thirds of the I (E♭-E) and V (B♭-B) chord in order to achieve the ambiguity that is part of the blues system. Note also that the vocal part contains elements of the blues mode that one might expect to find: neutral thirds, flatted fifths, and glissando.

The second version of the song, performed by Marvin Gaye and released a little over one year after the Gladys Knight version, exhibits a somewhat similar vocal style, except that the thirds are not neutral, but actually flatted. This comes about as a result of the fact that the piano and bass parts are clearly

EXAMPLE 34. Gladys Knight and the Pips, "I Heard It Through the Grapevine." CD track time 0:09–0:15. *Hitsville U.S.A.*, Motown CD 374636312-2, 1992. Originally released in 1967.

EXAMPLE 35. Marvin Gaye, "I Heard It Through the Grapevine." CD track time 0:21–0:28. *Hitsville U.S.A.*, Motown CD 374636312-2, 1992. Originally released in 1968.

performed in a minor mode (E♭ minor in this case). There is not much in this section of the music to suggest any melodic/harmonic ambiguity. However, later in the same song one finds that the pianist, and also the string section, plays major I chords while the vocalist sings the melody in a particularly bluesy manner. Songs like this paved the way for a whole body of R&B songs in a minor mode in the next decade and beyond.

Social commentary in song lyrics also became a significant trend in the R&B of the 1960s, especially toward the end of the decade. The Impressions were some of the first and most important artists to deal with issues of civil rights and black pride in the lyrics of their songs. One of their earliest hits that incorporated such subject matter was "We're a Winner" (1968). The lyrics of that song include the phrases: "We just keep on pushing" and "We're movin' on up, movin' on up, lord have mercy, we're movin', movin' on up." Another important song that spoke about a similar subject is "Choice of Colors," a number-one hit in 1969 by the same group. The lyrics of "Choice of Colors" ask such probing questions as: "If you had a choice of colors, which one would you choose, my brothers?"; "How long have you hated your white teacher?"; and "Who told you you love your black preacher?"

James Brown was also an important leader in the creation of rhythm & blues songs with social commentary. Cynthia Rose explains:

[In 1965] . . . the former Malcolm Little [Malcolm X] was dead. And, during the next three years, as *U.S. News & World Report* noted on November 13, 1967, 101 major riots had occurred in US cities, killing 130 people and injuring 3,673. The damage would total $714.8 million. And King's assassination quickly upped the ante: more cities were paralyzed, more people hurt, more homes and businesses and communities destroyed. Meanwhile, the body count from Vietnam was increasing.

When Brown entered the studio in Los Angeles during summer '68, all these things were on his mind. So was the expanding charisma of America's young, ultra-macho Black Power figure-heads—celebrities who used black style to animate their romance of revolution. Brown cut "Say It Loud-I'm Black and I'm Proud" as *his* statement, his answer record to Stokely Carmichael and company: it was his demonstration that JAMES BROWN still spoke from the heart of black America, and for the street.[19]

Against the backdrop of so much turmoil in American society—and in an industry whose product generally consisted of love songs or dance songs created for a young audience—James Brown created an anthem that appealed to all generations of blacks to proudly proclaim their race. No song with racial lyrics as blunt and to the point as "Say It Loud" had ever before become such a huge hit, and its message reverberated in the black community. Within a few years such message songs became a significant part of the R&B market.

TOP TWENTY-FIVE R&B SONGS OF THE 1960s

Tables 3 and 4 include record release and label information and song transcription data collected for this study of the top twenty-five rhythm & blues songs of the 1960s. As shown in table 4, the average tempo of the top twenty-five songs in the 1960s is 116 b.p.m., an increase of 10 over the average calculated for the top hits of the 1950s. Although such an increase may seem rather small at first glance, it leads us to an important discovery: namely, that there is only one song in the 1960s list that has a tempo below 80 b.p.m., while the 1950s list includes *nine* songs below that threshold. Based on the songs studied, one can come to the conclusion that slow songs were not as popular in the 1960s as they were in the 1950s, and that the 1960s saw an increase in the popularity of faster dance songs. The number of different chord types used in the 1960s group averages 4.24 per song as compared to 4.68 in the 1950s. This represents a change perhaps not as significant as that observed in the average song tempo of the two decades. We see that the slowest song, "Tell It Like It Is," with a tempo of 63 b.p.m., also has the most chord types, eight.

The columns showing the average incidence of the I, IV, and V chords in the top R&B songs of the 1960s reveal that there was no change in the use of the I chord as compared to the 1950s. However, the table shows that there was a 3 percent increase in the use of the IV and a 4 percent decrease in

TITLE	DATE	ARTIST	LABEL & NO.
Baby (You've Got What It Takes)	2/8/60	Dinah Washington & Brook Benton	Mercury 71565
Kiddio	8/29/60	Brook Benton	Mercury 71652
He Will Break Your Heart	11/14/60	Jerry Butler	Vee-Jay 354
Shop Around	1/16/61	The Miracles	Tamla 54034
Tossin' and Turnin'	7/3/61	Bobby Lewis	Beltone 1002
Please Mr. Postman	11/13/61	The Marvelettes	Tamla 54046
I Can't Stop Loving You	5/26/62	Ray Charles	ABC-Para. 10330
Fingertips, Part 2	8/3/63	Little Stevie Wonder	Tamla 54080
My Girl	1/30/65	The Temptations	Gordy 7038
I Can't Help Myself	6/5/65	Four Tops	Motown 1076
Papa's Got a Brand New Bag, Part 1	8/14/65	James Brown and the Famous Flames	King 5999
I Got You (I Feel Good)	12/4/65	James Brown and the Famous Flames	King 6015
Uptight (Everything's Alright)	1/22/66	Stevie Wonder	Tamla 54124
634-5789 (Soulsville, U.S.A.)	3/12/66	Wilson Pickett	Atlantic 2320
Ain't Too Proud to Beg	6/25/66	The Temptations	Gordy 7054
Beauty Is Only Skin Deep	9/24/66	The Temptations	Gordy 7055
Tell It Like It Is	1/7/67	Aaron Neville	Par-lo 101
I Never Loved a Man (The Way I Love You)	3/25/67	Aretha Franklin	Atlantic 2386
Respect	5/20/67	Aretha Franklin	Atlantic 2403
Soul Man	10/14/67	Sam and Dave	Stax 231
I Heard It Through the Grapevine	12/2/67	Gladys Knight and the Pips	Soul 35039
Say It Loud—I'm Black and I'm Proud	10/5/68	James Brown	King 6187
I Heard It Through the Grapevine	12/14/68	Marvin Gaye	Tamla 54176
Too Busy Thinking about My Baby	6/7/69	Marvin Gaye	Tamla 54181
I Can't Get Next to You	10/4/69	The Temptations	Gordy 7093

TABLE 3. Top 25 rhythm & blues singles of the 1960s: artist and label information.

—Adapted from Joel Whitburn, *Top R&B Singles: 1942–1999* (Menomonee Falls, WI: Record Research Inc., 2000).

the incidence of the V chord. This seems to support the notion that the V chord, already used sparingly in many rhythm & blues songs, was threatening to disappear altogether. Note that the V chord, at 12 percent of the track time, is only 4 points higher than the "other" chords (8 percent).

A drastic change can be observed in the next category, use of the twelve-bar blues form. The data shows that only 12 percent of the songs in the table use the form to any degree. This is in stark contrast to the results shown in the corresponding table of 1950s songs, in which 60 percent of the songs used the twelve-bar blues form at least part of the time. Just as dramatic as the decrease in the twelve-bar blues form is the increase in the use of the cyclic form, which averages 33 percent of the track time on the 1960s songs analyzed, over six times more than in the 1950s songs (5 percent). When we compare the use of the twelve-bar blues form to that of the cyclic form, we might easily surmise that the latter began to replace the former during the 1960s. Songs using either of these forms often have a blues-based melody; one can therefore view the dominance of the cyclic form over the twelve-bar form in the 1960s as simply a different, perhaps more "modern" vehicle with which to express the blues. Interestingly, the incidence of use of blue notes is exactly the same, 2.4, in both the 1950s and 1960s songs, perhaps further supporting the statements offered above. It is also worth mentioning that the increase in the cyclic form and decrease in the use of the twelve-bar blues form challenges the notion of "progress" that some people view as proceeding from simple to complex.

The last column in table 4 shows the use of the triplet-swing feel in the 1960s songs studied. Here again a major change has taken place. Only 28 percent of the top twenty-five rhythm & blues songs of the 1960s exhibited a triplet-swing feel, as opposed to 92 percent in the 1950s. It is fair to say that triplet swing almost completely dominated 1950s R&B but became far less prevalent in the 1960s. What is perhaps even more revealing is that none of the songs on the chart that were hits from May 1967 or later had the triplet-swing feel. These statistics might have been predicted in light of the fact that funk music, which started to become popular toward the end of the decade, typically does not use a triplet-swing feel, but is more likely built upon a foundation of straight sixteenth notes.

Based on our data, it is apparent that some significant changes took place in rhythm & blues during the 1960s. The statistics on the cyclic form typify just how deep these changes really were. The songs on table 4 that were hits in the 1961 through 1965 period exhibit an average of 21 percent incidence of the cyclic form, while those from 1966 onward show a 43 percent use of the same structural element. Similarly, there is not one single song listed on the table after 1965 that uses the twelve-bar blues form. Thus, not only were there significant changes in R&B during the entire decade of the 1960s, but also it appears that the process was ongoing and perhaps even accelerating in the second half of the period.

TITLE	TEMPO	CHORDS	I	IV	V	OTHER	12-BAR	CYCLE	SCALE	3-SWING
Baby (You've Got What It Takes)	132	4	47%	33%	18%	2%	Y	0%	3	Y
Kiddio	110	5	59%	34%	4%	2%	N	45%	3	Y
He Will Break Your Heart	130	6	40%	11%	16%	33%	N	0%	1	N
Shop Around	130	4	43%	39%	10%	8%	N	18%	3	N
Tossin' and Turnin'	140	4	46%	32%	20%	3%	N	0%	2	N
Please Mr. Postman	121	4	27%	24%	23%	27%	N	0%	1	N
I Can't Stop Loving You	80	3	50%	28%	22%	0%	N	0%	3	Y
Fingertips, Part 2	142–145	2	51%	50%	0%	0%	N	99%	3	N
My Girl	102	6	50%	24%	10%	15%	N	50%	1	N
I Can't Help Myself	125–128	4	37%	10%	31%	21%	N	0%	1	N
Papa's Got a Brand New Bag, Part 1	128	3	72%	18%	10%	0%	Y	27%	3	N
I Got You (I Feel Good)	145	3	61%	27%	12%	0%	Y	13%	3	N
Uptight (Everything's Alright)	130–135	2	100%	0%	0%	0%	N	100%	3	N
634-5789	102	4	60%	18%	13%	3%	N	21%	3	Y
Ain't Too Proud to Beg	121	3	64%	29%	7%	0%	N	55%	2	N

TABLE 4. Top 25 rhythm & blues singles of the 1960s: song transcription data. (*Continued*)

TITLE	TEMPO	CHORDS	I	IV	V	OTHER	12-BAR	CYCLE	SCALE	3-SWING
Beauty Is Only Skin Deep	117–120	5	48%	27%	16%	9%	N	17%	1	Y
Tell It Like It Is	63	8	24%	5%	27%	44%	N	0%	1	Y
I Never Loved a Man (The Way I Love You)	91	4	41%	6%	30%	1%	N	23%	3	Y
Respect	110–113	5	28%	49%	20%	3%	N	19%	3	N
Soul Man	112	6	74%	5%	3%	18%	N	50%	3	N
I Heard It through the Grapevine	112	5	51%	41%	5%	4%	N	14%	3	N
Say It Loud—I'm Black and I'm Proud	112	2	73%	27%	0%	0%	N	100%	3	N
I Heard It through the Grapevine	113–116	5	65%	27%	5%	3%	N	35%	3	N
Too Busy Thinking about My Baby	115	4	60%	35%	6%	4%	N	69%	3	N
I Can't Get Next to You	108	5	82%	14%	1%	1%	N	61%	3	N
Average	116	4.24	54%	25%	12%	8%	12%	33%	2.4	28%

TABLE 4.

CHAPTER FIVE

FUNK AND DISCO REIGN: 1970-1979

The major stylistic shifts in rhythm & blues that began to occur in the second half of the 1960s continued in the 1970s. Not only did the decade see several important genres come to the forefront—funk, disco, and rap—but there was also a shift in the business of R&B, as major labels, such as CBS, Warner Brothers, RCA, and ABC, began to gain a greater foothold in the market. But Atlantic and Motown, independent labels that emerged as major players in R&B in the 1950s and 1960s respectively, continued to be the most successful and influential producers of rhythm & blues records. These two independent labels accounted for 44 percent of the top twenty-five R&B singles of the 1970s. This fact is especially impressive when one realizes that artists such as Wilson Pickett, Sam and Dave, the Four Tops, the Supremes, and the Temptations—who had been a big part of the success of the labels in the 1960s—had by the mid-1970s either moved to other labels, or were suffering dwindling radio airplay and record sales. Both Atlantic and Motown were able to thrive by keeping step with the changing times and musical tastes of the black record-buying public.

Stax Records also continued its string of successes in the first half of the decade with singles by artists such as Johnnie Taylor, Jean Knight, the Staple Singers, and Isaac Hayes. However, the label had severed its distribution deal with Atlantic in 1968 and in 1972 entered a new agreement with CBS. By 1973

Stax had begun a long, slow spiral toward bankruptcy. It has been rumored that CBS Records—a major label that began to build a huge presence in the R&B market during this period—may have precipitated the destruction of Stax by engaging the smaller company in business practices that it could not sustain financially. According to this interpretation of events, CBS desired to gain a bigger share of the rhythm & blues market, and so it commissioned the Harvard Business School to conduct a study that would help the record company realize its goals. Speculations have spread over the years that CBS took the information learned from that report and intentionally derailed the success of Stax.[1] However, Rob Bowman's research indicates that *The Harvard Report*, as the above-mentioned study is sometimes called, does not actually contain the predatory suggestions with which it is often credited. The report recommends that one possible course of action for CBS was to create its own soul music company and not to become affiliated with an existing company. Another stated strategy implies that CBS should acquire licensing for some already existing soul music product.[2] Regardless of how one might tend to view this turn of events, the fact remains that not long after their agreement with CBS, Stax found itself in serious financial trouble from which it never recovered.

For many people rhythm & blues "became" soul music in the 1960s. Since 1949 the terms "rhythm & blues" or "R&B" had been used in the titles of the *Billboard* black music charts. However, in 1969, apparently bowing to the name of the new style that had swept the field throughout the decade, the chart was renamed "Best Selling Soul Singles."[3] By the 1970s R&B had splintered into several somewhat distinct styles, some of which were quite far removed from the type of soul music created by Ray Charles and Sam Cooke. The precursors of these new styles can, of course, be found in the music of the 1960s. An analysis of the music of the early 1970s should begin with the most important artist of both the 1960s and the 1970s, James Brown.

MAJOR STYLES AND ARTISTS

Simply to say that James Brown was influential in the rhythm & blues of the 1960s and 1970s would be a gross understatement. As was stated in the last chapter, Brown, whose career began in the mid-1950s, was far and away the most successful R&B artist of the 1960s. Yet more impressive is the fact that, according to Whitburn's tabulations, Brown was even more dominant in the 1970s, and easily ranks as the top R&B artist in that decade as well.[4] James Brown was able to perform a feat to which most musical artists can only aspire: *to successfully change musical styles in order to appeal to a new generation of record buyers.* In the 1950s Brown specialized in emotion-draining songs, usually slow in tempo, which the artist would sing in a pleading manner. In the early 1960s he alternated between this "cry" style and the newer soul music style. However, by the mid-1960s Brown, more than any other artist, had made the move to a style called "funk."[5]

In the early 1970s Brown perfected the funk style (or one might say *his* version of it), and it quickly spread throughout the R&B field. A few of Brown's most successful and influential funk hits from the early 1970s are: "Get Up (I Feel Like Being a Sex Machine), Part 1" (1970); "Super Bad, Parts 1 & 2" (1970); "Soul Power, Part 1" (1971); "Hot Pants, Part 1 (She Got to Use What She Got to Get What She Wants)" (1971); "Make It Funky, Part 1" (1971); "Get on the Good Foot, Part 1" (1972); and "The Payback, Part 1" (1974).

Such songs helped to pave the way for a number of groups who added their own innovations to the James Brown sound. A few examples of such artists and important singles are War, "The World Is a Ghetto" (1972) and "Low Rider" (1975); The Ohio Players, "Funky Worm" (1973), "Fire" (1974), and "Love Rollercoaster" (1975); Kool & the Gang, "Jungle Boogie" (1973) and "Hollywood Swinging" (1974); Rufus, "Tell Me Something Good" (1974); AWB (Average White Band), "Pick Up the Pieces" (1974); KC and the Sunshine Band, "Get Down Tonight" (1975); Brothers Johnson, "Get the Funk Out Ma Face" (1976); and the Commodores, "Brick House" (1977) and "Too Hot Ta Trot" (1977). Other groups that emerged in the late 1970s and had continued success in the 1980s are: Brick, "Dazz" (1976); Slave, "Slide" (1977); and Cameo, "I Just Want to Be" (1979).

Four other groups deserve mention in the discussion of 1970s funk music, Earth, Wind & Fire; the Isley Brothers; Sly & the Family Stone (also discussed in the previous chapter); and Parliament/Funkadelic. Earth, Wind & Fire, whose musical style crossed many boundaries, was one of the most important funk groups of the 1970s, with hits such as "Shining Star" (1975), "Getaway" (1976), "Serpentine Fire" (1977), and "September" (1978). The music of Earth, Wind & Fire is discussed further later in this chapter in regard to the influence of jazz harmony on 1970s R&B. The Isley Brothers have been one of the longest-running acts in R&B history and rank ninth on the list of most successful acts 1942–1999 according to Whitburn. The Isleys are among the few R&B artists who can rightly claim to have been a part of the creation of funk, and their 1969 number-one hit, "It's Your Thing," an early masterpiece of the slow-funk style, is offered as proof of this assertion. The Isley Brothers' chart success began in 1962 with "Twist and Shout" and includes twenty-five top-ten R&B singles through 1997. I discuss both Sly & the Family Stone and Parliament/Funkadelic in more detail later in this chapter.

An illustration of the style of funk created by James Brown in the early 1970s, which influenced all of the artists discussed in the previous paragraph, is presented in example 36. One can see in the illustration that interplay between the various parts creates a rhythmically complex, interlocked effect. Such rhythmic interlocking is one of the primary components of the funk style in this period. Another rhythmic feature to note in this example is the individual complexity of the drum part played by John "Jab'O" Starks. As the funk style developed over the first few years of the 1970s, the drum parts became less and less complex. However, Starks's performance in the example shown has a relatively high level of rhythmic complexity due to the inclusion of ragtime-like eighth- and sixteenth-note figures and accented offbeats. Another feature to note in the same example is James Brown's use of notes without definite pitch in the lead vocal part. The use of spoken or shouted

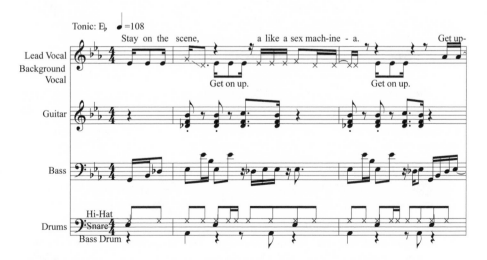

EXAMPLE 36. Funk style in James Brown's "Get Up (I Feel Like Being a Sex Machine), Part 1." CD track time 0:18–0:25. *Funk Power 1970: A Brand New Thing*, Polydor CD 31453 1684-2, 1996. Originally released in 1970.

words became a hallmark of Brown's style in the 1960s—for example, in "Say It Loud, I'm Black and I'm Proud" (1968)—and was important in the early development of rap music in the late 1970s. In fact, extended spoken sections of songs during the late 1960s and early 1970s, by James Brown, Isaac Hayes, Barry White, and others, were often called "raps."

The group Sly & the Family Stone was hugely influential not only in the R&B field but also in popular music in general. In many ways they were the group most responsible for bringing the funk style to the mass market. Sylvester "Sly Stone" Stewart put together an eclectic, racially mixed ensemble that included both male and female performers. Rickey Vincent describes the group and its influence:

> The impact of Sly Stone on *black* music was greater than anyone else from that era except for James Brown. Brown was identified with black folks *who would never be leaving the ghetto*, while Sly represented everyone else in the melting pot. It was much easier for studio musicians to imitate the infectious, upbeat innocence of Sly Stone's pop sounds than to try to capture the Godfather's serious race-conscious vibe. Following Sly's lead, dance music in the early seventies captured the soulful, funky polyrhythms and shouting riffs and shed the sixties soul sounds for good.
> ... Without Sly at the center, his lightweight imitators (such as the Jackson 5, Honey Cone, the Commodores, and Heatwave) could only imitate the loud colors, snappy dance steps over the choruses, and kicking funk licks. Yet everyone tried. The massive stage spectacles of Earth, Wind, & Fire, P-Funk, Michael Jackson, and Prince are all extensions of the glamorous, infectious, Sly Stone–united funk vibe.[6]

One point made by Vincent bears special discussion here: the statement that the music of James Brown would have been more difficult for a studio musician to play than that of Sly Stone because of Brown's more "race-conscious vibe." What the writer is apparently saying is that the music of James Brown was "blacker" and therefore less accessible to such musicians than the "pop" sounds of Sly Stone. There is some truth to this idea. Brown never made concessions to the white record-buying public. His personal musical style was built from the ground up by using elements long part of the African-American tradition, and he rarely wandered into the realm of mainstream popular music.

On the other hand, one should not get the impression that the music of Sly & the Family Stone is less authentic or that it was created strictly as commercial product. The band was highly innovative and arguably the most influential popular music group from 1968 through 1972. As Vincent suggests,

Sly moved the entire popular music field away from the soul music of the 1960s. The group led this movement toward a somewhat different style not only by creating new blends of elements that were already present in blues, rhythm & blues, gospel, and rock 'n' roll, but also through personal innovation. Sly & the Family Stone put their own stamp on funk music, as Example 37 shows. "Thank You (Falettinme Be Mice Elf Agin)" (1970) hit the number-one spot on both the R&B charts and the Hot 100, and it was for many people their first experience with a funk song that made use of the one-chord cyclic form. In fact, the song stays on the I chord for 100 percent of the track's duration. A less complex approach to drumming was typical of the brand of R&B created by Sly, and it had a great deal of influence on later funk groups, particularly Parliament/Funkadelic.

EXAMPLE 37. Funk style in "Thank You (Falettinme Be Mice Elf Agin)." CD track time 0:54–1:04. *Sly & the Family Stone: Greatest Hits*, Epic CD EK 30325, 1990. Originally released in 1970.

The bass part in "Thank You (Falettinme Be Mice Elf Agin)" includes slapped notes, a technique popularized by Sly & the Family Stone bassist Larry Graham. During the 1970s and 1980s this became an identifying feature of the funk style. Slapped bass is played in a variety of ways. In a November 2003 conversation, Nashville bassist Joe Murphy explained some of the techniques used to create the slapped-bass sound. These include: (1) striking the string with the thumb; (2) pulling the string with the thumb and one or more fingers away from the neck, with the resulting rebound causing the string to pop against the fretboard; and (3) using the open hand to literally slap the string. All of these techniques create a particularly loud and aggressive bass sound.[7]

No discussion of R&B in the 1970s could be complete without mentioning the contributions of George Clinton and his musical groups, which were variously named Parliament, Funkadelic, Parliament-Funkadelic, and P-Funk. The type of music created by bands under Clinton's sphere of influence was some of the most important in R&B from 1974 until the early 1980s. These groups started with the funk style created by Sly and James Brown and added elements of European music, electronic instruments, theatrical sets, and space-age stage outfits to build a style that continued to influence R&B well into the 1990s. The P-Funk entourage included conservatory-trained keyboardist Bernie Worrell and ex-members of the James Brown band Bootsy Collins, Phelps Collins, Maceo Parker, and Fred Wesley.[8]

Example 38 shows a portion of the P-Funk song, "Flashlight" a number-one R&B hit (number sixteen on the Hot 100 chart) for Parliament in 1978. We can identify a number of features in this section of music as traits of the blues system, such as the use of blue-note thirds (E♭s) and sevenths (B♭s) and offbeat phrasing. The formal structure of the song is built on a repeating two-chord cycle using the progression Cm7 to F7, as defined by the guitar and bass riffs. This is an example of the phenomenon described in the previous chapter in which the I chord is played as a minor, and replaces the C7 one might expect to find as the tonic chord in R&B from an earlier time period.

It is important at this point to further explain the minor mode used in this song, since the phenomenon appears more and more in R&B as time goes on. According to Western music standards, songs in C minor ("natural" minor) should have *three* flats, B♭, E♭, and A♭, written in the key signature. Here the As are not flat—yet the song still exhibits many characteristics of minor due to use of the ♭3 (E♭) and ♭7 (B♭). Because of this, many European music and jazz theorists would come to the conclusion that this song is in the *dorian mode*, a note set that includes the ♭3 and ♭7 of the scale, but not the ♭6.[9]

Making a distinction between natural minor and dorian is important because songs that incorporate the ♭3 and ♭7, but not the ♭6, are prevalent in much R&B of the 1970s onward; it would be misleading to indicate them as minor without some sort of explanation. So, where I indicate the tonic of these songs at the top of each musical example, I will also include in

EXAMPLE 38. Elements of funk style in "Flashlight." CD track time 0:30–0:40. *Parliament's Greatest Hits*, Casablanca CD 822 637-2, 1984. Originally released in 1978.

parentheses "minor," for songs that are in the natural minor (♭3, ♭6, and ♭7), or "dorian" for those that have the ♭3 and ♭7 present but not the ♭6. Use of the term dorian mode in this book is done with caution; I do not wish to imply that the musicians performing these songs would necessarily use such a term. However, many schooled jazz and R&B musicians are quite familiar with the dorian mode as a theoretical construct, and in fact this scale is taught extensively in jazz education.

A feature that does not appear in the transcription, but which is nevertheless present on the track, is triplet swing. This is a particularly significant inclusion in the song because the triplet-swing trait all but disappeared in R&B for much of the 1970s. In "Flashlight" the triplet swing is not found in the eighth notes as one might expect in much jazz, blues, or earlier R&B songs, *but in the sixteenth notes of the guitar, bass, and drum parts*. The eighth notes are noticeably *not* played with the triplet-swing feel. The fundamental shift from swing eighths to swing sixteenths occurs because the basic metronomic value of funk is the sixteenth note, not the eighth note as in many earlier styles of African-American music.

This was not the first time in the history of American popular music that the sixteenth note acted as the basic metronomic value, nor the first time such notes were played in triplet-swing style. For example, sixteenth-note triplet swing appears in Coleman Hawkins's famous 1939 version of "Body and Soul."[10] The song is played at a slow tempo, and the saxophonist's solo includes streams of triplet-swing sixteenth notes. In such cases the slower tempo increases the likelihood that a soloist will play sixteenth notes, thereby going into "double-time."

The implication of this phenomenon in the context of R&B of the 1970s is important because triplet-swing sixteenth notes became an important element in the R&B of the late 1980s and beyond. The 1969 recording of "Give It Up Or Turnit a Loose," by James Brown, presents one of the earliest examples of triplet-swing sixteenth notes in the funk style.[11] On that track one of the band's guitarists, Jimmy Nolen, plays a single-note figure with triplet swing in the sixteenth notes. However, the rest of the band plays straight sixteenths. One year later the band re-cut the song with all new members. The 1970 version of the song has triplet swing not only in the guitar part, but also in the bass and drum parts, giving the entire track a marked swing feel.[12] Figure 9A-B shows straight-sixteenth notes and a rough approximation of triplet-swing sixteenth notes.

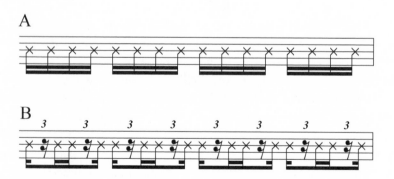

FIGURE 9. Comparison of straight and triplet-swing sixteenth notes.

Example 39 illustrates a phrase in the song "Tell Me Something Good" (1974), by the group Rufus. Although it is set to a tempo of 75 b.p.m., somewhat slow for the funk style, the rhythmic structure qualifies it as a funk song because of the implied sixteenth-note basis, offbeat phrasing, and interlocking parts. Other blues systems traits present in the song are the use of blue notes (lowered-third C and flatted-seventh G♭) and melisma.

EXAMPLE 39. Funk style in Rufus's "Tell Me Something Good." CD track time 0:25–0:35. *The Very Best of Rufus*, MCA CD MCAD-11543, 1996. Originally released in 1974.

Another important feature of "Tell Me Something Good" is the use of an electronic voice modification effect. Although the unique sound created in this manner is not illustrated in this example, it can be heard in the chorus of the song when one of the background vocalists answers the lead vocal with the phrase, "Tell me, tell me, tell me." The electronic sound effect is created when a vocalist sings a phrase while at the same time holding in his mouth a rubber tube that is connected to the driver of a loudspeaker. The loudspeaker in such a setup is driven by an amplifier that has an electric guitar, or another similar instrument, plugged into it. What occurs is that the sound of the guitar exits the loudspeaker driver, travels up the tube into the performer's mouth. The sound of the guitar and the voice are then "blended" by the performer who modifies the shape of the mouth, and thereby alters the timbre and envelope of the guitar sound. The resulting sound is an affected vocal that is metallic and "robotic."

The use of such an effect in this song is probably significant because over the course of the 1970s the use of electronics in rhythm & blues increased dramatically, adding new traits to the musical blends being created. "Tell Me Something Good" was one of the first hit songs in R&B to feature the electronic effect described above, but by the early 1980s use of this and other electronic sounds became widespread in R&B. Alan Stoker, Audio and Moving

Image Curator at the Country Music Hall of Fame and Museum in Nashville, Tennessee, explained to me that this particular effect had been used much earlier in country music.[13] One of the earliest recorded examples appears in the 1964 Pete Drake song "Forever."[14] In the 1970s the effect became popular enough for electronic musical instrument makers to create a marketable device—called the "talk box" or "talk bag"—that created the sound, without the need for a separate amplifier or loudspeaker.

In the early 1970s a wide variety of electronic instruments and effects began to be used in R&B, the above described "talk box" technique being just one. The "wah-wah" pedal also became a vehicle for the creation of new sounds in R&B. The wah-wah sound is created by means of a pedal that allows the user to quickly alternate the tone quality of a guitar (or whatever else might be plugged into the pedal) from an emphasis on treble frequencies to those in the bass register.[15]

The incorporation of keyboard synthesizers into the music was also widespread and significant. Probably because of the limitations of the instruments themselves, synthesizers were at first used primarily to create melodic lines. At that time synthesizers were not polyphonic, but able to play only one note at a time. The Mini Moog, introduced in 1971 by Robert Moog and probably the most important synthesizer of the era, was monophonic. Other popular keyboards of the time period were produced by Arp and E-mu. It was not until 1978 and the production of the Prophet 5 keyboard by Sequential Circuits that true synthesizer polyphony was available to the mass market. This keyboard, which became a standard piece of equipment for cutting-edge keyboardists of the time, also was programmable: it allowed the musicians to create sounds and save them to a computer memory chip inside the unit, a major advance in both ease of use and reliability in live performance.[16]

Stevie Wonder is one of the most important pioneers in the use of electronic keyboards in rhythm & blues and popular music in general. His album *Talking Book* (1972) stands as one of the first to make significant use of the synthesizer as an integral voice in the overall musical landscape.[17] Wonder's next album, *Innervisions* (1973), took the use of the synthesizer to still another level.[18] The song "Too High" from that album, which was not released as a single, makes use of the synthesizer as the bass instrument. The advantages of using a "keyboard bass" are that the musician is able to play more rapidly and with a greater range than on a standard electric bass. In addition, many synthesizers include a pitch-bend feature that allows the keyboardist to bend notes in performance. The use of the synthesizer as a bass voice, and later as a polyphonic instrument, continued in the 1970s and beyond. By the 1980s the widespread use of electronic instruments at times threatened the very existence of electric guitar, bass, and drums in R&B.

The Jackson 5, a Motown Records family group that was phenomenally successful, emerged on the R&B scene in 1969. The group had particular appeal to young people due in part to the youth of the performers themselves. Five of their first six singles reached number one on the R&B charts, and four of these also reached the top spot on the Hot 100. The group continued its success over the next several years with a total of fifteen top-ten R&B hits and eight top-ten pop hits between 1969 and 1974. In 1976 the group left Motown to sign with Epic (CBS) and at the same time changed its name to the Jacksons. In the meantime, the lead singer for most of the group's hit songs, Michael Jackson, had several releases on his own: "Got to Be There" (1971), "Rockin' Robin" (1972), and "Ben" (1972). Michael Jackson went out on his own for good in the late 1970s and in 1979 released the album *Off the Wall*, a multimillion seller. The influence of Michael Jackson on R&B and popular music in the 1980s is explored in the next chapter.

Social commentary in R&B gained significant ground in the 1970s, and probably had its greatest voice in the early part of the decade in the person of Marvin Gaye. His hits in this style made important statements about a variety of subjects and were popular not only on black radio stations but also on the Hot 100 reporting stations. The most important of these songs are: "What's Goin' On," "Mercy Mercy Me (The Ecology)," and "Inner City Blues (Make Me Wanna Holler)" (all 1971). The early 1970s was also the era of the so-called "blaxploitation" films, movies that featured black actors playing hero roles such as that of an inner city private detective (*Shaft*, 1971) or a sophisticated drug dealer (*Superfly*, 1972). Because these movies typically offered a look—although at times a somewhat slanted Hollywood version—into black life in the city, the musical soundtracks often included songs with lyrics about social injustice, inner city crime, and drugs. Curtis Mayfield created the soundtrack for the movie *Superfly* featuring two songs that became radio hits, "Freddie's Dead" and "Superfly."

In spite of the general move to a new style of dance-oriented R&B, as described earlier, there were many highly successful performers in the 1970s that can best be described as soul singers. Some of these performers had been R&B stars in the 1960s, and their careers simply carried over into the 1970s.

The most important of these artists and some of their biggest hits are Aretha Franklin, "Spanish Harlem" (1971), "Daydreaming" (1972), and "Until You Come Back to Me (That's What I'm Gonna Do)" (1973); Marvin Gaye, "Let's Get It On" (1973) and "Got to Give It Up, Part 1" (1977); Bobby Womack, "Woman's Gotta Have It" (1972) and "Lookin' for a Love" (1974); Stevie Wonder, "Superstition" (1972), "Living for the City" (1973), "Boogie On Reggae Woman" (1974), and "I Wish" (1976); Joe Simon, "The Power of Love" (1972); and Johnnie Taylor, "I Believe in You (You Believe in Me)" (1973). It is probably important to note that three of these artists—Aretha Franklin (number two), Stevie Wonder (number four), and Marvin Gaye (number seven)—rank in the top-ten of the most successful R&B artists in the 1942 to 1999 period, according to Whitburn's tabulations (rankings shown here in parentheses).[19] Such success is due in part to the ability of these performers to sustain their careers over a long period of time by keeping pace with the changing tastes of the record-buying public.

Other performers were new to the R&B field in the 1970s but more or less held to the soul music vocal aesthetic. Some members of this new generation of soul singers, and also some of those who were stars in the previous decade, combined soul-based vocals with pop dance-oriented instrumental tracks. This fusion helped lead the way to the disco movement later in the decade (discussed later). One of the first and most influential of such singers was Barry White, who had a string of hits that combined his soulful bass voice with an orchestra comprised of strings and horns. A few of his hits during this period are "I'm Gonna Love You Just a Little More Baby" (1973), "Can't Get Enough of Your Love, Babe" (1974), "You're the First, My Last, Everything" (1974), and "It's Ecstasy When You Lay Down Next to Me" (1977). White's lead was followed by Johnnie Taylor, "Disco Lady" (1976), and Lou Rawls, "You'll Never Find Another Love Like Mine" (1976). These two artists had been successful in the 1960s and were able to alter their styles to fit the 1970s dance scene.

In the last years of the 1960s and into the 1970s there was a resurgence of the sophisticated, jazzy vocal style that had lost some of its popularity in the 1960s. The trend quickly became nothing short of a phenomenon, and over time replaced to a great extent the 1960s soul-vocal style of artists such as Otis Redding and James Brown, particularly in songs with slower tempos. Of course, each singer brought his or her own individuality to the music, but in general this jazz-influenced style can be defined as being refined, relaxed, highly arranged, clean (as opposed to dirty), and urban. Many of the songs in this category contain lyrics about man/woman relationships, although the type of mistreatment handed out by the opposite sex that often serves as subject matter for blues songs would not be typical of the 1970s fare being discussed here. This is not to say that each and every measure of such songs fits this profile, but simply that the music of a number of artists exhibits these general characteristics.

A complete list of singers who had success in this late 1960s and early 1970s version of the "Sepia Sinatra" style would be long indeed. Some of the singers already discussed, such as Lou Rawls and Barry White, fit into this category due in large part to their polished, orchestrated musical arrangements. A few other artists who should also be mentioned are Isaac Hayes, "Walk on By" (1969) and "Never Can Say Goodbye" (1971); Bill Withers, "Ain't No Sunshine" (1971) and "Lean On Me" (1972); Roberta Flack, "The First Time Ever I Saw Your Face" (1972), "Killing Me Softly with His Song" (1973), and "Feel Like Makin' Love" (1974); Roberta Flack and Donny Hathaway, "Where Is the Love" (1972) and "The Closer I Get to You" (1978); Luther Ingram, "(If Loving You Is Wrong) I Don't Want to Be Right" (1972); Billy Paul, "Me and Mrs. Jones" (1972); George Benson, "This Masquerade" (1976) and "On Broadway" (1978); Teddy Pendergrass, "Close the Door" (1978) and "Turn Off the Lights" (1979); and Peabo Bryson, "Reaching for the Sky" (1978) and "I'm So Into You" (1978). As is shown in upcoming chapters, this style has been one of the most enduring in R&B.

One last singer should be mentioned in the discussion of 1970s solo R&B singers. From 1971 through 1975 Al Green was one of the most successful solo vocalists in rhythm & blues, and even a brief overview of the music of that time period must include mention of him. Green's music, although somewhat related in style to that of the artists mentioned in the previous paragraph, has elements that put him in a class by himself. His vocal style is more closely related to the gospel-based Otis Redding–style soul music than that of many other singers of his era. Green was able to create a unique personal style by combining emotion-drenched vocals with a variety of more up-to-date elements. He wrote many of own hit songs, which often featured chord progressions unusual in R&B at the time. These songs were recorded with a Memphis-based rhythm section and often featured the addition of string and horn sections. A few of Green's biggest hits of the 1970s are "Tired of Being Alone" (1971), "Let's Stay Together" (1971), "I'm Still in Love with You" (1972), "Livin' for You" (1973), and "L-O-V-E (Love)" (1975).

There was also a highly visible, and very successful, movement in the 1970s toward a smooth and sophisticated vocal-group style. Many of the biggest of hits in this style have elements in common with the early 1950s doo-wop style. As in doo-wop, many early 1970s vocal-group songs featured slow tempos and lyrics about love. The lack of a unique and identifiable bass vocal part in the R&B vocal group sound, however, shows that such artists also borrowed from the stylistic changes made by black vocal groups in the 1960s.

Example 40 illustrates the first few bars of the chorus of the 1971 hit "Have You Seen Her," by the Chi-Lites. The vocal structure presents a unified, homophonic sound, although the lead vocal is mixed somewhat louder on the record than the rest of the vocals. The general style shown in the example—including the slow tempo, often called a "ballad" in the parlance of R&B musicians—is typical of many vocal group hits from the period, including the Jackson 5, "I'll Be There" (1970); the Moments, "Love on a Two-Way Street" (1970); the Temptations, "Just My Imagination" (1971); the Persuaders, "Thin Line Between Love and Hate" (1971); the Chi-Lites, "Oh Girl" (1972); the Stylistics, "Betcha By Golly, Wow" (1972), "I'm Stone in Love with You" (1972), and "You Make Me Feel Brand New" (1974); Harold Melvin and the Blue Notes, "If You Don't Know Me by Now" (1972); Gladys Knight and the Pips, "Neither One of Us (Wants to Be the First to Say Goodbye)" (1973) and "Best Thing That Ever Happened to Me" (1974); and the Manhattans, "Kiss and Say Goodbye" (1978).

EXAMPLE 40. Group vocals in "Have You Seen Her." CD track time 1:23–1:31. *The Chi-Lites Greatest Hits*, Brunswick CD BRC 33002-2, 1998. Originally released in 1971.

Two distinct approaches to harmony dominated the 1970s R&B musical landscape. One of these, as we have seen in the songs that use the cyclic form, is the trend toward use of less complex or nonfunctional harmony in the Western sense. These songs, for example "Thank You (Falettinme Be Mice Elf

Agin)" (ex. 37), often make use of one or two chords only. However, another vein of R&B developed at about the same time which incorporated complex jazz-like harmonies. The group that best exemplifies this trend is Earth, Wind & Fire, an eight-to-ten member group led by singer/percussionist Maurice White. Example 41, of one five-measure section of music, contains twelve different chords,[20] some of which are themselves complex structures of thirds stacked up to the ninth degree of the scale. Such complex chords were used a great deal not only by Earth, Wind & Fire, but also by Stevie Wonder, as in "Living for the City" (1973), "Too High" (1973), and "All in Love Is Fair" (1973), and also by many of the "jazzy" vocalists—Isaac Hayes, Luther Ingram, George Benson, Teddy Pendergrass, and others—mentioned earlier.

EXAMPLE 41. Harmonic complexity in "After the Love Has Gone." CD track time 0:47–1:04. *Earth, Wind & Fire: The Definitive Collection.* Columbia CD 480544 9, 1995. Originally released in 1979.

The influence of jazz in the R&B market was not only manifested in the many R&B groups with a jazz flair. A number of highly successful groups and individual performers who could be labeled "jazz" artists regularly appeared on the R&B charts. Just a few of the musicians of the 1970s that might be considered part of this general category, along with the number of charted R&B singles they had in the 1970s (shown in parentheses), are the Crusaders (eleven), George Benson (ten), Grover Washington (six), and Stanley Turrentine (two). Another important jazz musician who had success in 1970s R&B was Herbie Hancock. His 1974 release, "Chameleon," rose to number eighteen on the rhythm & blues chart and was based in great measure on his desire to emulate the sound of Sly & the Family Stone: "I started thinking about Sly Stone and how much I loved his music and how funky 'Thank You For Letting Me Be Myself' [sic] is. . . . I knew I had to take this idea seriously. Would I like to have a funky band that played the kind of music Sly or someone like that was playing? My response was, 'Actually, yes.' "[21]

The trend in 1970s rhythm & blues that was most visible to the general public, and which had the broadest commercial appeal, was disco. This genre of music has been demonized by many writers over the years who point to its highly commercialized approach to dance music as destructive to rhythm & blues in general. Nelson George states that the emergence of disco in the mid- to late 1970s helped to "destroy R&B."[22] Discotheques themselves began in Europe and spread to the U.S. Earlier in the decade, a lot of the music one might have heard in an American disco was created by R&B artists such as the Ohio Players and Kool & the Gang. Many of the songs by such artists, having extended playing times and being built on riff-oriented cyclic forms, were perfect for dance clubs.

Also present early in the development of disco was CBS's Philadelphia International label. The sound created by the label's producers, Kenny Gamble and Leon Huff, became an important ingredient in R&B when they released a number of hits using a formula that included a rhythm section playing a generally funky dance beat, sometimes also incorporating a Latin-based rhythmic feel, along with an orchestra of strings and horns. The sound was similar to that created by Barry White and his Love Unlimited Orchestra, which had a number-one R&B hit in 1973 with "Love's Theme." Philadelphia International was particularly successful with an Ohio-based group, the O'Jays, who had a string of hits including "Back Stabbers" (1972), "Love Train" (1973), and "I Love Music, Part 1" (1975). In 1974 the label scored a number-one R&B hit with the instrumental song "TSOP (The Sound of Philadelphia)," by MFSB (the studio band at Philadelphia International). The song served as the theme for *Soul Train*, one of the most watched black music and dance programs on TV at the time. In 1975 Van McCoy's "The Hustle," a song that introduced a particular line-dance, hit number one on both the *Billboard* R&B and Hot 100 charts. The widespread success of the song signaled that disco had arrived as a major musical force.

Nelson George's hypothesis about the death of R&B includes the idea that the crossover potential in disco music caused many black artists to abandon the core R&B style in order to cash in. He cites statistics that show the huge success of Johnnie Taylor's "Disco Lady" (2.5 million copies sold), Chic's "Good Times" (5 million copies sold), and Michael Jackson's *Off the Wall* album (9 million copies sold). But, as George states, there existed a "feast-or-famine" syndrome in which the artists either struck gold, as in the examples listed above, or were almost totally unsuccessful.[23]

The disco music scene was responsible for the emergence of a number of solo and group female artists. These vocalists, held up as "divas" by many in the metropolitan gay communities who were attracted to the disco lifestyle and music, were visible symbols of the disco movement to many Americans. Just a few of these artists are LaBelle, "Lady Marmalade" (1974); Thelma Houston, "Don't Leave Me This Way" (1976); Donna Summer, "I Feel Love" (1977), "Last Dance" (1978), "Hot Stuff" (1979), and "Bad Girls" (1979); Gloria Gaynor, "I Will Survive" (1979); and Sister Sledge, "We Are Family" (1979).

By the late 1970s, disco had lost a lot of the funk edge that groups like Ohio Players and others had earlier brought to the genre. Often the music was built on a highly repetitive, inhumanly perfect beat with precious little other musical content. A group that helped define disco toward the end of its period of greatest popularity was the New York–based Chic, produced by Bernard Edwards and Nile Rodgers. The music created by this ensemble could perhaps be described as minimalist in nature due to its economical use of musical resources, often bordering on the simplistic. Edwards and Rodgers found a formula that was hugely successful and enjoyed phenomenal airplay and sales in both the R&B and broader popular market. Their biggest hits from the years 1977 through 1979 are "Dance, Dance, Dance (Yowsah, Yowsah, Yowsah)" (1977), "Le Freak" (1978), "I Want Your Love" (1979), and "Good Times" (1979).

The last few years of the 1970s saw the emergence of a genre that began as an underground style, most likely in the Bronx area of New York, became a national phenomenon due to a song that many people assumed was a novelty record, and has continued its popularity up through the 1990s and into the early 2000s. Despite predictions to the contrary, rap music has remained a vital force in American popular music for over twenty years. The exact beginnings of the genre are difficult to trace, but it is likely to have gotten off the ground at block parties and clubs in the Bronx in the mid-1970s with DJ Kool Herc, Afrika Bambaataa, and Grandmaster Flash, among others. These record deejays spun funk and disco records at parties and over time developed stage personas and raps in order to become more popular. After a while, the deejays themselves became the artists and the development of the genre began to pick up speed.[24]

Rap came to the popular music forefront in 1979 with the hit "Rapper's Delight" by the Sugarhill Gang (ex. 42). The single reached number four on the R&B chart and thirty-six on the Hot 100, and at the time the song seemed

EXAMPLE 42. Sugarhill Gang, "Rapper's Delight." CD track time 1:53–2:02. *Sugarhill Gang Hits,* Flashback CD R2 75956, 1999. Originally released in 1979.

to be omnipresent. Significantly, the music on this very first hit rap record was not original but was an almost exact copy of the song "Good Times," a hit for Chic earlier that year. The section of "Rapper's Delight" shown here illustrates the four-bar harmonic progression that is repeated for the entire length of the track. Other than this one hit, rap did not enjoy extensive success either in the general market or on the R&B charts in the 1970s. But in the 1980s and beyond, it became one of the most important genres in the R&B category.

TOP TWENTY-FIVE R&B SONGS OF THE 1970s

Tables 5 and 6 contain the data for the top twenty-five R&B songs of the 1970s. Table 6 illustrates that during the 1970s there were significant changes in the incidence of a number of the traits being investigated. On the other hand, some traits seem to show a marked resistance to change from the 1960s through the 1970s. The average tempo of the top twenty-five songs is 105 b.p.m. in the 1970s, a significant reduction from the average of 116 b.p.m. in the top songs of the 1960s. The body of songs analyzed seems to be large enough to gain some sense of a trend in tempo, and it should be pointed out that the average tempo of the 1970s group is almost exactly the same as that from the 1950s. In other words, the 1960s group, having a faster tempo by ten or eleven b.p.m. than the 1950s or 1970s songs, exhibits a significant spike in tempo as compared to other decades. Probably more important to our immediate discussion of the 1970s songs is the fact that the tempos are

TITLE	DATE	ARTIST	LABEL & NO.
Thank You (Falettinme Be Mice Elf Agin)	2/7/70	Sly & the Family Stone	Epic 10555
Love on a Two-Way Street	5/16/70	The Moments	Stang 5012
The Love You Save	6/20/70	The Jackson 5	Motown 1166
Signed, Sealed, Delivered I'm Yours	8/1/70	Stevie Wonder	Tamla 54196
I'll Be There	10/10/70	The Jackson 5	Motown 1171
What's Goin' On	3/27/71	Marvin Gaye	Tamla 54201
Mr. Big Stuff	7/3/71	Jean Knight	Stax 0088
Family Affair	12/4/71	Sly & the Family Stone	Epic 10805
Let's Stay Together	1/8/72	Al Green	Hi 2202
I'll Be Around	10/14/72	The Spinners	Atlantic 2904
Let's Get It On	8/18/73	Marvin Gaye	Tamla 54234
Feel Like Makin' Love	8/3/74	Roberta Flack	Atlantic 3025
Disco Lady	3/13/76	Johnnie Taylor	Columbia 10281
I Wish	1/15/77	Stevie Wonder	Tamla 54274
I've Got Love on My Mind	2/26/77	Natalie Cole	Capitol 4360
Got to Give It Up, Part 1	4/30/77	Marvin Gaye	Tamla 54280
Float On	8/13/77	The Floaters	ABC 12284
It's Ecstasy When You Lay Down Next to Me	10/1/77	Barry White	20th Cent. 2350
Serpentine Fire	11/19/77	Earth, Wind & Fire	Columbia 10625
Use Ta Be My Girl	5/27/78	The O'Jays	Philadelphia I. 3642
One Nation Under a Groove	9/30/78	Funkadelic	Warner 8618
Le Freak	12/2/78	Chic	Atlantic 3519
Ring My Bell	6/16/79	Anita Ward	Juana 3422
Good Times	7/28/79	Chic	Atlantic 3584
Don't Stop 'Til You Get Enough	9/8/79	Michael Jackson	Epic 50742

TABLE 5. Top 25 rhythm & blues singles of the 1970s: artist and label information.

much more bunched around one speed, 100 b.p.m., than in previous decades, a startling "sameness" of tempo. Of the twenty-five songs studied from that decade, only five have a beginning tempo outside the 80–120 b.p.m. range. Compare this to the number of songs outside that range in the 1960s, eleven out of twenty-five, and for the 1950s, eighteen out of twenty-five. Perhaps this phenomenon is due in part to the fact that songs in the funk genre are

TITLE	TEMPO	CHORDS	I	IV	V	OTHER	12-BAR	CYCLE	SCALE	3-SWING
Thank You (Falettinme Be Mice Elf Agin)	106	1	100%	0%	0%	0%	N	100%	3	N
Love on a Two-Way Street	70	9	29%	23%	18%	29%	N	18%	1	N
The Love You Save	113	7	16%	0%	8%	60%	N	0%	1	N
Signed, Sealed, Delivered I'm Yours	108	4	58%	15%	15%	11%	N	0%	3	N
I'll Be There	90	10	45%	9%	19%	27%	N	0%	2	N
What's Goin' On	98–102	6	21%	26%	23%	30%	N	0%	1	N
Mr. Big Stuff	91	5	47%	31%	19%	3%	N	94%	3	N
Family Affair	108	5	22%	38%	2%	37%	N	49%	3	N
Let's Stay Together	99	8	12%	9%	2%	77%	N	0%	2	N
I'll Be Around	110	2	55%	0%	0%	45%	N	75%	1	N
Let's Get It On	81	5	21%	30%	25%	23%	N	76%	3	N
Feel Like Makin' Love	94	9	9%	9%	9%	71%	N	0%	1	N
Disco Lady	102	5	90%	0%	0%	11%	N	90%	3	N
I Wish	106	6	45%	43%	5%	7%	N	54%	3	N
I've Got Love on My Mind	78	9	13%	15%	38%	30%	N	46%	2	Y
Got to Give It Up, Part 1	121	4	74%	11%	8%	6%	N	35%	3	N
Float On	94–98	2	50%	50%	0%	0%	N	100%	1	N
It's Ecstasy When You Lay Down Next to Me	102	6	63%	0%	23%	14%	N	35%	3	N
Serpentine Fire	140	7	91%	3%	2%	3%	N	74%	3	N
Use Ta Be My Girl	109–112	5	25%	28%	28%	19%	N	22%	3	N
One Nation Under a Groove	121	8	24%	61%	12%	4%	N	64%	3	N
Le Freak	120	3	50%	31%	0%	19%	N	100%	3	N
Ring My Bell	125	3	50%	25%	24%	0%	N	100%	3	N
Good Times	110	4	51%	50%	0%	0%	N	100%	3	N
Don't Stop 'Til You Get Enough	119	2	96%	0%	0%	0%	N	96%	2	N
Average	105	5.40	46%	20%	11%	21%	0%	53%	2.4	4%

TABLE 6. Top 25 rhythm & blues singles of the 1970s: song transcription data.

typically based on sixteenth notes (as explained earlier), and thus tempos in such songs are generally moderate.

The average number of chord types used in the 1970s songs studied was 5.40, a significant increase from 4.24 per song in the 1960s. This increase exists in spite of the fact that many of the songs in the 1970s group are in cyclic form and use a very limited number of chords. Thus, one can come to the conclusion that the remaining songs have a very significant increase in chord types over the previous decade. This fact can be observed in table 6, in which eight songs make use of seven or more chord types, a dramatic increase from the 1960s (which had only one such song). Many of the 1970s songs that exhibit a high number of different chord types are those of the jazz-influenced variety, such as "Feel Like Makin' Love," "I've Got Love on My Mind," and "Serpentine Fire."

There was also a shift in the incidence of the I, IV, V, and "other" chords in the 1970s songs investigated. The most striking change occurs in the use of the I chord, which fell from 54 percent in both the 1950s and 1960s, to 46 percent in the 1970s. The reduction in use of the tonic chord is balanced by an increase in the use of chords in the "other" category, implying an overall trend toward the use of more chord types, as was discussed above. The marked decrease in the use of the I chord is, however, also related to the disappearance entirely of the twelve-bar blues form in the 1970s songs analyzed. Along with the increase in chord types used in these songs, we can also observe that the incidence of the V chord has decreased, although only slightly (from 12 percent in the 1960s to 11 percent in the 1970s). The 1970s represent the first of the decades studied in which the incidence of the V chord has dropped below that of the "other" category.

In the 1970s the cyclic form became a major structural feature in R&B, as indicated in Table 6. As the table shows, the top twenty-five songs use the cyclic form for an average of 53 percent of the track time, a significant increase over the 33 percent figure for the 1960s songs. What is even more important is that the individual song data reveal that a number of songs rely almost entirely on the cyclic form for structure: *eleven songs in the 1970s group use the cyclic form for over 70 percent of the track time.* Compare this figure to that of the 1960s, in which only three songs extensively used the cyclic form. The cyclic form is used extensively in the funk and disco genres, and this is likely the reason that it emerged in this decade as a major structural feature.

The table indicates that the incidence of the use of blue notes, at 2.4 on a scale of 3, has remained unchanged from previous decades. The fact that blue-note use has remained constant, even through a change in rhythmic style, the use of electronics, and increased jazz influence in R&B suggests that this trait is part of the core style of rhythm & blues. Whether or not the use of blue notes continues in the 1980s and 1990s at such a level is explored in the next two chapters. In any case, the trait can at this point be considered an important and enduring feature of rhythm & blues for at least the 1950–1979 period.

The final feature to be discussed is triplet swing. Although there was a somewhat lengthy discussion of the topic offered earlier in this chapter concerning the emergence of sixteenth-note swing, the data in the table imply that triplet swing all but disappeared from R&B during the 1970s. In fact, the decline of triplet swing from the 1950s, through the 1960s and 1970s, is dramatic: 92 percent to 28 percent to 4 percent. Based on the data from the sample group, I conclude that eighth and sixteenth notes were not played in triplet swing style in a large portion of the successful R&B music created in the 1970s. However, it has been pointed out that sixteenth-note triplet swing was beginning to emerge (or re-emerge) during this period as an important feature, and its continued presence in the music of the 1980s is traced in the next chapter.

CHAPTER SIX

THE OLD AND THE NEW: 1980–1989

In many ways the 1980s were a transitional period in the development of rhythm & blues. The title of this chapter alludes to the fact that during the 1980s a number of older artists—many of whom had been popular as far back as the early 1960s—enjoyed continued success alongside a new generation of musicians. African-American music had made great strides from the 1950s through the 1970s in acceptance by the general population of the United States. In the 1980s this trend became even more conspicuous with the worldwide success of two black artists, Michael Jackson and Prince, who were the number-one and number-four American popular music artists of the 1980s.[1] Although these artists were the leaders in post-soul black popular music and were highly visible symbols of the era, a number of other artists began to develop styles that, toward the end of the decade, would change the musical landscape dramatically.

As the 1980s began, many of the independent labels that had been the most important sources of R&B in earlier decades either had been absorbed by larger concerns or were out of business entirely. Stax Records, the most important voice of southern soul music, had been forced into receivership in 1975. Syd Nathan's King Records, the label of superstar James Brown among others, was purchased in 1971 by Polydor, a European record conglomerate. In a series of corporate moves that began as far back as the mid-1960s and continued into the 1970s, Atlantic Records became part of the WEA music corporation. WEA is an acronym for Warner-Elektra-Atlantic music group, one of the largest music conglomerates in the world, and it included the Atlantic Group, Elektra Entertainment Group, Rhino Entertainment, Warner Bros. Records Inc., and Word Entertainment.[2] Over time, the Atlantic label began to produce more and more music outside the rhythm & blues category. Atlantic's emphasis on artists such as ABBA, the Bee Gees, Black Oak Arkansas, the J. Geils Band, and Led Zeppelin caused the company to lose its original focus on the music of African Americans. Perhaps predictably, no single by an Atlantic artist made the list of the top twenty-five R&B songs of the 1980s.

Motown Records, however, enjoyed tremendous success in the 1980s rhythm & blues market, as it had in the previous two decades. Motown and its subsidiaries were responsible for twelve of the top twenty-five singles of the decade. This level of success matches the phenomenal achievement of Motown in the 1960s and is an increase from the 1970s, when seven of the top twenty-five R&B songs were produced by the label. Many of the Motown artists who enjoyed success in the 1980s, such as Stevie Wonder, Smokey Robinson, and Diana Ross, were holdovers from the 1960s. Other 1980s Motown artists, including Rick James and Lionel Richie, had emerged in the 1970s, either as soloists or as group members, and continued their popularity in the 1980s. Motown was doing so well with these and other artists, such as DeBarge and Rockwell, that the label probably did not even suspect that the next decade would find it struggling to keep a viable roster of artists.

The so-called "major" labels continued to make serious inroads in the mainstream R&B market during the 1980s, a trend that had begun to accelerate in the 1970s. As mentioned above, the WEA group had already spread its umbrella over Atlantic Records. Warner Records, another subsidiary of WEA, was responsible for music by such artists as Ashford and Simpson, Atlantic Starr, George Benson, Prince, Rufus, and Karyn White. CBS continued to make progress during the 1980s in its bid to gain market share in African-American music sales. One of the label's biggest coups during this period was to sign Michael Jackson away from Motown and onto the company's Epic label. The result was a series of record-breaking, multimillion-selling albums by Jackson that ushered in a new era in music marketing. Marvin Gaye also left Motown and signed with Columbia, another CBS label.

It seemed for a time during the 1980s that big business might take over the R&B market entirely, and that the small entrepreneur might never again be able to produce records for the national market. Rap, originally an underground musical style, was the vehicle by which a number of small local and regional labels, often owned by black entrepreneurs, eventually took a significant portion of the music business back from the major labels. The rap genre is explored to a much greater extent later in this chapter. Three of the earliest labels to produce and distribute rap records in the late 1970s and early 1980s were Sugarhill, Def Jam, and Jive Records.

MAJOR STYLES AND ARTISTS

Some of the brightest stars in rhythm & blues in the 1980s were musicians who were able to continue the success they had enjoyed in the 1960s and 1970s. Eight of the top twenty-five artists of the 1980s had first charted an R&B single in the 1960s[3]—a significant increase from previous decades, when far fewer artists had the staying power to produce a significant number of hits in three consecutive decades. For example, there is just one such artist in the 1970s, James Brown.[4] Why this phenomenon occurred in the 1980s is open to speculation, of course. One possible cause is that when disco suffered its precipitous loss in popularity in the early 1980s, the artists who had remained loyal to the older soul- and funk-based styles became the recipients of the affection of the R&B record-buying public, specifically because they represented black music as it had been before the disco era.

The most successful of the artists to enjoy the career longevity described above, and their biggest singles from the 1980s, are Stevie Wonder, "Master Blaster" (1980), "That Girl" (1982), "I Just Called to Say I Love You" (1984), "Part-Time Lover" (1985), "That's What Friends Are For" (1985) (with Gladys Knight, Dionne Warwick, and Elton John), "Skeletons" (1987), and "You Will Know" (1988); Kool & the Gang, "Celebration" (1980), "Joanna" (1983), "Fresh" (1985), and "Cherish" (1985); the Isley Brothers, "Don't Say Goodnight (It's Time for Love), Parts 1 & 2" (1980) and "Caravan of Love" (1985); Smokey Robinson, "Being with You" (1981); Diana Ross, "Endless Love" (1981) and "Missing You" (1984); Aretha Franklin, "Jump to It" (1982), "Get It Right" (1983), and "Freeway of Love" (1985); and Gladys Knight & the Pips, "That's What Friends Are For" (1985) (same single listed above for Stevie Wonder) and "Love Overboard" (1987). Michael Jackson could also be included in the above list since the Jackson 5, the family group of which he was the lead singer, released their first single "I Want You Back" in late 1969 when Michael was just eleven years old. However, due to the level of Jackson's success and overall importance in the R&B of the 1980s, he is discussed separately. The Whispers, whose first single was released in 1969 and who enjoyed continued success well into the 1980s and beyond, are also to be dealt with later in a section concerning vocal groups.

By far the most popular and influential of the younger breed of solo R&B artists of the 1980s were Michael Jackson and Prince. Their level of success in the general popular music chart (Hot 100), as mentioned in the introduction to this chapter, is almost exactly reversed in the R&B chart, where Prince is calculated to be the number-one R&B artist and Michael Jackson the number-three artist of the 1980s. These tallies are based on Whitburn's method of calculation, which takes into account both airplay and sales of singles *but not album sales*, a significant point to keep in mind.

One of the most important factors in the rise to superstardom of Michael Jackson, and many other artists for that matter, was the emergence of the music video and MTV. Clearly, the release of Michael Jackson's *Thriller* album in 1982, and the subsequent release of a string of videos including those for the songs "Beat It" and "Thriller," changed the way American popular music was marketed. Due in part to the popularity of Jackson's music videos, the album sold an astounding forty million copies (yet the single "Thriller" would reach only the number-three position on the R&B chart).

The music of Michael Jackson is difficult to characterize, other than simply to say that the artist borrows elements from the broad spectrum of American popular music, including the blues system. Both as a member of the Jackson 5 and in his solo career, Jackson has offered an eclectic mix of musical styles ranging from smooth and sophisticated ballads, such as "Ben" (1972) and "She's Out of My Life" (1980), to pop-disco dance songs like "Don't Stop 'Til You Get Enough" (1979), "Beat It" (1983), and "Bad" (1987).

Jackson's biggest hit single, based on *Billboard* R&B chart success, is "Billie Jean" (1983), a song that remained at the number-one position for nine weeks. Example 43 shows measures three through six of the first verse of "Billie Jean." The song uses a minor (dorian) version of the twelve-bar blues form, with the V chord left out entirely (a iv chord is used in its place). This is the only top twenty-five R&B song of the 1980s which uses the twelve-bar blues form, and since it is in dorian mode, the flatted third (A natural) is present throughout. However, it is probably significant that Jackson does

EXAMPLE 43. Excerpt from "Billie Jean." CD track time 0:37–0:42. Michael Jackson, *Greatest Hits: HIStory*, vol. 1, Epic CD EK 85250, 1991. Originally released in 1983. Notehead shown with an asterisk (*) indicates a characteristic "hiccupping" vocal effect often used by the artist.

not give special emphasis to the blue notes in the melody, as indicated in the example. In fact, the second and fourth degrees (G♯ and B) of the scale generally are given more weight than the third. The seventh is absent from the vocal part in our example. The topic of minor modes and their use in 1980s rhythm & blues is further discussed later.

Prince, the stage name for Prince Rogers Nelson, arrived on the R&B scene in 1978 and had his first big hit with "I Wanna Be Your Lover" in 1979. Although the music created by Prince is often more "dangerous" than that of Jackson, due in part to the explicit or implicit sexual themes of the song lyrics, he nevertheless became a huge popular music icon. His string of top-five hits in the 1980s includes: "When Doves Cry" (1984), "Let's Go Crazy" (1984), "Purple Rain" (1984), "Raspberry Beret" (1985), "Kiss" (1986), "Sign O' the Times" (1987), and "Batdance" (1989).

Music videos were a significant factor in the success of Prince from mid-decade on. However, the artist also gained fame by starring in the movies *Purple Rain, Under the Cherry Moon*, and *Sign O' the Times*. The music popularized by Prince is, like the work of Michael Jackson, difficult to categorize due to his use of a wide variety of styles. Both of these artists exhibits stylistic traits, in both music and stage persona, which hearken back to those of earlier R&B stars such as Little Richard, James Brown, and Jackie Wilson. Despite any "sweetening" of the sound that Jackson and Prince may have employed in order to appeal to a wider popular market, the artists nevertheless retained a connection to the blues-system tradition.

A number of other solo artists achieved star status for the first time in the 1980s. Lionel Richie, former lead singer of the Commodores, was one of the most successful crossover R&B/popular music artists of the 1980s. His number-one R&B hits from that period include: "Endless Love" (duet with Diana Ross) (1981), "All Night Long (All Night)" (1983), "Hello" (1984), and "Say You, Say Me" (1985). For a time in the mid-1980s it seemed as if Richie was about to take the "king of pop" crown away from Michael Jackson. However, Richie's career began to fade significantly by the late 1980s.

Among the many female artists of the new generation who had success in 1980s rhythm & blues, two stand out for their consistent appeal in the black record market, Stephanie Mills and Janet Jackson. Although Mills is seldom mentioned as a "superstar," she was in fact the ninth most successful R&B artist of the decade according to Whitburn. Mills, who had played Dorothy in the Broadway version of *The Wiz*, had a big hit in 1980 with "Never Knew Love Like This Before," one of the last of the disco anthems. By the mid- to late 1980s she began to specialize more in the funk ballad, a style of slow song which typically uses the sixteenth note as its basic metronomic value. This style is closely related to, or one might say a part of, what is usually referred to as "quiet storm," to be examined later. Mills had a string of five number-one R&B hits from 1986 through 1989: "I Have Learned to Respect the Power of Love" (1986), "I Feel Good All Over" (1987), "(You're Puttin') A Rush on Me" (1987), "Something in the Way (You Make Me Feel)" (1989), and "Home" (1989).

Janet Jackson, sister of Michael Jackson and actress in the TV shows *Good Times, Different Strokes,* and *Fame,* became an R&B star in her own right in the 1980s. She does not rank in Whitburn's list of the top twenty-five R&B artists of the 1980s, probably due to the fact that Jackson released only thirteen singles in the decade. However, seven of these singles eventually reached the number-one spot on *Billboard*'s charts. Her 1986 album *Control* is important in the development of R&B for a number of reasons. The primary producers of *Control,* Jimmy Jam, Terry Lewis, and Jackson herself, crafted a new sound that fuses the rhythmic elements of funk and disco, along with heavy doses of synthesizers, percussion, sound effects, and a rap music sensibility. The tracks often feature cyclic form with limited harmonic movement. In addition, the production imparts a decidedly "metallic" or "industrial" sound caused by the inclusion of an assortment of sound effects reminiscent of some rap records released in the mid-1980s. Jackson's album was one of the first to create an identifiable bridge between rap and mainstream R&B.

The success of *Control* in the R&B and greater popular music market led to the incorporation of many of the stylistic traits of rap over the next few years, and Janet Jackson was to continue to be one of the leaders in that development. Five of the six singles released from *Control* reached number one on the *Billboard* R&B charts: "What Have You Done for Me Lately" (1986), "Nasty" (1986), "Control" (1986), "Let's Wait Awhile" (1987), and "The Pleasure Principle" (1987). The one single released from *Control* that did not reach the chart's top position was the only slow song of the group, "When I Think of You" (number three in 1986).

Creating a similar blend of rap and mainstream R&B were a number of other new 1980s artists. In the later part of the decade a style called "new jack swing" emerged that took the fusion of mainstream R&B and rap to a new level. Probably the most important innovator of this style was Teddy Riley, a young Harlem-born musical prodigy. Riley was involved in a number of projects in the last few years of the 1980s, and his influence earned him the title "king of new jack swing."[5] Three important late 1980s albums that Riley was involved with, and that incorporated the new jack swing style, are Keith Sweat, *Make It Last Forever* (1987); Guy, *Guy* (1988); and Bobby Brown, *Don't Be Cruel* (1988).[6]

The word "swing" in the term "new jack swing" comes from a button on the Linn drum machine that Teddy Riley often used to create a particular beat.[7] Previous chapters of this work have discussed the decline in the use of triplet swing in R&B over the course of the 1960s and 1970s. In the mid-1980s and beyond, however, triplet swing made a comeback of sorts, especially in the new jack swing style. Music produced by Riley often uses a triplet-swing rhythm in the sixteenth notes, and good examples of this effect can be witnessed in the songs "My Prerogative" (1988), which he composed for the Bobby Brown album *Don't Be Cruel*, and "Off on Your Own" (1988) from the Al B. Sure album *In Effect Mode*. As is typical of songs in the new jack swing style, rhythmic figures consisting of eighth notes or greater durational values in "My Prerogative" and "Off on Your Own" are played "straight," in other words, evenly spaced in time.[8] Of course, one should not get the impression that Riley was the only musician or producer using triplet swing in this manner in rhythm & blues of the 1980s. In fact, one can find a conspicuous example of this trait in the song "Nasty" from the Janet Jackson album, *Control*. Since Jackson's album was released in 1986 and was hugely successful, it is not unreasonable to assume that it had at least some impact on the new jack swing creations of Teddy Riley.

A style of R&B that developed in the mid- to late 1970s and became a significant factor in the 1980s is "quiet storm." The name for the style is borrowed from the song "Quiet Storm" from the 1975 album by Smokey Robinson entitled *A Quiet Storm*. Songs in this style are typically slow to moderate in tempo, romantic, sensual, sophisticated, sometimes jazzy, and can be viewed as the modern day equivalent of the "Sepia Sinatra" style of the 1940s and 1950s.[9] Apparently the style came to be regarded as an identifiable subgenre sometime after general manager of Howard University radio station, WHUR, Cathy Hughes, created this format for the station using Smokey Robinson's "Quiet Storm" as the theme song.[10]

One example of the quiet storm style is the 1982 hit "Sexual Healing" by Marvin Gaye. The tempo of the song is 95 b.p.m., giving the song a moderately slow, yet somewhat funky groove typical of the style. The subject matter of "Sexual Healing," basically a romantic plea by the artist for sex, is also commonly found in such songs. Gaye uses a number of elements of the blues system in his vocal approach to the first verse of "Sexual Healing" (ex. 44). His use of blue notes is evident in the example, with neutral thirds (lowered G's)—some of which are lowered considerably and others that are much closer to the major third of the Western scale—being particularly stressed in the vocal part. Measures one, three, and four of the transcription show

EXAMPLE 44. Marvin Gaye vocal style in "Sexual Healing." CD track time 0:18–0:27. From *Midnight Love and the Sexual Healing Sessions*, Columbia/Legacy CD C2K 65546, 1998. Originally released in 1982.

the vocalist singing a lowered third followed by a G natural. In each of these measures the singer then glides down past the lowered third to an F, the second degree of the scale. Heard in context this vocal riff, which is repeated throughout the song, imparts a particularly bluesy sound to the track. Gaye's vocal approach is also highly melismatic, a tendency which is evident in the example.

The quiet storm style became widespread by the mid-1980s, and numerous artists performed consistently in that manner throughout the decade. In addition to Marvin Gaye and Smokey Robinson, the following artists were also highly successful in the style during the 1980s: Luther Vandross, "Never Too Much" (1981), "There's Nothing Better Than Love" (1987), "Any Love" (1988), and "Here and Now" (1989); Freddie Jackson, "Rock Me Tonight (For Old Times Sake)" (1985), "You Are My Lady" (1985), "Tasty Love" (1986), "Have You Ever Loved Somebody" (1986), "I Don't Want to Lose Your Love" (1987), "Jam Tonight" (1987), "Nice 'N' Slow" (1988), and "Hey Lover" (1988); Anita Baker, "Sweet Love" (1986), "Caught Up in the Rapture" (1986), "Giving You the Best That I Got" (1988), and "Just Because" (1988); Teddy Pendergrass, "Joy" (1988); and Peabo Bryson, "Show and Tell" (1989).

The doo-wop-inflected vocal group style that had been popularized in the early 1970s by artists such as the Temptations, the Chi-Lites, the Dramatics, and the Stylistics largely waned in the 1980s. Although each of these groups ranks in the top twenty-five R&B acts of the 1970s, none was able to earn a number-one single in the 1980s. Although there were successful vocal groups in 1980s R&B, many of the elements of the classic 1950s and early 1960s doo-wop styles, such as a separate and identifiable bass vocal part and the use of nonsense lyrics, had all but disappeared. In fact, the two biggest 1980s R&B acts that could most reasonably be labeled "vocal groups," the Whispers and New Edition, performed a wide variety of musical styles that sometimes did not feature group vocals, as such.

The Whispers, a group that had been recording since the 1960s, are ranked by Whitburn as one of the twenty-one most successful R&B act of the 1980s, in spite of having just two number-one singles in the decade. Neither of these releases, "And the Beat Goes On" (1980) and "Rock Steady" (1987), is very closely related to the group vocal style we have witnessed in previous decades. Instead they are dance songs based on disco and funk rhythms. The Whispers did have a significant hit with a slow ballad, "Lady," a number-three record in 1980, and were able to chart a total of seventeen songs during the decade.

New Edition, a vocal group made up of five teenage boys from Boston, was the 1980s answer to the 1970s' Jackson 5. In fact, the group's first hit single, "Candy Girl" (1983), sounds very similar to the 1970 Jackson 5 hit, "ABC." New Edition had a string of rhythm & blues hits in the 1980s: "Cool It Now" (1984), "Mr. Telephone Man" (1984), "Count Me Out" (1985), and "Can You Stand the Rain" (1988). Generally speaking, the group's vocals consist of a lead singer and background harmony, with the lead part being sometimes shared among the different singers. Bobby Brown left the group in the mid-1980s to begin a highly successful solo career.

The funk style continued to be a driving force in the rhythm & blues of the 1980s, as it had been in the 1970s. The 1980s brand of funk, however, was not exactly the same as that created in the 1960s and early 1970s by such artists as James Brown, Sly & the Family Stone, and the Isley Brothers. By the early 1980s the use of electronics—including synthesizers, drum machines, MIDI (musical instrument digital interface), sequencing, and sampling—had become an essential element in much of the music under the funk umbrella. Electronic aspects of 1980s R&B are addressed later in the chapter.

To discuss funk in the 1980s one must first explain the difference between that style and disco. During the peak of its popularity in the 1970s, disco was a musical category that primarily included medium- to fast-tempo dance-oriented songs. As it developed over that decade, disco became simpler rhythmically, sometimes consisting of nothing more than a standard beat produced on a drum machine (or "rhythm box") with sparse instrumentation, electronic effects, and vocals overlaid. The disco style changed dramatically over the course of the 1970s, becoming in the minds of some critics inanely simple. For the most part disco was out of the picture by the early 1980s, although a few of its biggest artists, such as Donna Summer, continued to be successful in the field until at least 1983.

Funk music had emerged in America well before disco came to be a major force. As mentioned in chapter 5, it was the music of funk artists such as James Brown, Ohio Players, and Kool & the Gang that was played by the deejays at many of the first discos in the U.S. However, funk survived the "disco sucks" reaction of the early 1980s. It not only thrived throughout the decade, but also served as a musical style base from which many of the other music genres of the 1980s and 1990s borrowed heavily.

The most successful of the 1980s funk groups, according to the *Billboard* charts, was the Gap Band. Example 45, "You Dropped a Bomb on Me,"

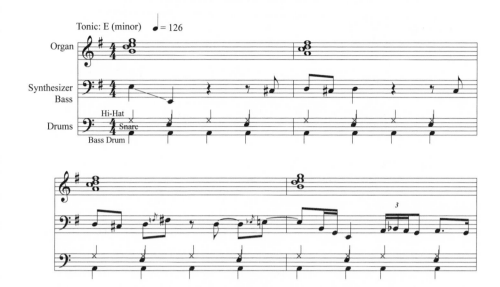

EXAMPLE 45. 1980s funk style in "You Dropped a Bomb on Me." CD track time 0:08–0:16. *Gap Band: The Ultimate Collection*, Hip-O CD 314 548 098-2, 2001. Originally released in 1982.

illustrates classic 1980s funk as performed by that group. I see five important stylistic elements in this excerpt: (1) the song is in E minor, so that blue-note thirds (Gs) and sevenths (Ds) are inherently part of the scale; (2) the bass part is performed on a synthesizer and includes complex rhythms, glissando, and melisma, (3) the flatted fifth (B♭) is present in measure four of the bass part (and elsewhere in the song); (4) the drum part is rhythmically very simple, a characteristic that had become popular in funk in the mid- to late 1970s; and (5) the only two chords used in the segment shown (Em7 and D7 in the organ part) continue for the entire track.

The vocal style in much 1980s funk includes the use of traditional elements of the blues system such as melisma, glissando, blue notes, and gravelly timbre. Example 46 shows the vocal style in a verse of "You Dropped a Bomb on Me." Like much African-American music, the vocal part of this song is not sung strictly in time as the example seems to indicate, but rather has a swing that creates a tension by moving the melody forward or backward in time against the basic pulse. Though the swing effect is virtually impossible to illustrate using the Western system of notation, the example does help one visualize the use of offbeat phrasing in the melody, especially noticeable on the words "said you'd set me free." An important point to make is that the

EXAMPLE 46. Vocal style in "You Dropped a Bomb on Me." CD track time 1:15–1:20. *Gap Band: The Ultimate Collection.* Hip-O CD 314 548 098-2, 2001. Originally released in 1982.

vocalist makes characteristic blues-system use of the variable third degree of the scale. "You Dropped a Bomb on Me" is in a minor mode, and nothing in the instrumental parts suggests an E major chord (see ex. 45). The vocalist often sings a G natural, which matches the E minor chord, but he also uses a noticeably raised G in various places throughout the song (such as on the word "Eve" in example 46). At times the raised G approaches a G♯, making for an ambiguous tonality typical of much blues-system music from the early 1900s on.

In addition to "You Dropped a Bomb on Me," the Gap Band had several other hits in the 1980s, including: "Burn Rubber (Why You Wanna Hurt Me)" (1980), "Early in the Morning" (1982), "Outstanding" (1982), and "All of My Love" (1989). A number of other successful funk groups and solo artists in this decade had been widely accepted in the 1970s; others hit their stride in the 1980s. Just a few a these artists and their hits are Zapp, "More Bounce to the Ounce, Part 1" (1980) and "Dance Floor, Part 1" (1982); Earth, Wind & Fire, "Let's Groove" (1981) and "System of Survival" (1987); Rick James, "Give It to Me Baby" (1981), "Super Freak, Part 1" (1981), and "Cold Blooded" (1983); Dazz Band, "Let It Whip" (1982); Cameo, "She's Strange" (1984), "Word Up" (1986), and "Candy" (1986); and Maze, "Back in Stride" (1985).

The use of minor modes (both the natural minor and dorian) became so prevalent in 1980s funk, and much other R&B for that matter, that one is tempted to call it a fundamental style feature. Of the top twenty-five R&B songs of the 1980s, seventeen are in the minor modes, and all ten of those that might reasonably be labeled "funk" songs are minor. Example 47 shows how the dorian mode is used in a typical 1980s funk song, "Let It Whip," by Dazz Band (1982). The V chord often exists in the song as an Em7, thereby avoiding the use of the major seventh of the Western system scale (G♯). Such avoidance

EXAMPLE 47. Example of dorian mode in "Let It Whip." CD track time 0:53–1:01. *The Best of the Dazz Band*, Motown CD 314 556 771-2, 2001. Originally released in 1982.

of the major seventh is a trait identified earlier as one of the elemental features of blues-system music. Present in the fourth measure of the example is an F♯ (the major sixth of the scale of A) in the electric piano part—found throughout the song in the recurring riff shown—clearly indicating that the song is in A dorian mode. Such "modal" songs can be found across a wide spectrum of blues-system music. Two such examples are "So What" by Miles Davis[11] and "Cold Sweat, Part 1" by James Brown,[12] both of which use the same mode and almost exactly the same riff—though performed on horns—played by the electric piano player in "Let It Whip."

The use of electronics in rhythm & blues spread quickly in the 1970s; by the early 1980s it had become a common feature of the core style. As shown in some of the examples above (exs. 45 and 47), the synthesizer had come to be used as the bass instrument on a regular basis in funk and other styles of R&B. By the early 1980s the keyboard synthesizer was no longer simply a monophonic instrument. Polyphonic, user-programmable synthesizers had come to the forefront in 1978 with the Sequential Circuits Prophet 5 keyboard. Within just a few years, similar keyboards were marketed by several manufacturers, such as Oberheim, Yamaha, Roland, Korg, and others.[13] Some of the funk artists mentioned above, particularly Zapp, Rick James, the Gap Band, and Dazz Band, used synthesizers to such an extent—often with multiple overlapping parts—that they sometimes overshadowed, or entirely replaced, the electric bass and guitars.

The invention of MIDI—an acronym for musical instrument digital interface—in 1983 paved the way for the further use of electronics in R&B, and music in general. In short, MIDI is a system by which two or more synthesizers, or other compatible devices, can communicate through the use of electronic signals sent over a cable. Once this system was in place, a whole new world opened up to R&B musicians: for the first time, several electronic devices could be easily controlled by one person playing a single keyboard. Cooperation among major synthesizer manufacturers led to a universal MIDI standard, and nearly any brand of synthesizer could be controlled by a synthesizer made by a competitor.

One advantage of such technology is that a musician may control many devices at once, thereby creating a huge wall of synthesized sound. Another important aspect of the invention of MIDI is the fact that the system can incorporate other devices such as sequencers and drum machines (sometimes called drum boxes, rhythm boxes, or beat boxes). Sequencers—basically electronic devices that enable the user to program a given rhythm pattern—have been around since at least the early 1970s, when Oberheim introduced the DS-2. These machines allow a complex mix of parts to be created, stored electronically, and used to trigger any number of keyboards or other electronic instruments.

When electronic instrument manufacturers began to produce drum machines, technology took R&B by storm. Basically, a drum machine is an electronic device that is able to reproduce electronically the sounds of any number of drums and other percussion instruments. The first important drum machines were the Roland TR-808 and TR-909, the LinnDrum, and the E-mu Drumulator, all of which were produced in the late 1970s and early 1980s. One of the best known early uses of this technology can be heard in the Marvin Gaye hit, "Sexual Healing," a number-one R&B song in 1982.

EXAMPLE 48. Roland TR-808 in "Sexual Healing." CD track time 0:00—0:05. Marvin Gaye, *Midnight Love and the Sexual Healing Sessions*, Columbia/Legacy CD C2K 65546, 1998. Originally released in 1982.

Example 48 shows the multilayered drum parts created for that record using the Roland TR-808 drum machine.[14]

Use of sampling technology was another important new element in 1980s R&B. A sampler is an electronic device that allows the user to digitally record and subsequently manipulate a sound. In 1980 the E-mu company came out with the Emulator, the first affordable and successful sampler, followed by Ensoniq's Mirage and several models by the Akai, Roland, and Yamaha companies.[15] At first, samplers were primarily used to borrow a particular sound, for example that of a snare drum, from a pre-existing record. By the late 1980s, however, sampling had become one of the main compositional tools of R&B as artists and producers used the technology to record entire sections of previously recorded songs for reuse in a new context.

One of the most significant uses of sampling is in the creation of a so-called "loop," a short section of a song or other pre-existing material which is sampled and then made to play repeatedly. Example 49 shows a portion of "Me Myself and I," released by De La Soul in 1989. The segment illustrates how the sample loop of synthesizers, piano, and drums taken from the 1979 Funkadelic song "(Not Just) Knee Deep, Part 1" is used in the instrumental track of the De La Soul song (beneath the newly created rap). Over the course of the 1980s such use became controversial, and a number of lawsuits were initiated by original creators of music claiming copyright infringement.

Some critics believe that using sampling in the way described here is not only ethically wrong but also a contributing factor in an overall lack of creativity in R&B and other categories of popular music. But use of repeating musical figures (riffs or cycles) is a feature we have followed in R&B

EXAMPLE 49. Sample loop in "Me Myself and I." CD track time 0:10–0:15. *De La Soul Timeless: The Singles Collection*, Tommy Boy/Rhino CD R2 73680, 2003. Originally released in 1989. Instruments sampled from "(Not Just) Knee Deep, Part 1." Funkadelic, Warner 49040, 1979.

throughout the course of this study, specifically because it is a trait of the blues system. I suggest that the use of a digitally recorded sample loop that serves the same basic purpose as a cycle is nothing more than an extension of an important element of the blues system in a modern context.

Rap first appeared on the national scene in the late 1970s, as was briefly discussed in the previous chapter. Some writers prefer to use the term "hip hop" to describe the music I label here as rap. "Hip hop culture" or the "hip hop community" are the generally accepted terms for the overall urban cultural setting that includes not only rap music, but also break dancing, graffiti, and b-boy clothing styles. To avoid confusion, "rap" is used in this chapter when discussing the late 1970s and 1980s musical genre and "hip hop" is used when referring to the general cultural environment that includes rap music.

The African-American technique of rapping can be traced as far back as one would care to go, possibly even to ancestral African roots.

> Whatever the disagreements over lineage in the rap hall of fame or the history of hip hop, there is one thing on which we all are agreed. "Rap is nothing new," says Paul Winley. Rap's forebears stretch back through disco, street funk, radio DJs, Bo Diddley, the bebop singers, Cab Calloway, Pigmeat Markham, the tap dancers and comics, The Last Poets, Gil Scott-Heron, Muhammad Ali, *a capella* and doo-wop

groups, ring games, skip-rope rhymes, prison and army songs, toasts, signifying and the dozens, all the way to the griots of Nigeria and Gambia. No matter how far it penetrates into the twilight maze of Japanese video games and cool European electronics, its roots are still the deepest in all contemporary Afro-American music.[16]

In addition to the points made in the above quotation by David Toop, it should be noted that some of the earliest rappers, for example Kool Herc, were of Caribbean origin. When rapping over drum breaks, funk grooves, and sample loops, Herc and some other deejays may have been adapting the "toasting" technique that had been in use since the late 1960s by deejays who "rapped" improvised lyrics over reggae "dub" records in Jamaican dance halls. The dub style incorporates specially created, instrumental-only B-sides of records that, because there is no vocal part, allow for the improvised rap.[17]

In the 1980s rap music went through a series of changes that had a lasting effect on the genre and on rhythm & blues in general. The first change is exemplified by the song "Planet Rock" by Afrika Bambaataa, which incorporates a heavy dose of electronic music into the rap style. Bambaataa sampled "Trans-Europe Express" from the German techno-rock group Kraftwerk, and also added the sounds of the Roland TR-808 drum machine. This song broke the ground for further use of electronics in rap music over the rest of the decade.[18] After the release of "Planet Rock" many rap songs came to be more and more like musical collages. In other words, they were created as collections of elements—raps, background vocals, drum machine beats, sound effects, and a variety of musical samples—pasted together to make a whole.

Another important milestone in rap was the emergence of the group Run-DMC, who brought to the genre a style that was far more aggressive musically. Run-DMC, considered to be the first "hardcore" rap artists and the first of the "new school" of rap, often included in their tracks powerful rock drum beats and biting heavy metal guitar riffs. The most obvious example of the rock tendencies of Run-DMC can be heard in their mega-hit "Walk This Way" (1986), which was a remake of a song originally released by the rock group Aerosmith in 1977. To further emphasize the connection between Run-DMC's brand of rap and hard rock, the singer and lead guitarist of Aerosmith, Steven Tyler and Joe Perry, were featured on the rap video of the song. The minimalist musical approach of Run-DMC exhibits both a general lack of rhythmic complexity in the instrumental parts and also the use of very few different parts overall. Yet at the same time it strikes a decidedly aggressive stance because of the presence of elements such as: (1) an

EXAMPLE 50. Rap style of Run-DMC, "It's Like That." CD track time 0:17–0:25. *Run-DMC's Greatest Hits*, Arista/BMG Heritage CD 07822 10607-2, 2002. Originally released in 1983.

emphasis on bass drum and snare drum in the mix; (2) a rap that, because of its gravelly timbre, high pitch, and loudness, verges on yelling; and (3) the use on some songs of hard-edged rock guitars, as mentioned above. Example 50 shows a segment of the first charted single by Run-DMC, "It's Like That" (1983). The portion shown is the first verse of the song and includes all of the parts being played at that point in the track. The sparseness illustrated here— the synthesizer having just one quarter-note chord every other measure and the bass and drum parts consisting of simple two-measure cycles—is typical of the music created by Run-DMC. Note that the rap itself is somewhat more rhythmically complex than the rest of the parts and uses many of the offbeat rhythms seen in earlier African-American music.

The next important change in rap occurred in 1988 with the release of the album *It Takes a Nation of Millions to Hold Us Back*, by Public Enemy.[19] The rap style of Public Enemy borrows heavily from that of Run-DMC. The group's lead rapper, Chuck D. (Carlton Ridenhauer), typically raps with a very raspy vocal timbre and in a high-pitched quasi-yell that implies frustration and anger. The musical collages that had been created by early rappers such as Afrika Bambaataa and other artists were brought to a new level of sophistication by Public Enemy. A number of its songs—for example, "Don't Believe the Hype" and "Night of the Living Baseheads"—make extensive use of sampling. Some of the samples are taken from musical sources (older recordings), some from speeches by public figures such as Nation of Islam leader Louis Farrakhan.

The following key musical features are found on *It Takes a Nation of Millions to Hold Us Back*: (1) very short samples used as cycles to achieve basic grooves; (2) little or no harmonic function in the Western music sense; and (3) music moving rapidly from one section to the next, sometimes in an apparently "disorganized" or "haphazard" fashion. In reality, creating such musical collages is anything but disorganized or haphazard. It takes a significant amount of time and skill with electronics and recording studio equipment to create such works by cutting and pasting parts from different sources.

The last important movement in rap of the 1980s was the emergence of so-called "gangsta rap," a subgenre born out of the gang culture of the Los Angeles and Oakland areas near the end of the decade. Subject matter in gangsta rap songs typically includes drugs, prostitution, misogyny, crime, and violence by and against police, other gangs, and even other rap groups. N.W.A (Niggaz with Attitude) was the group that first exploded onto the scene in 1988 with "Straight Outta Compton" and "F**k Tha Police." Because of the nature of their lyrics, N.W.A was subject to police and F.B.I. investigations and parental advisory labels on their CDs.[20] The musical style of many gangsta rap artists can be viewed as a mixture of Public Enemy's electronic collage and Run-DMC's hard-edged rock style. N.W.A's "Straight Outta Compton" is a good example of this blend in that it includes not only musically austere sections built on one-chord samples with power-rock drums and rock guitar chords, but also stop-time sections with gunshots, casual conversations, ambulance sirens, and many other sound effects.

Also arriving on the rap scene toward the end of the 1980s were several artists sometimes labeled "pop-rap" due to their wide commercial appeal. As might be expected, both the song lyrics and musical presentation of such artists are somewhat less "dangerous" than those of many gangsta rap or political rap artists. A few of the most successful such artists and songs in the mid- to late 1980s were LL Cool J, "I'm Bad" (1987) and "I Need Love" (1987); Tone Loc, "Wild Thing" (1988) and "Funky Cold Medina" (1989); DJ Jazzy Jeff and the Fresh Prince, "Parents Just Don't Understand" (1988) and "A Nightmare on My Street" (1988); and Young MC, "Bust a Move" (1989).

The influence of rap on R&B in general cannot be overstated. Although none of the rap artists mentioned here had radio airplay or single sales on the level of artists such as Michael Jackson or Prince, the overall musical style, use of electronics, and studio production values of rap had a huge impact on rhythm & blues throughout the 1980s and beyond. Because many media outlets were unwilling to play the music or videos of rap artists for a variety of reasons, the genre retained its underground appeal for much of the 1980s. Many rap artists were produced by small independent labels such as Def Jam, Jive, Priority, Sugarhill, and Tommy Boy, although at some point many independents entered into distribution deals with major labels.

Songs with social or political messages also were prevalent in 1980s R&B, especially as part of the second wave of rap music. One of the most influential of such early rap songs is "The Message" by Grandmaster Flash and the Furious Five (1982), a single that reached number four on the R&B chart. "The Message" was one of the first rap songs to make a social statement about the realities of life in the ghetto. Partly because of the success of that song, rap artists such as Run-DMC began to address social issues in rap lyrics, such as those found in "It's Like That" (ex. 50), discussed above.

The power of social and political commentary in rap was fully unleashed by the group Public Enemy in the late 1980s. Many of the decade's artists used rap music to send messages of political, economic, and social injustice, but critics often consider this group to be the one by which all others are measured. One of the best early examples of Public Enemy's message raps is the song "Black Steel in the Hour of Chaos," an excerpt of which is shown below (ex. 51). Message raps with strong political points of view had a powerful influence on the inner-city black community in the late 1980s, and were important in the resurgence of the ideas of Malcolm X.[21] Public Enemy continued to produce politically charged songs well into the 1990s.

I got a letter from the government the other day.
I opened it and read it.
It said they were suckers.
They wanted me for their army, or whatever.
Picture me givin' a damn—I said never.

EXAMPLE 51. Excerpt from "Black Steel in the Hour of Chaos." CD track time 0:28–0:39. Public Enemy, *It Takes a Nation of Millions to Hold Us Back*, Def Jam CD 314 527 358–2, 1988.

TOP TWENTY-FIVE R&B SONGS OF THE 1980s

Tables 7 and 8 contain the data for the top twenty-five R&B songs of the 1980s. Table 8 shows that the average tempo of the 1980s songs is 113 b.p.m., an increase of eight over the 105 b.p.m. average of the top twenty-five songs of the 1970s. However, the 1980s figure is very close to that shown in the corresponding table for the 1960s (table 4), where the top R&B songs averaged 116 b.p.m. Thus, it is difficult to determine whether there is any trend developing here, or simply that the average song tempo in all three decades has remained in a general range around 110 b.p.m.

There was a significant increase in the number of chord types used in the top R&B hits of the 1980s, where the average of 6.92 is well above the 5.4 chord types per song average of the 1970s. At first glance this point might seem contradictory to the fact that the use of the cyclic form also increased in the 1980s songs to 57 percent from 53 percent in the 1970s hits. One might expect that because of the increase in the use of the cyclic form there would be many more songs in the table with just one or two chords, similar to some of the funk songs discussed earlier by artists like James Brown, Sly & the Family Stone, and others. Table 8, however, shows that only one of the top twenty-five R&B songs of the 1980s has three or fewer chord types and that most of them have between four and eight chord types. Thus, one can conclude that by the 1980s many songs using the cyclic form were using a more harmonically complex cycle that included a significantly greater number of chords, as opposed to the earlier one or two chord varieties.

The incidence of the I, IV, V, and other chords in the 1980s songs also relates to the increase in the number of different chord types used. The table shows that there was a significant decrease in use of both the I chord (from 46 percent in the 1970s to 39 percent in the 1980s) and IV chord (20 percent in the 1970s, 13 percent in the 1980s) in the biggest R&B hits of the 1980s, while the incidence of the V chord remained stable at 11 percent. Perhaps

TITLE	DATE	ARTIST	LABEL & NO.
Rock With You	1/5/80	Michael Jackson	Epic 50797
And the Beat Goes On	3/1/80	The Whispers	Solar 11894
Let's Get Serious	5/17/80	Jermaine Jackson	Motown 1469
Take Your Time (Do It Right), Part 1	6/28/80	The S.O.S. Band	Tabu 5522
Master Blaster	11/1/80	Stevie Wonder	Tamla 54317
Celebration	12/20/80	Kool & the Gang	De-lite 807
Don't Stop the Music	2/28/81	Yarbrough and Peoples	Mercury 76085
Being with You	4/4/81	Smokey Robinson	Tamla 54321
Give It to Me Baby	6/13/81	Rick James	Gordy 7197
Endless Love	8/22/81	Diana Ross and Lionel Richie	Motown 1519
Let's Groove	11/28/81	Earth, Wind & Fire	ARC 02536
That Girl	2/20/82	Stevie Wonder	Tamla 1602
Let It Whip	5/29/82	Dazz Band	Motown 1609
Love Come Down	10/2/82	Evelyn King	RCA 13273
Sexual Healing	11/6/82	Marvin Gaye	Columbia 03302
Billie Jean	2/12/83	Michael Jackson	Epic 03509
Juicy Fruit	6/4/83	Mtume	Epic 03578
Cold Blooded	9/3/83	Rick James	Gordy 1687
All Night Long (All Night)	10/22/83	Lionel Richie	Motown 1698
Time Will Reveal	10/15/83	DeBarge	Gordy 1705
Somebody's Watching Me	3/3/84	Rockwell	Motown 1702
When Doves Cry	6/30/84	Prince	Warner 29286
Operator	12/22/84	Midnight Star	Solar 69684
Rock Me Tonight (For Old Times Sake)	6/1/85	Freddie Jackson	Capitol 5459
Part-Time Lover	10/19/85	Stevie Wonder	Tamla 1808

TABLE 7. Top 25 rhythm & blues singles of the 1980s: artist and label information.

—Adapted from Joel Whitburn, *Top R&B Singles: 1942–1999* (Menomonee Falls, WI: Record Research Inc., 2000).

predictably, the "other" category rose 7 percent from the 1970s. Table 6, from the previous chapter, shows the level of use of the twelve-bar blues form in the top R&B hits of the 1970s to be 0 percent. However, table 8 reveals a small, probably statistically insignificant, increase to 4 percent in the 1980s hits due to the presence of this form in one 1983 song by Michael Jackson, "Billie Jean."

TITLE	TEMPO	CHORDS	I	IV	V	OTHER	12-BAR	CYCLE	SCALE	3-SWING
Rock with You	114	12	28%	18%	28%	22%	N	0%	2	N
And the Beat Goes On	110	6	24%	5%	38%	28%	N	77%	3	N
Let's Get Serious	110	7	52%	18%	4%	11%	N	49%	3	N
Take Your Time (Do It Right), Part 1	120	6	36%	26%	0%	38%	N	85%	3	N
Master Blaster	131	5	34%	32%	13%	18%	N	50%	3	Y
Celebration	121	8	50%	6%	1%	14%	N	87%	3	N
Don't Stop the Music	99	7	43%	4%	4%	48%	N	76%	3	N
Being with You	106	5	39%	17%	4%	40%	N	51%	1	N
Give It to Me Baby	120	4	44%	45%	3%	5%	N	87%	3	N
Endless Love	93	6	46%	21%	21%	12%	N	0%	1	N
Let's Groove	125	9	48%	1%	25%	26%	N	95%	2	N
That Girl	107	14	36%	10%	5%	33%	N	28%	2	N
Let It Whip	132	5	58%	6%	34%	3%	N	77%	3	N
Love Come Down	115	7	36%	0%	1%	53%	N	46%	2	N
Sexual Healing	95	7	27%	6%	24%	20%	N	97%	3	N
Billie Jean	116	5	30%	20%	1%	48%	P	24%	2	N
Juicy Fruit	96	4	28%	0%	0%	36%	N	59%	3	N
Cold Blooded	118	4	45%	46%	2%	0%	N	86%	3	N
All Night Long (All Night)	109	4	39%	0%	0%	43%	N	64%	2	N
Time Will Reveal	64	18	18%	4%	5%	39%	N	0%	1	N
Somebody's Watching Me	125	3	55%	0%	0%	43%	N	79%	3	N
When Doves Cry	126	6	21%	5%	8%	44%	N	37%	3	N
Operator	121	5	93%	2%	2%	4%	N	93%	3	N
Rock Me Tonight (For Old Times Sake)	72	8	20%	6%	27%	47%	N	78%	3	N
Part-Time Lover	174	8	27%	18%	19%	33%	N	0%	3	Y
Average	113	6.92	39%	13%	11%	28%	4%	57%	2.5	8%

TABLE 8. Top 25 rhythm & blues singles of the 1980s: song transcription data.

If the form were making a comeback, we might expect to see it appear in more songs later in the decade. This is not the case, however, and its appearance in "Billie Jean" seems to be an anomaly.

The use of blue notes also shows a slight (also probably statistically insignificant) increase, from 2.4 in the 1970s to 2.5 in the 1980s. The discussion presented in this chapter about the dramatic increase in the use of the minor modes should be kept in mind when evaluating the use of blue notes. Because the natural minor and dorian modes include the flatted third and flatted seventh (compared to the major mode of the Western system), our evaluation of the level of blue-note use on such songs did not rest simply on whether the pitches were present in the song, but also on whether or not they were used in an emphatic way. In some songs, such as Michael Jackson's "Rock With You," there does not seem to be any emphasis placed on blue notes, and in fact they seem to be avoided on strong beats. However, in other songs in a minor mode, such as Rick James's "Cold Blooded," blue notes are used in a more traditional, emphatic way, and thus were given a higher rating in that category.

Triplet swing experienced an increase in use in the 1980s, as was discussed above in the section concerning the new jack swing style. However, this trend is not particularly evident in table 8 where the level of triplet swing is 8 percent, an increase of just 4 percent over that found in the 1970s. There are two likely reasons why this trait, which was in fact an important feature in R&B during the late 1980s, does not appear prominently in the table. One is that the style of R&B that most used this element, new jack swing, did not enjoy a strong presence on radio until late in the decade. The second reason is that no song in table 8 was released after September 1985, a phenomenon due in part to fluctuations in *Billboard*'s chart tabulation system, and also to the methods used by Whitburn to calculate the top twenty-five hits of the decade. Our discussion of the possible long-term resurgence of triplet swing in R&B continues in the next chapter.

CHAPTER SEVEN

RAP GOES MAINSTREAM:
1990–1999

If the 1980s were a decade of change in rhythm & blues, then the 1990s represent a period of consolidation of those changes. By the early 1990s a noticeable transformation had taken place in R&B, which blended the elements of older styles such as soul and funk with those of rap. Key features of the rap music style—the use of drum machines, synthesizers, and sampling, emphasis on percussion and sound effects, and the rap itself—were absorbed into mainstream R&B, and the result was that new artists began to dominate the field. The chart successes of the number-one and number-two R&B artists of the 1990s, R. Kelly and Mariah Carey, underscore the dramatic changes that had taken place; neither artist had charted a R&B record in the 1980s (both were less than twenty-one years of age as the 1990s began).

The musicians who had dominated the 1970s and 1980s R&B scene were all but nonexistent at the top of the 1990s R&B charts. In fact, only two artists who had charted records in the 1970s, Prince and Luther Vandross, were among the top twenty-five artists of the 1990s (8 percent), a figure in contrast to the 32 percent of top R&B artists (eight of twenty-five) of the 1980s who had been successful in the 1960s.[1] Perhaps even more revealing is the drop-off by the early 1990s of success experienced by the top funk artists of previous decades. Of the nine funk-oriented R&B acts who had made the list of top twenty-five artists of the 1970s or 1980s—James Brown; Kool & the Gang;

Rick James; Earth, Wind & Fire; Parliament/Funkadelic; the Ohio Players; the Isley Brothers; Cameo; and the Gap Band—none had a number-one single after 1990.

Some of the most important independent labels in the R&B category from the 1950s through the 1970s were, by the 1990s, not the powerhouses they once had been. This phenomenon was likely the result of many factors, including poor business decisions made by the labels and their unwillingness or inability to meet the shift in the tastes of the record-buying public. The most obvious example of such decline can be seen in the loss of prominence of Motown Records. In the 1990s only one single produced by Motown made the list of the top twenty-five of the decade. This figure translates to just 4 percent of the total, a percentage far below the 48 percent Motown enjoyed in the 1980s. Over the years Motown had also seen a huge decline in the number of R&B superstars on its roster. Of those artists who made the list of the top twenty-five R&B artists of each decade, Motown had 24 percent in the 1970s, but that number fell to 16 percent in the 1980s, and then plummeted to 8 percent in the 1990s. Other important once-independent labels—most notably Atlantic Records—were by the 1990s part of international entertainment conglomerates. Atlantic, which had been part of the WEA group for many years, produced just one top twenty-five R&B single in the 1990s.

Throughout the 1980s and 1990s, many of the labels previously considered "majors"—CBS and RCA are two examples—were themselves absorbed into even larger concerns such as the Sony Corporation and the Bertlesmann Group (BMG). To understand the extent of such consolidations, one might consider the expansive nature of BMG, a company that has under its umbrella "more than 200 record labels in 42 countries including Ariola, Arista Records, J. Records, RCA Label Group–Nashville, and RCA Records."[2] The list of the top twenty-five R&B songs of the 1990s includes at least twelve hits (48 percent) released either on one of the BMG labels listed above, or on affiliated labels such as Jive and LaFace. Other corporate music giants Sony/CBS, WEA, and EMI were also well represented with a cumulative total of six songs making the top twenty-five hits of the decade. When one combines the figures discussed here, it is revealed that over 70 percent of the top twenty-five R&B songs of the 1990s were produced or distributed by BMG, Sony/CBS, WEA, or EMI.

The figures presented above might lead one to speculate that R&B had by the 1990s become so corporate that it was at risk of losing its connection with its core audience. Such a concern is not necessarily ill-founded. Rhythm & blues artists themselves typically monitor the authenticity of their own music and attempt to "keep it real." A similar sensibility is often echoed in the general community. For example, some O.G.s (original gangsters) consider gangsta rap artists such as N.W.A (and its members, Dr. Dre, Eazy-E, Ice Cube, and MC Ren) to be "Hollywood hype" because of their lack of real participation in the black gang community.[3]

However, despite the involvement of multinational music corporations, much 1990s R&B was—and still is in 2005—generally created at the street level, and retains a blues-system sensibility. It must be kept in mind that the Bad Boy, LaFace, Ruthless, Jive, and EastWest labels together were responsible for eleven of the top twenty-five R&B hits of the 1990s (even though many of these songs were distributed by the bigger corporations). Much of the music created by these smaller labels—and others such as Death Row, Def Jam, Interscope, Priority, and Tommy Boy—was produced by the artists and owners (or co-owners) of the labels themselves, not by some faceless corporate executive.

MAJOR STYLES AND ARTISTS

Due in part to the stylistic transformation discussed above (but probably for marketing reasons as well), the number of names for musical genres, sub-genres, and styles included in the R&B spectrum proliferated greatly during the 1980s and early 1990s. As rap music splintered into a host of regional styles and also blended with older R&B styles and genres, new names were created to define the categories, just a few of which are dirty rap, dirty south, gangsta rap, g-funk, hardcore rap, alternative rap, jazz rap, East Coast rap, West Coast rap, bass music, contemporary R&B, new jack swing, neo-soul, and urban.[4] Of course, creating a specific name for a style makes it much easier to identify and discuss that category separately from the rest of the field. However, such differentiation also can mislead one into thinking that there are clear-cut, immutable boundaries between the categories where such lines of division do not in fact exist.

In order to remain consistent with the terminology used throughout this book, I continue to use the name "R&B" for music that earned a spot in *Billboard*'s R&B charts. However, for the sake of clarity the term "hip hop" is at times used when discussing the broad range of newer styles in R&B of the late 1980s and 1990s. Use of this nomenclature, it must be admitted, is somewhat problematic in that the term is used by some writers to describe the entire cultural setting of which music is a part, and which also includes graffiti, break dancing, and clothing styles. However, "hip hop" has come to be a term accepted by many writers in the R&B field to describe the body of 1990s music that blends the styles of rap, soul, funk, urban, and others.

To begin to understand the variety of R&B blends of the 1990s we can point to an important record that came out just as the decade began, "Rhythm Nation," by Janet Jackson. The song, from the album *Rhythm Nation 1814,* was released in November of 1989 and first hit the number-one spot on the R&B chart on January 13, 1990. As shown in example 52, "Rhythm Nation" makes use of elements from across the R&B spectrum, including use of a sample loop, triplet swing, rapped vocal parts and blue notes (D naturals and G naturals). However also present in this example is a higher pitched scale third in the vocal part in measure four, beat two. Throughout most of the track the G is sung or played very close to a G natural, but in this particular instance the pitch is noticeably raised, toward a G♯. This creates ambiguity at the third degree of the scale similar to that found in "You Dropped a Bomb on Me," discussed in the previous chapter (ex. 46).

The basic groove of the song is built upon a one-measure sample taken from the bridge of the Sly & the Family Stone song "Thank You (Falettinme Be Mice Elf Agin)" (1970) and can be seen in this example in the combined guitar and clavinet part. This digitally sampled measure is played in a loop for the majority of the track length. The compositional technique of using a sample loop as the basis for a song's cyclic form, as seen in this example, was discussed in chapter 6, primarily in reference to rap music.[5] In the early 1990s and beyond, however, sample loops came to be used in such a manner across the entire range of R&B styles. The presence of triplet swing is also evident in "Rhythm Nation," as indicated in the sixteenth notes in the snare drum part. As discussed later, triplet swing was somewhat common in R&B of the early 1990s. A feature that by the early to mid-1990s became widespread in R&B was that of alternating rapped and sung vocal sections within the body of a song. As we see in our example—the first chorus of the song—the vocal part in measures one and two is a group rap, but in measures three and four the vocalists *sing* in octaves.

The mix of features found in "Rhythm Nation" is closely related to the late 1980s and early 1990s new jack swing style. The popularity of new jack

EXAMPLE 52. Blended R&B style in "Rhythm Nation." CD track time 1:05–1:14. Janet Jackson, *Rhythm Nation 1814*, A&M CD 3920, 1989.

swing peaked in the first few years of the 1990s and then faded dramatically by mid-decade as elements from the style were absorbed across the spectrum of R&B. Among the important artists in the new jack swing style during the early 1990s, and some of the hits they created, are Bell Biv DeVoe, "B.B.D.

(I Thought It Was Me)?" (1990); Keith Sweat, "Make You Sweat" (1990); Al B. Sure, "Missunderstanding" (1990); Johnny Gill, "Rub You the Right Way" (1990) and "Wrap My Body Tight" (1991); Color Me Badd, "I Wanna Sex You Up" (1991); and Mary J. Blige, "Real Love" (1992). One of the most successful groups in the new jack swing style was Bell Biv DeVoe, a trio made up of former members of the 1980s vocal group New Edition. Example 53 is taken from their song "Poison," a classic of new jack swing, and shows some of the important features of the style, particularly the triplet-swing rhythm that exists in the snare drum part. As described earlier, this feature came to the forefront in new jack swing and other R&B in the late 1980s. Other key style traits of new jack swing found in "Poison" are sparse production, driving bass part, and upbeat dance tempo (112 b.p.m.).

EXAMPLE 53. Example of 1990s new jack swing style in "Poison." CD track time 1:12–1:17. *The Best of Bell Biv DeVoe*, MCA CD MCAD088 112 870-2, 2002. Originally released in 1990. It is unknown whether the part labeled "synthesizer" was played at the time of the recording, or if it was sampled from a previously existing source.

"Urban," or "urban contemporary," another R&B sub-category that emerged in the 1980s and 1990s, includes under its umbrella not only the smooth and soulful ballads formerly associated with the quiet storm style, but also uptempo dance and funk songs. One notable aspect of songs in the urban category is the polished, hi-tech production quality of the recordings. Taking these style factors into consideration, it is not difficult to imagine why these songs appealed to urban blacks of the late twentieth century. For ease of discussion, I continue to use the term "quiet storm" when referring to the style of romantic songs defined in the previous chapter. An important distinction that perhaps should be pointed out is that rap music typically is *not* included in the urban category.

Some of the most important quiet storm artists of the 1980s continued their success into the first few years of the 1990s, for the most part retaining their earlier style. The most visible of these were Freddie Jackson, "Love Me Down" (1990) and "Do Me Again" (1991); Whitney Houston, "All the Man That I Need" (1990) and "I Will Always Love You" (1992); Luther Vandross, "Power of Love/Love Power" (1991); Peabo Bryson, "Can You Stop the Rain" (1991); and Teddy Pendergrass, "It Should've Been You" (1991). Other than Whitney Houston, who was able to successfully change her style to meet the tastes of the mid-1990s R&B record-buying public, none of these artists was able to earn a number-one chart record in rhythm & blues after 1992.

Mariah Carey, an eclectic artist who had her first chart record in 1990 and went on to become one of the biggest stars in 1990s R&B, carried on the quiet storm tradition in the early part of her career with hits such as "Vision of Love" (1990) and "Love Takes Time" (1990). However, Carey's records are often a showcase for her extraordinary vocal ability, which in some cases makes them almost too dynamic and emotionally draining to be classified as quiet storm. Example 54 illustrates Carey's vocal style in a section of the song "Vision of Love." Note the extreme use of melisma and blue notes (lowered E, G♭, and B♭)

EXAMPLE 54. Vocal style in "Vision of Love." CD track time 2:55–3:11. *Mariah Carey*, Columbia CD CK 45202, 1990.

that are hallmarks of Carey's style, and are reminiscent of the gospel vocals of Mahalia Jackson, among others.[6]

By the mid-1990s newer blends of R&B had become more popular, and slow songs in R&B developed a tendency toward the inclusion of new jack swing and rap elements such as the use of triplet swing, sample loops, sparse production, hard-edged instrument sounds, and rapping itself. As explained earlier, these blends also made use of many traits of older R&B styles, particularly soul and funk. It was during this time that the term "hip hop" came to be widely used to describe a whole range of newer R&B styles. Because many of these songs had sixteenth notes as the basic metronomic value, the tempi were commonly very slow, often in the 60–70 b.p.m. range. These newer hip hop ballads largely replaced the more polished and sophisticated quiet storm style at the top of the charts by the middle of the 1990s.

Example 55 shows how both sung and rapped vocal parts are blended in Usher's "Nice and Slow" (number one R&B, number two pop in 1998), a song that typifies the R&B ballad style that became widely popular in the second half of the decade. When comparing the two vocal excerpts, taken from different locations in the track, it is important to keep in mind that the music accompanying each consists of a very simple two-measure chord sequence that is played in a loop along with sparse drum and bass parts. It probably goes without saying that, due to the presence of thirty-second notes, the rap

EXAMPLE 55. Comparison of sung and rapped vocals in "Nice & Slow." Vocal, CD track time 0:39–0:48; rap, CD track time 2:14–2:23. Usher, *My Way*, LaFace CD 73008-26043-2, 1997.

would be almost impossible to perform if the tempo of the song were much faster than indicated (61 b.p.m.).

Many artists released songs in the 1990s that fit somewhere in the range of styles between quiet storm/urban on the one hand and rap-inflected hip hop on the other. It seems futile to try to strictly categorize such artists, especially given the fact that it was (and continues to be in 2005) common practice for artists to perform in various styles from album to album, and from song to song. Just a few of the solo artists—some of whom have been mentioned above—who achieved considerable chart success in the 1990s are Tevin Campbell, "Tell Me What You Want Me to Do" (1991), "Alone With You" (1992), and "Can We Talk" (1993); Al B. Sure, "Right Now" (1992); Mary J. Blige, "Real Love" (1992) and "You Remind Me" (1992); R. Kelly, "Honey Love" (1992), "Slow Dance" (1993), "Bump N' Grind" (1994), and "Down Low (Nobody Has to Know)" (1996); Toni Braxton, "Seven Whole Days" (1993) and "You're Makin' Me High" (1996); Janet Jackson, "Anytime, Anyplace" (1994) and "I Get Lonely" (1998); Brandy, "I Wanna Be Down" (1994) and "Baby" (1995); Whitney Houston, "Exhale (Shoop Shoop)" (1995) and "Heartbreak Hotel" (1999); Keith Sweat, "Twisted" (1996); Usher, "You Make Me Wanna" (1997); and Erykah Badu, "On and On" (1997). It seems significant that all of the songs listed above reached the top spot on the R&B charts, and that none has a tempo greater than 95 b.p.m. In fact, the average tempo of all twenty-one songs listed here is just 76 b.p.m. The topic of tempo in 1990s R&B is discussed later in this chapter.

One artist/producer whose name should be singled out as an important creator of R&B in the late 1980s and throughout the 1990s is Kenneth "Babyface" Edmonds. This multi-instrumentalist/singer/songwriter and his partner L.A. Reid created their own record label, LaFace, and began producing top R&B hits for a number of artists, including several for Babyface himself. His own singles were in the style of the smooth and sophisticated crooners, and can be viewed as a continuance of the Sepia Sinatra tradition that stretches back to Charles Brown and Johnny Ace in the 1950s and Isaac Hayes and Luther Ingram in the 1970s. Some of Babyface's biggest rhythm & blues hits include "It's No Crime" (1989), "Tender Lover" (1989), "Whip Appeal" (1990), "My Kinda Girl" (1990), and "Give U My Heart" (with Toni Braxton) (1992).

On his own records and those he produced for other artists, Babyface, along with Reid, was able to effectively combine musical elements from a wide range of R&B styles into a modern, yet highly popular, sound. To say that the productions of Babyface and Reid define mainstream rhythm & blues in the 1990s is not an overstatement. Just a few of the artists, R&B and otherwise, that Babyface either produced or wrote songs for in the late 1980s and 1990s are Bobby Brown, Sheena Easton, Johnny Gill, Whitney Houston,

Celine Dion, Mariah Carey, Madonna, Boyz II Men, Gladys Knight, Aretha Franklin, En Vogue, Mary J. Blige, and Eric Clapton. In addition, Babyface was involved in the musical production of the films *My Bodyguard* and *Waiting to Exhale* and won three successive Grammy Awards in the 1990s for Producer of the Year, among numerous other achievements.[7]

Vocal groups, which had been somewhat less prominent in the 1980s than in earlier decades, experienced a marked resurgence in 1990s. In fact seven of the top twenty-five R&B artists of the decade were vocal groups (28 percent). In addition to this level of success on the R&B charts, four of these groups are also listed in the decade's top twenty-five artists in the popular music charts (Hot 100).[8] In rap music a tendency developed over the 1980s and into the 1990s to create performing groups which came to be known collectively as "clans," "crews," or "posses." Such ensembles are, from one point of view, "vocal groups," but a discussion of them is postponed until later in this chapter when rap music of the 1990s is explored.

The most successful mainstream 1990s R&B vocal groups typically created music across the same stylistic lines as did solo artists. Of course, the particular blend of R&B that each group created was more or less unique and was made up of various musical features of rap, soul, funk, quiet storm, and older African-American styles and genres such as blues, jazz, and gospel music. Just a few of the numerous R&B vocal groups of the 1990s and their biggest hit songs are: En Vogue, "Hold On" (1990), "Lies" (1990), "You Don't Have to Worry" (1990), "My Lovin' (You're Never Gonna Get It)" (1992), "Giving Him Something He Can Feel" (1992), and "Don't Let Go (Love)" (1996); Tony! Toni! Tone!, "The Blues" (1990), "Feels Good" (1990), "It Never Rains (in Southern California)" (1990), and "Whatever You Want" (1991); Boyz II Men, "It's So Hard to Say Goodbye to Yesterday" (1992), "Uhh Ahh" (1991), "End of the Road" (1992), "I'll Make Love to You" (1994), and "A Song for Mama" (1997); Jodeci, "Forever My Lady" (1991), "Stay" (1991), "Come and Talk to Me" (1992), "Lately" (1993), and "Cry for You" (1993); TLC, "Baby-Baby-Baby" (1992), "Creep" (1994), and "No Scrubs" (1999); Xscape, "Just Kickin' It" (1993), "Understanding" (1993), and "Who Can I Run To?" (1995); SWV (Sisters with Voices), "Weak" (1993), "Right Here/Human Nature" (1993), and "You're the One" (1996); BLACKstreet, "No Diggity" (1996) and "Don't Leave Me" (1996); and Destiny's Child, "No, No, No, Part 2" (1997) and "Bills, Bills, Bills" (1999).

The vocal arrangements used by many 1990s groups are similar to those of the 1980s vocal groups. This is to say that they often feature a lead vocalist singing the melody while the other voices provide harmonic support, often functioning more or less as a group of background singers whose parts harmonize the melody. By the mid-1990s vocal groups began to incorporate sample loops as the underpinning for an entire song layered over with multiple overlapping instrumental and vocal parts.

However, despite all the technical innovations and stylistic blends that had emerged since the 1980s, the gospel music tradition still held considerable influence on the vocal group style of the 1990s. The number-one hit by Boyz II Men, "It's So Hard to Say Goodbye to Yesterday" (1991), is a case in point. Example 56 illustrates the last few bars of the first verse of the song, and reveals traits of the gospel style, including a highly melismatic lead vocal and gospel quartet–based vocal harmonies. The song also makes extensive use of other features of the style not illustrated here, including use of vocables in harmony parts, emphasized lowered thirds, and the sixteen-bar gospel song form. It seems significant that this song was released by Motown Records, a label with a historical connection to gospel-influenced African-American popular music.

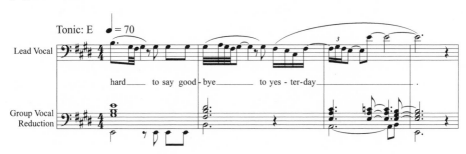

EXAMPLE 56. Gospel influence in "It's So Hard to Say Goodbye to Yesterday." CD track time 0:40–0:53. *Boyz II Men Legacy: The Greatest Hits Collection*, Universal CD 440 016 083-2, 2001. Originally released in 1991.

Rap music's rise in popularity during the 1990s is due in part to the tendency of the overall market to incorporate stylistic features of the genre. In other words, rap music no longer sounded so musically distant to many R&B listeners because many of its traits were commonly heard in songs by mainstream artists such as Janet Jackson, Mary J. Blige, Keith Sweat, and others. By the late 1980s and early 1990s some rap artists themselves had begun to move closer to mainstream R&B by incorporating older rhythm & blues styles into their music. The title of this chapter, "Rap Goes Mainstream: 1990–1999," refers not only to the fact that the rap musical style was blended into mainstream R&B styles during the decade, but also that the genre enjoyed considerable chart success on its own. Although rap flourished in the underground community in the 1980s, there was no rapper who finished that decade on the list of the top twenty-five R&B artists. In contrast there were four such artists on the 1990s list: Puff Daddy, LL Cool J, Jay-Z, and 2Pac. In addition, other R&B musicians in the top twenty-five of the decade may have released one or more rap-style records, but are not usually considered "rappers."

A number of important rap records released over the course of the late 1980s and 1990s moved the style closer to mainstream R&B and popular music in general. Perhaps the most visible of these was the song "U Can't Touch This," a 1990 release by MC Hammer that used a sample loop from Rick James's 1981 song "Super Freak, Part 1" as its musical foundation. Although some members of the rap community might not have taken Hammer seriously as a rap artist—due in part to his comical stage outfits and eccentric dancing style—there is little doubt that "U Can't Touch This" opened doors in the entertainment industry that many other rappers were later able to walk through.[9]

Other rap artists in the 1990s were widely successful in the broader R&B market, some of them continuing the popularity they had enjoyed in the late 1980s. Just a few of the most important of these were LL Cool J, "Around the Way Girl" (1990) and "Hey Lover" (1995); Queen Latifah, "Fly Girl" (1991), "Latifah's Had It Up 2 Here" (1991), and "U.N.I.T.Y." (1993); D.J. Jazzy Jeff and the Fresh Prince, "Summertime" (1991); Sir Mix-a-Lot, "Baby Got Back" (1992); and Salt-N-Pepa, "Shoop" (1993) and "Whatta Man" (1994).

A group that helped to popularize the use of samples of older R&B tracks for the musical underpinning of their raps was Digital Underground. Beginning in the late 1980s this group from Oakland repopularized the music of Parliament/Funkadelic and other funk artists by using it as the musical foundation for many of its rap records. Shock-G, the lead rapper and founder of Digital Underground, "made a deliberate attempt to bridge the gap between hip-hop and P-Funk. A lot of his New York buddies were true to the game with respect to hip-hop, he said, but they constantly fronted on George Clinton. . . . [Shock] was attracted to P-Funk because he felt that George Clinton was heavy on the Black side in both his concepts and lyrics."[10] Just a few of the hit songs produced by Digital Underground in the 1989–1991 period, and the samples they made use of, are "Doowutchyalike" (1989, rereleased in 1990) (sample taken from "Flashlight," Parliament, 1978),

"Same Song" (1991) (sample taken from "Black Hole," Parliament, 1979), and "Kiss You Back" (1991) (sample taken from "[Not Just] Knee Deep, Part 1," Funkadelic, 1979).

As was discussed in the previous chapter, gangsta rap came to the forefront in the late 1980s with the emergence of a number of artists. The West Coast gangsta rappers of the early 1990s, particularly Ice-T, Dr. Dre, MC Ren, Ice Cube, Eazy-E, Snoop Doggy Dogg, and 2Pac, continued to depict the culture of drugs, sex, violence, poverty, and social injustice that existed in many inner-city areas. Although the musical style of these artists is varied, it can generally be stated that until 1992 they exhibited many characteristics of what had been called "hardcore" rap, for example, the use of a variety of hard-edged instrumental sounds such as a highly-emphasized deep bass drum, aggressively-mixed snare drum, and use of industrial sound effects.

One of the leaders of gangsta rap in the very early 1990s was Ice-T. In addition to his success as a rapper, Ice-T starred in several movies, most visibly *New Jack City* (1991). The album *Rhyme Pays*, released in 1987, was an important early West Coast rap release. Perhaps his best album was *O.G.: Original Gangster* (1991), a release that has been called his "finest hour."[11] The release of "Cop Killer" from the album *Home Invasion* (1993) so much angered police groups across the country that they called for Ice-T's censorship. This, and other controversial songs, eventually led to his being dropped from the Warner record label.[12]

A new rap style emerged with the 1992 release of *The Chronic*, an important album by Dr. Dre on Death Row Records. The musical style unveiled on this record, which came to be called "g-funk," typically featured a slower tempo than in much previous rap, a deep-bass groove (often a sample loop), retro synthesizer sounds, and minimal instrumentation. The song, "Nuthin' but a 'G' Thang" from that album provides a good example of the g-funk style in that it (1) uses a sample from Leon Haywood's 1975 song, "I Want'a Do Somethin' Freaky to You," (2) consists of a sparsely instrumented two-bar repeating cycle, and (3) has a tempo of 94 b.p.m. Some of the songs on *The Chronic*, not only "Nuthin' but a 'G' Thang" but also "Let Me Ride," "Lil' Ghetto Boy," and "The Roach (The Chronic Outro)," among others, make use of elements one might associate with the quiet storm or urban styles of the 1970s and 1980s, especially the slow, mellow grooves borrowed from older R&B artists such as Donny Hathaway, Isaac Hayes, and Parliament/Funkadelic.[13] Layered on top of such mellow musical tracks are the nihilistic, menacing, and often misogynistic gangsta raps of Dr. Dre and Snoop Doggy Dogg, which overall make for a seemingly incongruous mix of elements. However, this album, which sold four million copies,[14] is considered one of the most influential rap albums of the 1990s, and the slow-tempo grooves it showcased became a hallmark of 1990s R&B in general.

Another rap group that made a big impact in the 1990s was Wu-Tang Clan, an assemblage of nine MCs.[15] The group's first effort *Enter the Wu-Tang: 36 Chambers* (1993) was perhaps its biggest critical success. The album presents an array of sonic styles, but generally the tracks are extremely sparse, at times consisting of only one or two instruments (often sampled). Because of this minimalist approach and also because of the use of overlapping samples taken from different sources, some of the songs present an ambiguous key center, or perhaps imply none at all. The creation of such a large group of performers may have been the predictable outcome of the tendency of rap artists since the 1970s to congregate into crews and posses—a group of local individuals with shared life experiences, more or less, and the musical equivalent of a gang.[16] Perhaps such a group concept has a precedent in the various collective musical ensembles of the 1970s, such as Sly & the Family Stone and Kool & the Gang.

Even a brief overview of the stylistic traits of rap music in the 1990s must include mention of perhaps the most successful artist/producer/entrepreneur in the field, Sean "Puffy" Combs, otherwise known as Puff Daddy or P. Diddy. During the decade, Combs built a rap music empire from his record label, Bad Boy, with total sales of over 100 million dollars. Combs's production style involves extensive use of sample loops from older tracks, a technique that, although causing him some criticism, resulted in several successful songs.[17] Three such tracks from his 1997 album *No Way Out* are "Can't Nobody Hold Me Down" (sample taken from Grandmaster Flash, "The Message," 1982), "Don't Stop What You're Doing" (sample taken from Yarbrough and Peoples, "Don't Stop the Music," 1980), and "I'll Be Missing You" (sample taken from the Police, "Every Breath You Take," 1983).

The next two examples illustrate some of the stylistic traits of rap as it existed in the mid-1990s music of one group, Public Enemy. Example 57 shows part of the first verse of the song "Thin Line Between Law and Rape" from the 1994 album *Muse Sick-N-Hour Mess Age.* In the segment shown, and for the entire verse thereafter, the music remains on the I chord, as implied by the bass part. The transcribed organ part reveals the use of blue-note thirds

EXAMPLE 57. Rap style in "Thin Line Between Law and Rape." CD track time 0:21–0:27. Public Enemy, *Muse Sick-N-Hour Mess Age*, Def Jam CD 314 523 362-2, 1994.

and sevenths (F♭ and C♭) in a one-measure repeating riff. The drum part is also made up of a one-measure-long repeating figure. Therefore, the bottom three parts shown on the score (organ, bass, drums) constitute the cycle that is the basis for the song's cyclic form. The moderately slow tempo and relatively mellow underlying track are stylistically similar to the g-funk style popularized by Dr. Dre.

The synthesizer part, as shown in the example, is a two-measure riff that repeats throughout the majority of the track. Although it cannot be seen in the printed example, the timbre of the synthesizer is that of a hollow-voiced, out-of-tune, synthesized choir, and coupled with the somewhat unusual pitches played, gives the part an almost ghostlike effect. The F♭ *could* be viewed as a blue-note third, of course, but in its movement down to the D natural (a pitch that strongly conflicts with the key center of D♭ in the Western music sense) it somehow tends to sound not so much "bluesy" as simply ambiguous. Chuck D., the rapper of the segment shown, often conveys anger, frustration, and moral indignation in his raps. Fittingly, his vocal timbre is typically very strident and the delivery usually high-pitched and declamatory, as it is in "Thin Line Between Law and Rape."

Example 58, a four-measure segment from later in the same song, helps to show how a sung vocal part can change the listener's perception of such

EXAMPLE 58. Vocal style in "Thin Line Between Law and Rape." CD track time 2:11–2:17. Public Enemy, *Muse Sick-N-Hour Mess Age.*

music. In this example the instrumental background is basically the same as before, although at this point in the track the music has moved up a fourth to hang on the IV chord for an extended period of time, and the organ part has become less active. However, the lead vocal part is now pitch-oriented and has a less gritty and aggressive timbre than the rapped portion. This lead part seems to convey a much less confrontational stance by the performer. The vocal excerpt shown here can be described as a hybrid style between singing and rapping, due to the fact that it has elements of both: a sequence of related pitches that make a discernable melody and also a highly dense, offbeat rhythmic quality that implies a rap. The combined effect of these two vocal performances in one rap song shows the connection between such songs and some mainstream R&B songs from the decade that use a similar technique of alternating sung vocals with raps. An example of such an R&B hit is "Nice & Slow," discussed earlier (ex. 55).

As it had been in the 1980s, rap music in the 1990s was again responsible for a significant amount of music that presented a social or political message. Numerous artists either specialized in message raps, such as Public Enemy, or released such songs as part of a body of work that also included less politically motivated subject matter. One of the most important of the new breed of message rap artists of the 1990s was 2Pac (Tupac Shakur). The son of Black Panther members, 2Pac began his professional career as a dancer with Digital Underground.[18] He eventually ended up as a rapper with N.W.A and over time became one of the most respected solo artists in the field. Although many of his lyrics focused on thuggish topics, 2Pac also produced songs that spoke poignantly about the hopelessness of ghetto life in the United States. Good examples of message lyrics can be found in such songs as "Words of Wisdom" and "Young Black Male" from *2Pacalypse Now* (1991) and "Keep Ya Head Up" and "The Streetz R Deathrow" from *Strictly for My N.I.G.G.A.Z.* (1993).

TOP TWENTY-FIVE R&B SONGS OF THE 1990s

Tables 9 and 10 contain the data for the top twenty-five R&B songs of the 1990s. Although previously in this study we have witnessed changes in average tempo from one decade to the next—for example, the increase from an average of 106 b.p.m. in the 1950s to 116 b.p.m. in the 1960s—we have not seen such a dramatic difference in two consecutive decades as exists between the 1980s and 1990s. As table 10 shows, the average tempo of the top twenty-five R&B songs of the 1990s is 79 b.p.m., a drop of 34 b.p.m. from the 1980s figure. The data reveals that very slow songs, those at a tempo of 70 b.p.m. or less, were far more prominent in the 1990s (52 percent of the total) than in the previous decade (4 percent). This major shift is related to a number of factors discussed in this chapter, including the difficulty of rapping sixteenth or thirty-second notes at a moderate or fast tempo and the use of sixteenth notes as the basic metronomic value. The g-funk style of Dr. Dre, which emerged in the early 1990s and typically featured slow song tempi, also had much to do with the overall phenomenon of decreased tempo in R&B during the decade.

The average number of chord types also dropped substantially during the 1990s (5.04) when compared to the 1980s figure (6.92). The 1990s average is actually much more in line with figures from the 1950s through the 1970s, as seen in tables 2, 4, and 6. This information suggests that at least one feature of the music of the 1980s, its dramatically higher average number of chord types, represents a significant departure from long-term trends in rhythm & blues. It may also indicate a return in the 1990s toward a more traditional blues-system harmonic sensibility.

The average track time of the I chord in 1990s R&B (38 percent) almost exactly matches the figure from the 1980s (39 percent), apparently indicating that the incidence of this chord has stabilized. When looked at together, the averages of IV, V, and other chords reveal more than when studied separately. The increase in use of the IV (up 5 percent) and V (up 3 percent) chords is, for example, offset in part by the drop in use of other chords (down 5 percent). It should be noted that the averages for the IV and V chords have in

TITLE	DATE	ARTIST	LABEL & NO.
I Will Always Love You	12/5/92	Whitney Houston	Arista 12490
Freak Me	3/13/93	Silk	Keia/Elektra 64654
Right Here/Human Nature	8/28/93	SWV (Sisters with Voices)	RCA 62614
Gangsta Lean	11/13/93	D.R.S.	Capitol 44958
Bump N' Grind	2/26/94	R. Kelly	Jive 42207
Anytime, Anyplace	6/11/94	Janet Jackson	Virgin 38435
I'll Make Love to You	8/20/94	Boyz II Men	Motown 2257
Creep	12/10/94	TLC	LaFace 24082
This Is How We Do It	4/1/95	Montell Jordan	PMP/RAL 851468
One More Chance/Stay with Me	6/24/95	The Notorious B.I.G.	Bad Boy 79031
Exhale (Shoop Shoop)	11/25/95	Whitney Houston	Arista 12885
Down Low (Nobody Has to Know)	3/9/96	R. Kelly	Jive 42373
Tha Crossroads	5/11/96	Bone Thugs-N-Harmony	Ruthless 6335
I Believe I Can Fly	12/21/96	R. Kelly	Jive 42422
Can't Nobody Hold Me Down	3/8/97	Puff Daddy	Bad Boy 79083
I'll Be Missing You	6/14/97	Puff Daddy and Faith Evans	Bad Boy 79097
You Make Me Wanna	9/6/97	Usher	LaFace 24265
My Body	11/22/97	LSG	EastWest 63132
Nice & Slow	1/24/98	Usher	LaFace 24290
The Boy Is Mine	6/6/98	Brandy and Monica	Atlantic 84089
The First Night	9/5/98	Monica	Arista 13522
Nobody's Supposed to Be Here	11/7/98	Deborah Cox	Arista 13550
Heartbreak Hotel	2/12/99	Whitney Houston	Arista 13619
Fortunate	5/15/99	Maxwell	Columbia 79135
Bills, Bills, Bills	7/10/99	Destiny's Child	Columbia 79175

TABLE 9. Top 25 rhythm & blues singles of the 1990s: artist and label information.

—Adapted from Joel Whitburn, *Top R&B Singles: 1942–1999* (Menomonee Falls, WI: Record Research Inc., 2000).

the 1990s risen almost to their 1950s levels. The topic of long-term harmonic trends in R&B is explored in greater depth in the final chapter of this book.

We should perhaps not be surprised to see that the twelve-bar blues form is entirely absent in the top twenty-five R&B songs of the 1990s. The form had been present in only one of the top twenty-five songs of the 1980s, and none of the top songs of the 1970s. Use of the cyclic form, however, has

TITLE	TEMPO	CHORDS	I	IV	V	OTHER	12-BAR	CYCLE	SCALE	3-SWING
I Will Always Love You	66	7	36%	17%	21%	18%	N	21%	3	N
Freak Me	67	7	0%	14%	28%	34%	N	100%	3	N
Right Here/ Human Nature	94	6	0%	20%	26%	26%	N	34%	2	Y
Gangsta Lean	55	3	41%	19%	0%	10%	N	100%	3	Y
Bump N' Grind	65	8	22%	14%	24%	29%	N	81%	3	N
Anytime, Anyplace	64	12	3%	4%	11%	66%	N	15%	1	N
I'll Make Love to You	47	7	17%	0%	20%	41%	N	0%	1	Y
Creep	93	2	50%	50%	0%	0%	N	100%	2	Y
This Is How We Do It	102	2	66%	0%	0%	22%	N	83%	2	Y
One More Chance/Stay with Me	93	1	98%	0%	0%	0%	N	98%	1	N
Exhale (Shoop Shoop)	69	7	47%	23%	2%	28%	N	84%	1	N
Down Low (Nobody Has to Know)	54	3	27%	24%	49%	0%	N	98%	2	N
Tha Crossroads	72	4	25%	31%	18%	26%	N	100%	1	N
I Believe I Can Fly	60	5	36%	0%	9%	53%	N	16%	2	N
Can't Nobody Hold Me Down	94	1	100%	0%	0%	0%	N	100%	1	N
I'll Be Missing You	110	4	50%	12%	12%	26%	N	100%	1	N
You Make Me Wanna	82	8	22%	21%	22%	28%	N	89%	3	N
My Body	60	5	18%	24%	29%	30%	N	80%	3	N
Nice & Slow	61	2	50%	0%	0%	50%	N	100%	2	N
The Boy Is Mine	93	2	50%	50%	0%	0%	N	100%	3	N
The First Night	76	9	46%	21%	2%	30%	N	85%	3	N
Nobody's Supposed to Be Here	128	7	22%	15%	7%	49%	N	51%	3	N
Heartbreak Hotel	67	5	48%	44%	3%	5%	N	90%	2	N
Fortunate	63	3	44%	25%	19%	0%	N	100%	3	N
Bills, Bills, Bills	128	6	23%	16%	46%	16%	N	81%	3	N
Average	79	5.04	38%	18%	14%	23%	0%	76%	2.2	20%

TABLE 10. Top 25 rhythm & blues singles of the 1990s: song transcription data.

continued to increase. The 1990s figure for that form (76 percent) is considerably higher than that of the previous decade (57 percent). This increase is probably due to a variety of factors, one of which is the widespread use of the sample loop—itself a cycle—to create a song. But the cyclic form is a long-term feature of African-American music that came to the forefront in R&B in the 1960s and 1970s, *before* digital sample loops were in use.

According to table 10, the use of blue notes in 1990s R&B has diminished to a figure of 2.2 from that of 2.5 in the 1980s. Part of the reason for this drop is the increase in popularity of rap music over the decade. Because rapping is typically performed without (or with few) specific pitches, blue notes, in the way they have been defined in this study and by numerous other writers, often do not exist in such songs. Therefore, songs in table 10 which consist primarily of rapped vocals, such as "One More Chance/Stay with Me" and "Can't Nobody Hold Me Down," show a relatively low incidence of blue notes.

Triplet swing experienced a pronounced increase in the 1990s to such a level that 20 percent of the songs studied exhibit the trait, up from 8 percent in the 1980s. However, table 10 appears to understate the phenomenon as it existed early in the 1990s, probably because of the fact that no song from 1990

YEAR	NO. 1 SINGLES	3-SWING	% OF TOTAL
1990	37	20	54%
1991	38	13	34%
1992	31	11	35%
1993	13	5	38%
1994	9	4	44%
1995	12	2	17%
1996	17	3	18%
1997	11	1	9%
1998	11	1	9%
1999	11	0	0%

TABLE 11. Incidence of triplet swing in number-one R&B songs, 1990–1999.

or 1991 made the top twenty-five of the decade. During the first few years of the decade (continuing from the late 1980s) there was a significant increase in triplet swing due in part to the popularity of the new jack swing style discussed earlier in this chapter (and in chapter 6). However, the popularity of this rhythm seems to have faded a great deal by mid-decade. Table 11 shows a total of all the number-one R&B singles in *Billboard* for each year of the 1990s (second column) and follows that with the number of those songs that clearly incorporate the triplet-swing element (third column). The percentage of the number-one songs of each year that use triplet swing is shown in the far-right column. The data clearly show that use of this feature diminished over the course of the decade.

CHAPTER EIGHT

THE TRANSFORMATION OF RHYTHM & BLUES

The body of rhythm & blues music is a collection of various blends that draw from a common pool of elements of musical style, form, and content, which I have labeled "the blues system." Using the data I have collected as evidence, we can examine the validity of the blues system concept while at the same time evaluating the influence of European and African musical traditions on the styles of R&B. Additionally, we can determine the relationship of the rhythm & blues music studied here to earlier African-American music, both folk and popular, and American popular music in general.

It has been my goal to add to the body of scholarship in African-American music. Thus, an effort is made in this chapter to relate key findings of this study to important earlier works by scholars in the field. I offer factual data that serve to support certain arguments while perhaps also suggesting that others might benefit from modification. I do not mean to imply, however, that any findings presented here are exhaustive or conclusive. A study, such as this, of music at the elemental level paints only part of the overall picture. To gain a truer understanding of such important questions as "*What outside factors caused the music to change?*" or "*What is the role of the music in society, and how has its function changed?*" one would need to look more closely at the social and cultural setting in which the music exists.

R&B AS A COLLECTION OF STYLES AND GENRES

Some writers seem to perceive rhythm & blues primarily as a 1940s and 1950s genre, and see soul music, funk, rap, and other styles of the 1960s and beyond as not truly R&B.[1] But it seems more accurate to think of rhythm & blues as a collection of different, yet related styles and genres. There is little doubt about the origin of the term "rhythm & blues" as it came to be used in society: it was created in the late 1940s as a label for the African-American record market and replaced the term previously used, "race records."

Rhythm & blues might more easily be defined as a genre if it were a limited group of very closely related musical styles. However, this is not what our research suggests. As we saw in chapter 3, the 1950s R&B charts included such stylistically diverse number-one R&B songs as "You'll Never Walk Alone" (from the Broadway musical *Carousel*); "I Almost Lost My Mind" (Sepia Sinatra style); "Honey Love" (Latin-influenced doo-wop); "I'm In the Mood" (blues); and "I Got a Woman" (fast-paced gospel style). I would suggest that the 1950s R&B category exhibited at least as broad a range of styles as the category did in any of the later decades studied. In fact, it is possible to argue that the 1950s R&B charts included songs from an even *wider* spectrum than the charts from the 1960s onward. Proof of this contention might be found in the large number of 1950s hits that can easily be labeled "jazz," "blues," "novelty," or "white crossovers," and the apparent decline of these types of song in R&B over the course of the next few decades.

The above argument—that somehow the body of 1950s R&B is overall less cohesive than the music of later decades—is hypothetical, and I offer it simply to illustrate the dangers in trying to define rhythm & blues as a genre instead of as a broad category that includes styles and genres. I am in no way seriously suggesting that 1950s R&B is less "pure" or "authentic" than later black popular music. The real question is: if soul, funk, quiet storm, urban, neo-soul, Philly-soul, new jack swing, rap, and hip hop are not "rhythm & blues," what are they? Due to the reliance of these genres on elements of style, form, and content of the blues system, there is an important relationship between them. But all such musical types exist as distinct blends of blues-system traits (and those from outside the system) and are simply part of a broad spectrum that is the body of African-American popular music.

One could suggest that there exists a fundamental difference between rap music and the other styles mentioned in the previous paragraph, regardless of its reliance on elements of the blues system. Although in the 1990s rap became more accepted into mainstream R&B, it was for much of its early history an underground music that went largely unnoticed, or unappreciated, by the public at large. Rap has maintained a separate existence outside the mainstream while developing its own special traits of musical and lyrical style. Yet these same traits eventually became the most important stylistic influences on modern R&B in general. In this way rap held a position in the R&B market of the 1980s and 1990s much like the blues and jazz genres did in the 1940s and 1950s. Eventually, the mass-market appeal of rap will decline, as did that of blues and jazz. It will be interesting to see if rap is able to maintain a separate, ongoing tradition as those other genres did after their commercial success began to wane.

The name given by *Billboard* to the chart I have been calling "rhythm & blues" has actually changed many times throughout the second half of the twentieth century. Some truths might be inferred just by understanding when and under what conditions these changes occurred. The term "R&B" was discarded by *Billboard* in 1969 and a new name, "Soul Singles," came into use, in apparent response to the popularity of that musical style throughout the 1960s. Then in 1982 *Billboard* changed the chart name to "Black Singles," perhaps indicating that the soul era had run its course. In 1990 the chart name was changed once more, and this time *Billboard* chose the familiar name "R&B Singles."

Over the years, *Billboard* modified the chart name to reflect the stylistic changes that had occurred and the way in which the black record-buying public perceived the music. In 1990 the magazine apparently came to the conclusion that the whole category was just as correctly labeled "R&B" as anything else it had been using. It should come as no surprise that in 1999 *Billboard* once again changed the chart name, this time to "R&B/Hip-Hop." One can only wonder how long the current name will remain, and if it will at some future date once again become simply "R&B."

R&B AND POPULAR MUSIC

R&B began the 1950s largely separate from the wider category of popular music. This is not to say that no black artists achieved success on the more general charts. As we have seen, Louis Jordan, Nat "King" Cole, the Mills Brothers, and other black musicians had been enjoying hits on the popular music charts since the 1940s. But the level of success experienced by such artists was greatly eclipsed by that of later black artists. In fact, some writers have suggested that musicians such as Jordan were not nearly as successful on mainstream popular radio stations as has often been assumed. David Brackett's research has led him to the conclusion that although Jordan is widely regarded as one of the first big crossover artists, his success is based more on jukebox charts than popular radio airplay. Therefore it is debatable as to how much of Jordan's music was actually heard on mainstream popular radio.[2]

The number of black musicians in the list of top twenty-five popular music artists of each decade waxed and waned over the years, as table 12 shows. Looking at the data from a long-term point of view, it might be said that the music of African Americans became generally more acceptable in the U.S. mainstream over the time period studied. These statistics imply that either (1) over the course of the second half of the twentieth century American popular music incorporated more traits of the black musical style, thereby moving closer to the African-American musical tradition, or (2) during the period studied African-American musical styles acquired elements of style, form, and content found in the general popular music field to such a degree that they became more acceptable to the mass market, or (3) a combination of both of the above phenomena occurred. In other words, either mainstream popular music moved toward the black musical tradition, or vice versa, or the two style pools converged. Of course, one recognizes that there are other possibilities and that these are not the only ways to interpret the facts at hand.

DECADE	BLACK ARTISTS IN TOP 25	%
1950–1959	5	20%
1960–1969	12	48%
1970–1979	9	36%
1980–1989	7	28%
1990–1999	18	72%

TABLE 12. Number of black musicians among the top twenty-five American popular music artists of each decade, 1950–1999, based on singles success.

—Adapted from Joel Whitburn, *The Billboard Book of Top 40 Hits*, 7th ed. (New York Billboard Books, 2000), 819.

But we can look at the above three points in order to gain an understanding of how our research addresses the overall question of how R&B fits into the broader popular music field.

Point one in the preceding paragraph could be thoroughly investigated by conducting the kind of research done in this study, but by using the Hot 100 charts instead of the R&B charts as the source for songs to be analyzed. I am suggesting that transcribing the top twenty-five *popular* music songs of each decade specifically for the incidence of traits such as blue notes, melisma, twelve-bar blues and cyclic form, and triplet swing—in other words, elements of the blues system—would go a long way toward proving whether American popular music 1950–1999 was gradually more influenced by black music. Of course, this has not been the focus of the present study, and therefore one can only speak in the broadest of terms concerning this topic. That being said, the fact that such a large percentage of the top twenty-five artists on the 1990s popular music charts are black (72 percent) carries much weight. Common sense seems to lead one to the conclusion that popular music must have gained an acceptance of black music traits over the time period studied simply due to the presence of so many top black artists.

Point two, the possibility that black music acquired traits from the popular music market and thereby became more "mainstream" *can* be specifically addressed with the results of our research. If it were true that black music began to abandon the African-American musical tradition and replace it with a more European-based, popular music sensibility, one should be able to identify related trends in the tables included in chapters 3 through 7. In such a case one would expect the key traits of the blues system to have largely disappeared over time.

R&B AND THE BLUES SYSTEM

Table 13 is a summary of the information collected from the rhythm & blues songs of the decades studied. One can clearly see that many of the features focused on in this study have changed significantly over time. Some have shown a decrease, or even disappeared entirely over the 1950 to 1999 time period, while others remained at more or less constant levels throughout the half-century, or increased dramatically. Though the elements of style, form, and content shown in the table were those specifically targeted for investigation,

DECADE	TEMPO	CHORDS	I	IV	V	OTHER	12-BAR	CYCLE	SCALE	3-SWING
1950–1959	106	4.68	54%	22%	16%	8%	60%	5%	2.4	92%
1960–1969	116	4.24	54%	25%	12%	8%	12%	33%	2.4	28%
1970–1979	105	5.40	46%	20%	11%	21%	0%	53%	2.4	4%
1980–1989	113	6.92	39%	13%	11%	28%	4%	57%	2.5	8%
1990–1999	79	5.04	38%	18%	14%	23%	0%	76%	2.2	20%

TABLE 13. Summary of data collected from top twenty-five R&B songs of each decade, 1950–1999.

the continued use of other blues-system traits was traced as well. The following discussion is intended to synthesize the collected data into a concise body of evidence that will help to define the stylistic spectrum of R&B and its reliance on blues-system traits.

The average tempo for the top twenty-five songs of each decade was originally calculated primarily for one reason: to determine if the R&B songs exhibited a tendency toward acceleration as described by Titon in his study of blues songs of the 1920s.[3] Our results (tables 2, 4, 6, 8, and 10) show that acceleration of tempo greater than three b.p.m. existed in nine of the twenty-five R&B songs of the 1950s (36 percent), six of twenty-five in the 1960s (24 percent), three of twenty-five in the 1970s (12 percent), and none thereafter. One is compelled to conclude that this tendency has been largely abandoned in rhythm & blues, although it may exist in R&B songs not studied.

One can hypothesize some of the reasons that tempo acceleration is no longer a significant factor in R&B. It is likely that the development of the modern recording studio played a role in the production of fixed song tempi due to the use of the "click track," a reference track recorded with the use of a metronome that is fed into each musician's headphones during the recording. The idea is that if all musicians follow the click track, the overall tempo will be metronomic, in other words, mechanically perfect. This technique is widespread, one could even say standard practice, in the modern music industry.

Another factor that has had an impact on tempo "perfection" in R&B, and other types of music, is the emergence of music created with sequencers and drum machines.[4] These devices are typically used to create a rhythmic pattern that is played repeatedly throughout a song. Since the sequenced part serves as the foundation for the rest of the music that is overlaid, and due to the fact that its mechanical nature precludes the possibility for any sort of live interaction between it and the musicians, it is created in as rhythmically exact a fashion as possible. However, such rhythmic perfection often sounds stiff and unnatural, in which case the use of a feature sometimes called "humanize" comes into play. The humanize feature of a sequencer allows for a certain degree of rhythmic imperfection to be programmed into the sequenced track, thereby making it sound more "human."

Another possible reason for the abandonment of tempo acceleration in R&B is the increased level of musical sophistication of the performers themselves. Whereas in the 1920s blues songs studied by Titon we would expect to hear few, if any, trained musicians in the Western sense, by the 1960s and beyond the typical R&B performer was far more likely to have received a formal music education. For example, Stax Records artist Booker T. Jones, of Booker T. and the MG's, was a musical star in his high school band in Memphis and later studied music at Indiana University,[5] Roberta Flack graduated from Howard University with a music degree,[6] and Chic's Nile Rodgers "studied classical music and jazz before joining the house band at the Apollo Theater."[7] Such musicians would almost certainly have been trained to keep an even tempo, an ideal typically promoted in Western art music and jazz education, and they would have tended to continue the practice in R&B.

The steep drop in the average song tempo in the 1990s from the 1980s level is a topic that deserves considerable attention and perhaps warrants further research. As discussed in the previous chapter, the somewhat surprising magnitude of the decrease in tempo, 34 b.p.m., indicates that significant factors are at play here. As suggested in chapter 7, one of the reasons for this phenomenon is that such slower tempi are a result of the influence of rap music on R&B in general in the 1990s. Rapping often makes use of sixteenth note and even thirty-second-note rhythms, and fast tempi are typically avoided due to the difficulty of performing the rap.

A related factor is that much R&B of the 1990s uses the sixteenth note as its basic metronomic value. Use of this rhythmic feature is probably a direct influence of the funk music style of the late 1960s and 1970s, but antecedents can be seen at least as far back as the mid-nineteenth century in African-American folk music. Examples can be seen in such songs as "The Graveyard" and "Jesus, Won't You Come By-and-Bye?," found in *Slave Songs of the United*

States.[8] Likewise, one need only browse through a book of Scott Joplin rags to see the prevalence of sixteenth-note rhythms in one genre of late nineteenth- and early twentieth-century African-American popular music.

Joplin, it might be mentioned, exhibits what amounts to a near obsession when he includes instructions at the top of most of his printed piano compositions indicating that the music is not to be played fast. A few examples are: "not fast," "not too fast," "slow," "play a little slow," and "Notice: Do not play this piece fast. It is never right to play Ragtime fast."[9] I am not suggesting, of course, that there is any sort of direct musical link between Joplin's desire for a slow tempo and that witnessed in the 1990s R&B songs studied. However, we can at least recognize that the common use of the sixteenth note as the basic metronomic value in both types of music leads them typically to adopt a slow or moderate tempo.

Several significant findings have emerged from our study of the harmonic aspects of R&B, 1950–1999. First and foremost of these is one that was not predicted at the outset of the research: *the dramatic rise in prominence of the minor modes in R&B of the 1970s and later.* As I have shown, especially in the funk style of the 1970s and 1980s, the minor modes (both natural minor and dorian) came to be preferred over the major. Numerous examples have been presented to support this contention, such as "I Heard It Through the Grapevine" (1968) (ex. 35), "Flashlight" (1978) (ex. 38), "Let It Whip" (1982) (ex. 47), and "Poison" (1990) (ex. 53).

A major significance of the use of these minor modes is that the scales have inherent blue notes at the third and seventh degrees. Considering the keyboard and sequencer orientation of R&B in the 1980s, use of minor modes seems to be a reasonable solution to the old issue of how to avoid the major third and major seventh of the Western scale. I do not feel that the evidence supports an alternate theory that use of the minor modes is somehow a movement by R&B musicians toward the mainstream popular music style. To make such an assertion one would likely need to show that during the 1970s the minor modes were prominent in mainstream popular music, and that their use was then co-opted by black musicians. Such proof would probably be very hard to come by, especially since only 28 percent of the top twenty-five songs on the Hot 100 in the 1970s were in a minor mode, and of those most were either by black artists or were disco-oriented songs.[10] In any case, the trend toward the use of the minor modes in R&B seems to be an important topic that should be investigated into the 2000s and beyond.

Research into harmonic tendencies in rhythm & blues has been a major focus of the current study, namely the change in incidence of the I, IV, V, and "other" chords, and the overall number of chord types used in the songs analyzed. Table 13 indicates that the number of different triads used in R&B songs in the 1950s and 1960s is fairly consistent, remaining between four and five chords per song. However the level of chord types rose notably in the 1970s to 5.4 and then leapt to 6.92 the 1980s. Three songs from the 1980s top twenty-five (table 8), "Time Will Reveal," "That Girl," and "Rock with You," are so chord-laden (18, 14, and 12 chord types, respectively) that one might suspect that they skew the results. However, such is not the case entirely. Deleting those three songs from the calculations altogether still leaves an average of almost six chord types per song in the 1980s.

Why this phenomenon occurred is open for debate. One might speculate that some R&B artists of the 1970s and 1980s were consciously adding more chords in an attempt to bridge the gap between the black music aesthetic and the sensibilities of the larger popular-music market. To sustain such a theory one would have to show first that the popular music of the era made use of significantly more chord types than in previous decades, and then that R&B musicians were emulating the mainstream musicians in their use of more chord types specifically to appeal to the mass market. To my knowledge no such detailed study of this particular elemental aspect of 1970s and 1980s popular music and its relationship to R&B has been made. However, such research might prove rewarding.

In apparent contradiction to the idea that black artists made use of more chords in order to become more successful in the popular-music market, table 12 indicates that in the 1980s the number of black artists at the very top of the popular-music field was lower than in any decade since the 1950s. This implies that black music of the 1980s was somehow *less* acceptable overall to the mainstream popular music audience than it had been before, despite the tremendous success of a few superstars such as Michael Jackson and Prince. However, several releases that made the list of top twenty-five R&B hits of the 1980s also earned a spot on the corresponding list of Hot 100 songs, and some of these songs showed a marked tendency toward the use of more chord types. Records that fit into such a category are "Rock with You," "Endless Love," "Billie Jean," and "When Doves Cry."

The trend held up here for examination seems connected to what Nelson George describes in *The Death of Rhythm & Blues*. To summarize briefly,

George suggests that the lure of crossover success in the wider popular-music market caused many black artists to orient their music in that direction, thereby losing their core "blackness" in the process.[11] There appears to be some truth to George's contention, and the average number of chord types used in 1980s R&B songs supports his argument. If black musicians were going to "sell out" their musical heritage in order to make it big in the popular-music market, "sweetening" their sound with sophisticated, jazzy-pop chords might have been a good way to go about it. As we have seen, however, only a limited number of black artists were successful in making a move to a more general popular sound and broader commercial success.

It seems important to note that, of the traits specifically investigated in the present study, only the average number of chord types used and the changes in the incidence of the I, IV, and "other" chords show a sudden and marked difference in the 1980s from the previous decades. All other elements studied retained levels generally consistent with the trends established in previous decades. If a real attempt were being made by African-American musicians to make their music sound more palatable to the wider popular audience, it would be advantageous also to curtail the use of, for example, blue notes, melismatic vocals, and the cyclic form.

The incidence of the I, IV, V, and "other" chords went through important changes over the 1950 to 1999 period. Figure 10 is a summary of the chord

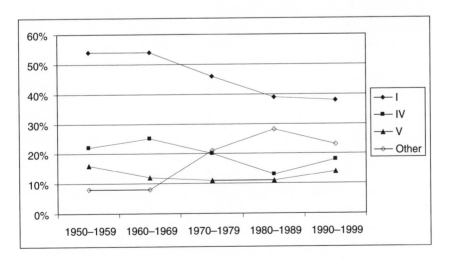

FIGURE 10. Graph of chord data from Table 13.

data from table 13. This graph allows us to see that after the 1960s there was a fundamental shift in the use of these chords. The factor that probably caused the greatest change in the incidence of the I, IV, and V chords was the dramatic decrease in use of the twelve-bar blues form in 1960s R&B. Because that form and its many variants has a basic chord ratio of 8 to 3 to 1 (I to IV to V), its widespread use in the 1950s and early 1960s caused the chord averages to hover at figures generally along those lines.

Van der Merwe's statement that twentieth-century American popular music has seen a "supplanting in importance of the dominant by the subdominant" (as discussed in chapter 2) is not supported by our research.[12] Based on the data in the graph shown above, one could conceivably make the argument that the IV chord began to replace the V chord in the 1960s. However, any hypothesis that this represents a long-term trend is immediately disproved by the fact that in no decade has the level of these two chords been closer than in the 1980s and 1990s.

It is probably significant that the "other" chord category experienced a sudden rise in the 1970s, and another in the 1980s, with a corresponding decline of the three primary chords. Perhaps the most striking change, however, is the loss in prominence of the I chord, a phenomenon related to the abandonment of the twelve-bar blues form and the increase in use of "other" chords. The upsurge in the use of "other" chords is also related to the earlier discussion about the average number of chord types in 1980s R&B; one would expect to see a rise in the use of "other" chords as the number of chord types rises. It should be noted that the "other" chord category rose above the level of the IV chord for the first time in the 1970s, and retained that advantage throughout the rest of the period studied. It is probably important to note that triads built on the flat third and flat seventh of the scale—both of which are included in the "other" category—became much more prominent in R&B from 1970 through 1999, probably due in part to the increased use of minor modes.

An interesting development in 1990s R&B is the return to a harmonic sensibility somewhat similar to that of the 1950s and 1960s. Table 13 indicates that the 1990s saw a decrease in the average number of chord types per song almost down to the 1950s level, far below that of the 1980s. We can also see that in the 1990s use of the IV and V chords rose nearly to the 1950s levels. The I chord, however, in the 1990s remained at an average similar to that of the 1980s, due no doubt in part to the persistence of the "other" chord category. Taken as a whole, this data seems to indicate a return by 1990s R&B

musicians, whether conscious or not, to an older harmonic aesthetic that was less reliant on complex chord structures.

Use of the cyclic form increased steadily from 1950 to 1999. Other than in the blues genre, it is very difficult to find any significant precedent for this form in mainstream American popular music or European music before 1950. Some Western music scholars might take exception to such a statement, however, and put forth the idea that some European musical forms, such as the canon or chaconne, make use of repeating harmonic, melodic, or rhythmic elements (or a combination thereof) in a similar way to the cyclic form defined here. However, there are two important differences: (1) the cycles of R&B, the repeated cells within the cyclic form, are often much shorter in length than those of the European forms mentioned, and (2) the cyclic form of R&B often has no functional harmony in the Western sense, and commonly uses what has been called "static" harmony in this study.

As indicated earlier, the cyclic form is common in African music as well as in nineteenth-century and twentieth-century African-American religious music.[13] Additionally, the static harmony that is often part of the cyclic form exists in the music of some twentieth-century African-American blues artists. Based on these facts, I hypothesize that the increasing use of the cyclic form in rhythm & blues from 1960 to 1999, led by James Brown and others, indicates that a reinterpretation of a traditional African-American form, based on an African musical sensibility, was taking place in a modern context. This reinterpretation—or "re-Africanization," the name given a similar phenomenon by Evans in a discussion about black fife and drum groups, gospel quartets, and mid-century blues artists[14]—of the cyclic form is one example of a movement by rhythm & blues of 1950–1999 further away from, not closer to, mainstream popular music and the European music tradition.

Coupled with the rise in the use of cyclic form is the dramatic decrease of the twelve-bar blues form. The graph in figure 11, based on data from table 13, shows that the two formal structures had an almost exactly negative correlation in R&B music over the second half of the twentieth century. As can be clearly seen, the twelve-bar blues form had all but disappeared by the 1970s. What is not revealed in either the graph or in Table 13 is that all of the top twenty-five R&B hits using the twelve-bar blues in the 1960s were released before 1966. Taken as a whole, our evidence suggests that, for all intents and purposes, the twelve-bar blues form was virtually abandoned in R&B after the mid-1960s.

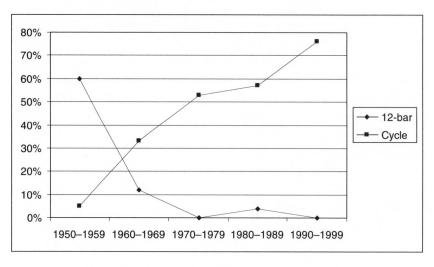

FIGURE 11. Graph of song form data from Table 13.

Why would the twelve-bar blues form, which dominated R&B in the 1950s and which had been a fundamental feature of popular black music since at least the 1910s, suddenly lose so much of its appeal? This question can probably never be completely answered, but I would suggest that the wholesale co-opting of the twelve-bar blues form by white rock 'n' roll musicians left many in the black community feeling as if their cultural property had been stolen. Black musicians who were early on labeled "rock 'n' roll" artists, such as Chuck Berry, Little Richard, and Fats Domino, consistently had hit records on the 1950s and early 1960s R&B charts. However, it was not long before rock 'n' roll came to be perceived by the general public as music made by and for white people. Additionally, it should be remembered that 1965 was the year that major victories in civil rights were won by blacks in the United States. Many African Americans may have associated the twelve-bar blues with a pre–civil rights way of life and turned away from the form. In any case, black musicians in the U.S., consciously or not, abandoned the twelve-bar blues form and focused on a different, perhaps even more African-influenced, construct, the cyclic form.

Table 13 also reveals that over the course of the half-century there was a consistent use of blue-note thirds and sevenths in the R&B hits. However, as presented in chapter 7 (the results of which appear in table 10), the 1990s saw a slight decrease in blue-note use due partly to the tendency toward the use of non-pitched vocal parts in rap and hip hop music. There are two points to be made regarding this phenomenon. The first is that, even though rapping obviously reduces the incidence of blue notes, it has been shown that when vocal parts are sung in 1990s R&B, blue notes are often preferred over the Western scale equivalent. The second point is that rapping itself can be viewed as the ultimate in melodic ambiguity, a trait that has been discussed throughout this study as another important component of the blues system. A rapped vocal part has no pitch relationship whatsoever to the harmonic structure below it and therefore floats over the chords in its ambivalence.

A fact that probably needs re-emphasizing is that the use of blue notes in African-American folk and popular music goes back as far as anyone can look.[15] For instance, one of the earliest collections of transcribed examples of African-American folk music is *Slave Songs of the United States*, and the first song in that book, "Roll, Jordan, Roll," makes use of both blue-note thirds (in the variation) and sevenths.[16] The continued use of blue notes in rhythm & blues over the period studied indicates that the trait is one of the most important elements of the blues system and perhaps is largely immutable. The data collected during this study provides conclusive evidence that the core style of R&B has not abandoned this important part of its traditional melodic sensibility.

Triplet swing, almost absent in the 1970s and 1980s R&B songs studied, made a comeback in the late 1980s and early 1990s. However, as was discussed in chapter 7 and shown in table 11, this was a short-lived phenomenon, which had run its course by the late 1990s. The overall decrease in use of the triplet-swing trait does not necessarily prove that a "Westernization" of rhythms in African-American popular music was taking place; other rhythmic features of the blues system remained basically intact throughout the 1950 to 1999 time period. But based on the findings, I would at least posit the theory that triplet swing is not a feature as universal and unchangeable in African-American music as, for example, the use of blue notes. The triplet swing is not insignificant in black music, of course, for it is a trait that has appeared quite regularly in blues, early rhythm & blues, and especially jazz, but over time there has been a general tendency to move away from the triplet-swing feel. Evidence for this trend is found in our data and in the widespread incorporation of straight-eighth Latin and funk rhythms in jazz, especially from the 1960s onward.[17]

Related to triplet swing is the use of compound rhythms such as 6/8, 9/8, and 12/8. As discussed in chapter 2, this trait can be found across a wide range of African-American folk and popular music and has been especially prevalent in gospel music. I have not created a special category for data collection on compound time signatures because, for the purposes of this study, such rhythms have been considered a subset of triplet swing. Obviously, a song that uses one of the compound time signatures mentioned above also can be said to have the triplet-swing trait because each beat is divided into three parts. Therefore, songs using the 6/8, 9/8, and 12/8 schemes have been included in the triplet-swing figure for each decade studied. The use of compound time signatures was fairly prevalent in the 1950s R&B songs studied, with several songs based on triplet rhythms, including "The Great Pretender," "The Things That I Used to Do," "It's Just a Matter of Time," and "Pledging My Love." Although the average number of songs using compound time signatures decreased over the period studied, the trait still was in use to some degree in 1990s rhythm & blues. For example, two R&B songs from the top twenty-five of the 1990s, "Gangsta Lean" and "I'll Make Love to You," make use of 12/8 time.

The use of offbeat phrasing has been consistently present in R&B from 1950 to 1999. Several examples held up for examination in the present study support this statement: "Get Up (I Feel Like Being a Sex Machine), Part 1" (1970) (ex. 36); "Tell Me Something Good" (1974) (ex. 39); "You Dropped a Bomb on Me" (1982) (ex. 46); and "Thin Line Between Law and Rape" (1994) (exs. 57–58). Throughout the period studied, dance songs with a fast or medium tempo commonly included offbeat rhythmic phrasing. However, by the 1990s slow songs in R&B were also regularly incorporating such rhythmic figures (in sixteenth notes and sometimes thirty-second notes). A good example of this is the 1998 song "Nice & Slow" (ex. 55). It is not being suggested that the slow songs of the 1950s and 1960s were completely lacking in offbeat rhythms, but by and large the use of the feature on such songs was much less prevalent in that era than later in the century.

The increased use of complex interlocked rhythms in R&B from the late 1960s onward is a phenomenon that, like the rise in use of the cyclic form, arguably demonstrates a reinterpretation of elements of the African musical tradition. The level of complexity and rhythmic interrelationship seen in much funk music constitutes a fundamental shift in the way that the rhythmic fabric of a typical R&B song is woven. Funk music and its stylistic descendents create a musical whole by making use of a number of interlocking rhythmic parts which fit together in a complementary way.

Of course, intricate rhythmic patterns have traditionally existed in many forms of African-American popular music, notably jazz, since at least the early twentieth century, but precedents in American music, R&B or otherwise, for such a dramatic shift toward interlocked rhythms are difficult to find. Such a feature is, however, common in much African music as described by any number of experts in the field.[18] Three songs included in this study that best exemplify the rhythmically complex, interlocked rhythms discussed above are "Papa's Got a Brand New Bag, Part 1" (ex. 30), "Cold Sweat, Part 1" (ex. 33), and "Thank You (Falettinme Be Mice Elf Agin)" (ex. 37). Because rap and mainstream hip hop of the 1990s often rely on sampled loops from songs such as these, interlocked rhythms have become a fundamental feature of much modern R&B.

The presence of swing, by which I mean the deliberate shifting of a rhythm backward or forward in time against a fixed pulse, has also remained a vital part of R&B. Although the incidence of this trait was not specifically measured here (other than triplet swing), its presence was noted in more than a few musical examples. Unfortunately, swing—other than in equal triplet subdivisions of the beat—is difficult to indicate accurately in Western music notation.[19]

Perhaps the most visible manifestation of swing in R&B 1950–1999 is the persistence of "rubato-swing." This trait was defined in chapter 2 as a rhythm performed in such a way that it "floats" above the basic pulse. Such swing was identified in several transcribed examples from each of the decades investigated: "Hobo Blues" (ex. 4), "Doodlin'" (ex. 6-B), "Papa's Got a Brand New Bag, Part 1" (ex. 18), "These Arms of Mine" (ex. 29), "You Dropped a Bomb on Me" (ex. 46), and "Vision of Love" (ex. 54). Rubato-swing is more or less universal in R&B and African-American folk and popular music in general. It is possible to view this feature as a combination of two separate elements that have been discussed in this study, offbeat phrasing and improvisation. It is improvised in the sense that when using rubato-swing the musician typically creates a new version of the song in each performance.

The rubato-swing vocal improvisations described above, which typically make use of a variety of other features such as melisma, glissando, emotional delivery, and "dirty" tone, were a reminder in the 1970s and beyond that R&B still had a strong connection with the black music tradition. Perhaps to offset the "perfection" of the sequenced music tracks, which had the potential to dehumanize the music, such stylistic vocal traits often became the most prominent identifying features of the music. The vocal styles of Whitney Houston and Mariah Carey, both of whom rely heavily on the gospel music vocal tradition, display an emphasis on melisma that increased in R&B generally over the 1980s and 1990s, but which had existed in R&B from the outset. The Mariah Carey song "Vision of Love" (ex. 54) exemplifies the sometimes extreme use of melisma in late twentieth-century rhythm & blues.

OVERALL CONCLUSIONS

According to some scholars, African-American music has over time become less African. The proof often given for such hypotheses is based on the widespread incorporation in American black music of European musical elements and the wholesale abandonment or radical transformation of those from the African tradition. There is little doubt that African-American music relies a great deal on the European musical tradition. The evidence for this includes, among other things, the use of fixed-pitch European instruments, dominant-to-tonic chord progressions, strophic form, and printed music. But is there any real proof that African-American music overall is becoming increasingly more European, as suggested by Richard Waterman? "The ease with which many European musical traits could be incorporated into the African patterns simply permitted, through the processes of reinterpretation and syncretization, a retention of African musical formulae in the bodies of New World Negro music which have become, if we start with African music, more and more European with each generation as the blending progressed."[20]

I do not doubt that the process theorized by Waterman in the above quotation did in fact take place early in the development of African-American music. One can easily understand, even in the absence of data that might prove such a conclusion, that early on the music of the enslaved Africans took on European traits. However, the evidence collected for the present study suggests that in late-twentieth-century African-American popular music there was a movement toward the incorporation, or reincorporation, of elements of style, content, and form that are African in nature. In 1953, when the paper by Waterman was published, it was probably unclear that the re-Africanization of African-American music had begun, and its effects were not noted.

One of the main focal points of this study has been the work of Nelson George, especially these remarks in his 1988 book *The Death of Rhythm & Blues*:

> ... I can't shake off the feeling that in the enormous groundswell of change in the black community since World War II, something crucial *has* been lost. In the twenty years since the Great Society, which marked a high point in R&B music, the community that inspired both social change and artistic creativity has become a sad shell of itself. . . . The truth is that since white values were held up as primary models, many blacks, through no fault of their own, lost contact with the uniqueness of their people, and with their own heritage. . . .
>
> As a result of these broad social changes, black culture, and especially R&B music, has atrophied. The music is just not as gutsy or spirited or tuned into the needs of its core audience as it once was.[21]

Based on the findings of the present study, it seems that George's comments are proven true, at least in part. There does appear to have existed in the mid-1970s and 1980s a tendency for some R&B artists to produce music that was sweeter, more sophisticated, and less gritty than in the 1960s. Proof that this phenomenon occurred is seen in our data for that era, and is specifically indicated by the increases in the average chord type per song and the use of "other" chords.

However, the core style of R&B, and its reliance of the traits of the blues system, was not completely abandoned in the 1970s and 1980s. Although changes in the harmony might indicate a conciliatory move by *some* R&B artists toward the popular music market, persistence in the use of (among other traits) blue notes, melisma, gravelly timbre, offbeat phrasing, improvisation, and rubato-swing, along with increased use of the cyclic form, indicate the continued strength of black music tradition. Some of these elements were nurtured in the musical underground, especially the hip hop community, during the era under discussion. However, many were also retained in mainstream R&B, as shown in our data.

It seems that one true test of the authenticity of R&B music, and also its connection with black music tradition, is whether or not it is accepted by black record buyers and radio listeners. Thus, it might be enlightening to look at those artists who were successful in R&B in the 1980s but *did not* appeal significantly to the wider popular music market. One can surmise that the music of some of these artists, for example, funk musicians such as the Gap Band, Cameo, and Rick James, was somehow "too black" for the mass market. These artists, the fifth, seventh, and fourteenth most successful musicians on the R&B charts of the 1980s, together were able to produce only one top-twenty single in the larger popular music market during that decade. One can come to the conclusion that even though the lure of crossover into the popular market may have caused a change in the music of some R&B artists, and produced a handful of superstars, overall the blues-system tradition survived.

Rap uses many elements of the blues system, as I have maintained throughout this study. In some ways rap has been shown to be not only a continuation of the long-standing African-American tradition, but also a vehicle by which many African-derived elements, such as the cyclic form, were reinterpreted and reintroduced. In this way rap has served as fuel for the R&B fire. As mentioned earlier, because of its lack of widespread acceptance in the popular-music community for most of the 1970s and 1980s, rap remained an underground, folklike music during much of its early development. In his 1998 book *Hip Hop America*, George himself seems to have come to similar conclusions.[22] By the 1990s the incorporation of rap into mainstream R&B had breathed new life into the category and, based on our data, was partly responsible for a return to an older musical aesthetic.

Amiri Baraka's contention that the co-opting of the music of African Americans throughout the history of the country has caused black musicians to continually reinvent their music has also been one of the points of departure for this study. From a philosophical point of view Baraka's ideas ring true. One of the goals of this study has been to provide data on the presence of musical elements that either support, or disprove, his general hypothesis. One of the tenets presented by Baraka in *Blues People* is that each time a style of black music became part of mainstream popular music it eventually lost its emotional validity, which subsequently caused a reaction: "The result was a deliberately changing, constantly self-refining folk expression, the limbs of which grew so large that they extended into the wider emotional field to which all Western art wants constantly to address itself.... The fact that popular ragtime, Dixieland, swing, etc., were not Negro musics is important. They were the debris, in a sense, of vanished emotional references. The most contemporary Negro music to result afterward had absolutely nothing to do with this debris, except as a reaction to it."[23] Baraka's thoughts on the development of new styles as "reactions" in African-American music seem to be supported by our findings. This is not to suggest that all of what he says can be substantiated by our results, but simply that his conclusions about when and how African-American popular music changed coincide for the most part with our data.

For example, the late-1950s rise of soul music, which was closely related in style to black gospel music, was due in part to a reaction against the widespread popularization of late 1940s and 1950s rhythm & blues. In other words, when white doo-wop and rock 'n' roll became mass-market expressions of black musical tradition, some features of these styles became less popular in the black community. Thus, in the 1960s the twelve-bar blues form began to lose favor to the cyclic form, and triplet swing, a common feature of much doo-wop and early rock 'n' roll, became less prominent as well. However, the use of blue notes, melisma, gravelly timbre, rubato-swing, and other traits continued unabated. The alternative would have been a turn toward the use of the European scale and melodic approach.

In the late 1960s, as soul music became more accessible and easier to emulate by "blue-eyed soul" artists, funk music came into being. This style retained many features of the blues system, and put special emphasis on offbeat phrasing, interlocked rhythms, and cyclic forms, all three elements with strong connections to the African musical tradition. Funk developed in the early 1970s into a popular style that was used in discos, which eventually led to its simplification and loss of much that had made it part of the blues system.

In the late 1970s, an underground music, rap, began to develop as a reaction, in part, to the sometimes callously commercialized disco sound. Although there were a few crossover hits in rap, the genre remained largely underground into the mid-1980s. Like the other styles discussed above, rap music is created with reinterpreted elements of the African-American music tradition, especially the use of many of the traits of early funk such as offbeat phrasing and the cyclic form. However, rap adds a new "old" element in that it often features rhymed, spoken lyrics as opposed to sung vocals. As discussed in chapter 6, such rhymes are part of a long-standing black tradition as well. Rap music also features a ghetto sensibility, and this has been one of the features that helped to keep it from being co-opted by mainstream America for much of its history. What I mean to say here is simply that there is no authenticity in a performance by a middle-class, white suburbanite rapping about the "boyz 'n' tha hood." In this way, a certain reality check is maintained in rap music for the most part, as was witnessed by the demise of the career of white rapper Vanilla Ice when his middle-class roots were publicized.

One of the core features of rhythm & blues, and African-American musical style in general, is ambiguity. As a general cultural trait this tendency derives from the African tradition.

> While the whole European tradition strives for regularity—of pitch, of time, of timbre, and of vibrato—the African tradition strives precisely for the negation of these elements. In language, the African tradition aims at circumlocution rather than at exact definition. The direct statement is considered crude and unimaginative; the veiling of all contents in ever-changing paraphrases is considered the criterion of intelligence and personality. In music, the same tendency towards obliquity and ellipsis is noticeable: no note is attacked straight; the voice or instrument always approaches it from above or below, plays around the implied pitch without ever remaining on it for any length of time, and departs from it without ever having committed itself to a single meaning. The timbre is veiled and paraphrased and by constantly changing vibrato, tremolo and overtone effects. The timing and accentuation, finally, are not *stated*, but *implied* or *suggested*. The musician challenges himself to find and hold his orientation while denying or withholding all signposts.[24]

Although this quotation by Ernest Borneman was published in 1959 and was written in reference to the roots of jazz, his suggestions apply as well to the music studied here. Based on my research into the melody, harmony, rhythm, and form of rhythm & blues, 1950–1999, I have come to the conclusion that ambiguity is the single most important overall aesthetic.

Melodic ambiguity comes in a variety of guises in R&B, including the persistent use of blue notes, glissando, melisma, and pitch bends. By incorporating these techniques, individually or in tandem, the performer can imply a pitch without stating it precisely. Gaining a working knowledge of exactly how much ambiguity is appropriate, and where and when to use such effects, is a skill one learns by being a member of the cultural group that defines the acceptable use of such traits. For this reason it has remained difficult, as mentioned earlier, for any person outside the African-American community to produce an acceptable black vocal style.

Rhythm & blues of the 1970s and 1980s began to make consistent use of minor modes, thereby rendering the blue-note thirds less ambiguous due to the fact that there was no longer a major third also present. However, during that same time period rap developed, and with it came the non-pitched vocal, the ultimate in melodic ambiguity. It should be pointed out that improvisation itself is a type of melodic ambiguity in the sense that an improvised melody is by definition never restated in exactly the same manner.

Of course, harmonic ambiguity is related to the melodic tendency discussed above. It has been shown that a common feature of R&B in the 1950 to 1999 time period was that the melody and chords of a given piece of music were often seemingly "unrelated." In fact, this same phenomenon has always existed in blues where the melody and chords of the twelve-bar blues, for example, together do not "match" from a European music point of view.[25] Harmonic ambiguity is also related to the concept of static harmony, much discussed in this study, because such harmonies, by their very nature, do not adhere to the dominant-to-tonic rules of Western music theory.

Rhythmic ambiguity has also been a common feature. Offbeat phrasing in general has been found to be a fundamental element of all styles discussed in this paper, notably funk, rap, new jack swing, and 1990s hip hop. The consistent use of offbeat phrasing and rubato-swing in the vocal parts, as exemplified by the songs mentioned earlier in this chapter, has been a key trait in black popular music from the earliest music studied onward. Use of rubato-swing is very effective in creating a great deal of rhythmic ambiguity—one might call it "rhythmic dissonance"—in the music without totally upsetting the basic pulse.

FINAL THOUGHTS

This study of the elements of rhythm & blues has shown the reliance of that music upon the blues system, a pool of musical traits. In investigating the use of these traits in R&B over the half-century studied, I have identified certain features that have remained largely unchanged, such as the use of blue notes, melisma, glissando, rhythmic complexity, offbeat phrasing, and swing. The results of the research have also supported the concept of a "super-genre" that includes not only rhythm & blues, but also several other categories of American music, such as blues, jazz, country, rock 'n' roll, and gospel, that rely on the same body of elements of style, content, and form. Based on this study of rhythm & blues, 1950–1999, it seems that the blues system concept is useful and valid in describing the general style of much African-American music and its relationship to the broader category of American popular music.

It is hoped that the research conducted here leads to new lines of study in African-American music and American popular music in general, and that such work will help to give further weight to the blues-system concept. Much work remains to be done before the blues system can be said to be truly defined. For example, the R&B music of the 2000s will reveal whether the changes seen in the 1980s and 1990s, especially the use of minor modes and significantly slower tempi, will become part of the blues system, or whether these features will be discarded. A thorough study at the elemental level of the effects of R&B on popular music in the 1960s and 1970s would be a fruitful area of research as well, due to the widespread cross-pollination between the two categories during that period.

APPENDIX A

Record Data Collection Methodology

This study was conducted by transcribing a body of songs and then compiling the data gathered into tables. The 125 songs selected for data collection are the top twenty-five hits in the rhythm & blues category from each decade, 1950 through 1999. Song rankings are taken from Joel Whitburn's compilation, *Top R&B Singles: 1942–1999*, which is based on data derived from *Billboard* magazine's rhythm & blues charts. During the course of this research, data was collected for the following musical features:

I. Measures: all full and partial measures were counted for each song. For the purpose of this study, radio and retail versions were preferred when available over dance and disco mix versions.

II. Tempo: approximate beginning and ending tempi of the track in beats per minute were measured. Songs with tempi that are primarily rubato received an "NA" rating in this category. However, tempo was calculated in those examples that include a rubato section within a song that otherwise has a tempo. A tempo change of three beats per minute or less was considered insignificant for the purposes of this study.

III. Chord types: the total number of different chord types was calculated for each song. All triad qualities were considered as different chord types: majors, minors, augmented, diminished, and suspended fourths. For the purpose of this analysis, sixth, seventh, ninth, eleventh, and thirteenth chords were not considered as separate chord types.

    A. Chords were analyzed and notated using a numeric system, based on the intervallic relationship of the chord root to the tonic note of the key.

    B. The chord quality was designated by the following, more or less standard, symbols which were added as suffixes to the chord numeral. See Appendix B for more information on chord conventions used throughout this study.

no symbol = major

m = minor

+ = augmented

dim = diminished

sus = suspended fourth (see below)

C. The terms "suspended," "suspended fourth," and "sus" are often used to indicate chords with no third, but a fourth instead. These structures are utilized a good deal in jazz and rhythm & blues, among other types of American popular music. This type of chord can be constructed above a root at any step of the parent scale. The chord usually functions as would a major or minor chord on that scale step, and in fact, often resolves to one of those chords. This sort of chord suspension and resolution is also typical of much European music during the "common practice period," 1600–1900.

IV. I, IV, V, "other," and "passing" chords

A. Chords in each song studied were analyzed and categorized into one of the five groups: "I," "IV," "V," "other," or "passing." The primary goal of the categorization of these chords was to tally the occurrences of the chords for comparison. The "passing" category was created to contain those sections of music which for one reason or another do not belong in the I, IV, V, or "other" categories.

B. Chords with duration of less than 1.5 beats were included in the "passing" chords category.

C. Measures or partial measures with several fast moving chords were counted in the "passing" chords category.

D. Rhythmic sections of songs with no chords were included in the "passing" chords category. Since such sections do not include melodic or harmonic activity, including them in the tally for any particular chord type would have skewed the results.

E. Because major, minor, and suspended chords are often interchangeable in the music being studied, these chords were counted together in the I, IV, V, and "other" categories. In other words, a IV chord (major), a iv (minor), and a IVsus chord would all have been included under the general heading "IV chord" because each is built up from the fourth scale degree and they are often used interchangeably.

F. All chords not categorized as I, IV, V, or "passing" were counted in the "other" category.

V. Blues form: this form is considered to be somewhat fluid, often having more or less than twelve measures and with many variants possible. Each song was analyzed for the presence of the "twelve-bar blues" form and received one of the following designations.

    A. N = twelve-bar blues form or variant not used.

    B. P = twelve-bar blues form or variant used in portions of the music, but less than 50 percent of total track.

    C. Y = twelve-bar blues form or variant used in more than 50 percent of track.

VI. Blues scale

    A. 1 = very little or no incidence of blue notes: neutral or flatted thirds, flatted fifths, and flatted seventh degrees of the European equal-temperament scale.

    B. 2 = moderate presence of blue notes.

    C. 3 = marked presence of blue notes. Blue notes are used liberally in the songs in this category, and they also often receive a noticeable melodic emphasis.

VII. Cyclic form

    A. An important part of this research was to trace the use in rhythm & blues of an element called the "cyclic form." Such a form is typically an extended musical section that constitutes a significant portion of the song. In some styles of rhythm & blues, especially from the late 1960s onward, the cyclic form can comprise an entire song. The characteristics of the form are described briefly below.

    B. Characteristics

        1. Often involves a cessation of harmonic movement.

        2. Sometimes involves a short, repeated harmonic progression (e.g., I, vi, ii, V).

        3. Often features a solo performer.

        4. Sometimes includes a call-and-response element.

        5. Often begins at a low emotional level and builds to a high point.

6. Generally features the repeated use of a musical phrase or "cycle."

7. The cycle is the smallest unit of music that is repeated within the cyclic form, and is often two or four measures in length.

8. Cycles generally consist of riffs, which are short, repeated musical figures. The nature of a riff is melodic and rhythmic, sometimes with a harmonic element as well. Some cycles are composed of multiple riffs. Others are made up of harmonic patterns that lack an identifiable riff.

C. For a discrete section of music to have been considered cyclic form, the cycle must be repeated a minimum of three times within that section.

D. For a discrete section of music to have been considered cyclic form, its duration must be a minimum of 10 percent of the track time.

E. A single chord that continues from one section of a song to the next was not considered to be part of a section using cyclic form unless there was a continuation of the repeating cycle.

F. For the purposes of calculating a numerical value, cycles in two different keys or of two different types were counted together as if they were one cyclic form section. However, the presence of more than one cyclic form section in a song was noted.

G. The cycle number and percentage were calculated and then combined into cyclic form indices so that several sections of music using the cyclic form could be counted together as one longer cyclic form section. However, as stated above, each cycle section must have a duration of at least 10 percent of the track when calculated independently.

H. In some songs two short but somewhat different sections may be repeated consecutively in cyclical fashion (e.g., ABABABAB). Such repeated sections were considered cyclic form for the purpose of this study.

VIII. Triplet swing

A. Each song was analyzed for the presence of "triplet swing." This rhythmic feature is often associated with jazz and generally refers to the division of the beat into theoretical (or actual) triplets. In practice, triplet swing is rarely made up of exact triplets, but is usually a rhythm that is somewhere between triplets and evenly-spaced eighth (or sixteenth) notes.

B. Each song was given the designation of "triplet swing," or "not triplet swing," based on the predominance of the usage of triplet-swing eighth or sixteenth notes.

C. This element is not to be confused with the more universal term "swing," which I use in this study to include a variety of rhythmic movement backward or forward in time.

APPENDIX B

Chord Conventions and Diacritical Marks

I. Chord conventions: The following are explanations of the chord symbols used throughout this study. These chord names are based on those often used in printed American popular music, although many alternate systems are also employed. For more information on the "standard" chord nomenclature systems in use, see: David Baker, *David Baker's Jazz Improvisation*, Van Nuys, CA: Alfred Publishing, 1988; and Kenneth Baker, *Chords and Progressions for Jazz and Popular Keyboard*, New York: Amsco Publications, 1983.

C = major triad = C, E, G.
Cm = minor triad = C, E♭, G.
C2 = major triad with an added second = C, D, E, G.
C6 = major triad with an added sixth = C, E, G, A.
Csus = triad with no third, but with an added fourth instead = C, F, G.
C+ = augmented triad = C, E, G♯.
Cdim = diminished triad = C, E♭, G♭.
Cmaj7 = major triad with an added major seventh = C, E, G, B.
C7 = major triad with an added flat seventh = C, E, G, B♭.
Cm7 = minor triad with an added flat seventh = C, E♭, G, B♭.
Cdim7 = diminished triad with a diminished seventh = C, E♭, G♭, B♭♭.
Cm7♭5 = minor seventh chord with lowered fifth (sometimes called a "half-diminished" 7th chord) = C, E♭, G♭, B♭.
C/E = C major chord with an E bass note.

Other conventions:

1. Any 9th chord or higher includes the notes in the underlying chord that its name implies. For example, a C9 includes the notes: C, E, G, B♭ (from the C7 chord), and D. A Cmaj9 chord would include the notes: C, E, G, B, and D.
2. When a 7th is present (or implied) in a chord an added scale second is termed a "ninth."

3. Chord notes may be altered with a flat (♭) or sharp (♯) to raise or lower the pitch ½ step. Thus a C7(♯9) chord would include the pitches: C, E, G, B♭, and D♯.

II. Diacritical marks: The following are explanations of the diacritical marks used throughout this study.

A. Note performed noticeably lower in pitch than that of the equal-temperament scale.
B. Note performed noticeably higher in pitch than that of the equal-temperament scale.
C. Glissando down to a definite pitch.
D. Glissando down from a definite pitch.
E. Glissando up to a definite pitch.
F. Glissando up from a definite pitch.
G. Glissando from one definite pitch to another.
H. Note performed with exceptionally gravelly timbre.
I. Slapped bass note.
J. Note with indefinite pitch.
K. Strongly accented note.
L. Note performed with pronounced vibrato.
M. Rolled chord.

APPENDIX C

Interview with James Brown

October 20, 2001
Sam's Town Casino, Tunica, MS

The interview was conducted in a backstage dressing room in a trailer just behind the casino showroom. In attendance were James Brown; Hollie Farris, bandleader for James Brown's band and a band member since the mid-1970s; and Richard Ripani, interviewer. When the interview began, Brown and his manager were watching professional basketball on TV and remarking about the return of Michael Jordan to the National Basketball Association.

Portions of the interview proved somewhat difficult to transcribe with certainty. Words enclosed in brackets [ ] are "best guesses" made by the interviewer as to what Brown intended. Words in parentheses ( ) are additions that I have included in an attempt to clarify what is being portrayed in the text of the interview.

RR What type of music, growing up and coming up, influenced you the most?
JB Louis Jordan . . . "Choo Choo Ch'Boogie," "Run, Joe, Run," that sort of stuff.

RR Did you listen to that growing up?
JB When I was growing up, I didn't have no radio. We had to listen to someone else's radio. You know, with a battery. It played about two days, then run out.

RR What about the other music coming out then? Nat "King" Cole?
JB I love Nat "King" Cole.

RR In the late 1950s and '60s when you were creating a unique James Brown sound, what music were you influenced by? Church music mostly? Louis Jordan mostly?
JB I looked at these people, and I admired them and gave them a lot of respect, and I sang their songs. But, I knew I wasn't going nowhere.

RR With their songs?

JB I wasn't going nowhere with two and four. So I changed it to [section] the music.

RR To one and three?

JB Yeah . . . and that's all I had to do. 'Cause, although they wanted, they could never catch me. Now I play all in between the beats, which is really, you can't catch it. Right now, you'll hear tonight . . . Now you go back in them other years. It's nice to do that, but if you listen tonight, the music is better than I've ever had it in my life, 'cause of young people.

RR Energy?

JB No, young people adapt. Energy can come from anybody. Young people don't make energy, 'cause I'm sixty-eight and I got more energy than anybody else has got. So, we were talking about Michael Jordan now. I understand it, and I've been a very blessed person, and then I've always tried to outdo myself. We try that every night.

RR Try to make it a little better?

JB Oh, yeah. But let me say something, don't get me wrong, 'cause they're good people . . . ah, like Maceo, Fred, Jimmy Nolen . . . a fellow we had named "Country."

RR Kellums?

JB Yeah! Ah, and cats leave here some reason and I can't understand it, 'cause what we've got is so dominant. See there's kids out there, and this young man right here (Brown points to Hollie Farris). What we got is so dominant until people can forget about trying to outdo it, because you're almost gonna have to come back with a whole new thing on one and three. So, all that two and four music it's just there, and it's never gonna outdo what we're doin'.

RR A lot of people may not understand where your music comes from, how it was created.

JB And can't figure out how to write it. If you write it you almost can't check it. You can write it, but it's going to be all up to everybody to interpret. You almost gotta tell 'em, "Now it goes here and goes here," 'cause you're thinking two and four. That's where it was started. Now we're one and three. We're all the way away from you. We're the flip side of the coin.

RR What about the concept of the "one"?

JB People used to laugh at me. Thing about it was, "one, and TWO, three, and four." If you look at Lawrence Welk, that's what it was. Country and western people were hipper than all those other people ever tried to be, because they could play a shuffle. See, we're the only band out here who can play a shuffle today.

RR Help us understand the concept of the "one," of *landing* on the one?

JB Right there (conducts a downbeat with his right hand). And it's got to be in your brain.

RR And the funk comes after that, but you've got to land on one?

JB Uh, huh. But when other people get on the one they go, "one . . . two . . . three . . . four . . . ONE." But we say, "ONE," and go right into it. Other people got to set a tempo. The tempo is with us, when we hit it, that's it. But other people say, "one . . . two . . . three . . . four . . . ONE." I laugh at 'em, you know.

RR When I was young one of my favorite James Brown songs was "Think."

JB That was another kind of song, an old thing.

RR A different feel?

JB An old thing. (sings saxophone part from the introduction of his song "Think" in a swing style) Ba do dah do bah do bah dah. . .

RR And the rhythm that's on that. . .

JB But, that's not the normal one and three. It's different by itself. I didn't go back to that no more.

RR Some people might call that the "New Orleans" beat (Ripani taps the rhythm shown in example "A").

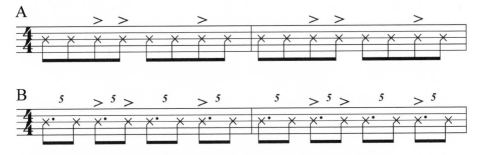

JB That ain't the way "Think" was though. You *thought* you had it. (Brown taps and sings the "B" version. This transcription is as accurate as the Western system of notation allows. However, what Brown actually tapped was somewhere between a triplet and straight-eighth rhythm.) You were going where we are *now*. That ain't the way "Think" was. See, we did it with the music, but the drummer was on a totally different thing.

RR I think I learned something there.

JB Him (points to Hollie Farris) and Dave Matthews, a fellow who played with me a long time ago, I had him and Dave Matthews scratching their chin at me.

Always scratching. I'd be looking, he'd be scratching. So, he gave up on trying to understand it. And he said to me, "I know you're gonna fix it." He wouldn't say . . . he walked away from it . . . I'd laugh and say, "Yeah, I'm gonna fix it, meanwhile, you gotta learn what I'm fixing 'cause when I be going you'll be left."

RR Hollie has told me before about you: "He knows what he wants and has an idea in his head, and you have to figure it out."

JB This man here (points at Farris). We got a lot of fellows that can do it the first time around. We got a few people, don't wanna name all the people, but once we show 'em, me and Hollie and Jeff, and a couple more, once we show 'em, they can play it better than anybody in the world. This man here plays songs better than people who cut the record. They are second time around, but in a lot of instances you gotta have the first time around, and everybody can't do that. You've been here how many years (asks Farris)?

HF About twenty-six years.

JB About twenty-six years. The first time around, that's hard. He used to go out and do something and *think* about it. Now, he *does* it (Brown and Farris laugh together). He don't wanna hear me say that. I know where you're at, yeah. He's (still referring to Farris) truly the leader now. He's truly the leader. Let me tell you another thing: directing is very important. See, there's a lot of tricks in direction! He learned that from me. A lot of tricks in direction. If you have to direct a band "do . . . dat . . . dat" or something like that "do . . . dat," that won't work in our group (here Brown seems to be emulating a Western art music band or orchestra director). Bam, unh, unh (here he illustrates the directing style he uses, in which all beats are downbeats). Right on the point. Don't mess around. See, when you leave it up for grabs they're thinking for themselves.

RR Do they think of written music?

JB Well, they think for themselves, and we don't want them to think for themselves. We want them to think for us. One thing about local bands . . . uh, musicians today, they don't have the knowledge and the know-how to watch the director. If they would watch him, anything he does . . . I used to get angry with 'em 'cause here's a cat knows all the music that you need to know. He knows all of it, and I told him that before. But, the band didn't know it and had attitudes, you know, think "whatever." And overcoming the color barrier . . . and music don't have no color. You either have it or you don't have it, whatever color you are. If it ain't right, it ain't right. I don't go along with a cat that ain't playing it right. I got my songs to play. But I don't hang with them. He has to learn from them.

RR Sometimes it takes a while?

JB *Sometimes?* Boy, all the music written and none of it what we're doing. We got everybody. We got people beat so bad, and thank God we do because he's (points at Farris) not a young man and I'm older. I'm about thirteen years older than him. We are the best at what we're doing 'cause we know what we're doing. What we're doing belongs to us! When I put it together it belongs to us. Nobody can beat us doing it. Take either one of these fellows gonna go to another band. It's gonna take 'em five years, six years, to know what he's talking about. So, ain't nobody gonna do it nowhere. They can forget about that. If you hear Maceo and them today, as good as Maceo was, they're twenty years behind us now. We're doing the funky . . . they're just . . . that's twenty years behind.

RR They're not going to be able to catch up?

JB Not now. Not unless they come back here, and then they're going to have to learn. Who was once the star will wind up being a sideman. You're not going to find a cat that played no more than Maceo, what he played.

RR He did some great solos.

JB Oh yeah, and still does some great solos. But the music has moved to a different place. And if you're gonna try to play James Brown, you got to be with James Brown, 'cause every day we're going to something new. Right now I don't need no hit records no more in my life . . . and still we got an album you wouldn't believe.

RR I'd love to hear it.

JB I know you would (laughs).

(Tour manager interrupts conversation.) Excuse me fellows, we're late for your dinner and I hate to cut you off, but you gotta eat then you gotta go to work.

JB God bless. I enjoyed the talk . . . and this is history, and . . . You should find when we're rehearsing and you come down. I know you'll do that. But as young as you are, and as old as I am . . .

RR I'm almost fifty.

JB Well God bless you! We can share that with you. You come down and Mr. Farris will set it up. We'll let you see some insights. Since you're in school you can broaden the scope for a lot of people.

RR Over the next thirty to forty years people are going to want to know exactly how you've created your music.

JB They'll never know that.

RR Yes, but they'll still *want* to know.

JB Yep. But it comes from within, and he's worked long enough for everything to come from within.

RR Thank you so much for your time.

JB God bless.
(After the tape machine was turned off)
HF You'll never guess who his favorite country star is.

RR Who?
JB Little Jimmie Dickens.

NOTES

Chapter 1: The New Blue Music and Rhythm & Blues

1. Another obvious, perhaps even more radical change of direction occurred in Western art music in the early to mid-twentieth century when twelve-tone music and its related musical techniques were fashioned and implemented.
2. In this book the term "art" music is used to signify the body of European music that is sometimes called "classical" or "serious." This usage of the word "art" is not intended to be exclusive, or imply that some other type of music is *not* art. Nor does use of the term mean to suggest that such music is of a higher quality than any other. It is simply used as a way of identifying a certain type of music that was developed in Europe and was prominent from the middles ages to the twentieth century.
3. Other observers have also suggested that a major musical revolution occurred around the beginning of the twentieth century. See, for example, Peter van der Merwe, *Origins of the Popular Style: The Antecedents of Twentieth-Century Popular Music* (Oxford: Clarendon Press, 1989), 1–14.
4. Robert M. W. Dixon and John Godrich, *Recording the Blues* (New York: Stein and Day, 1970), 17.
5. Joel Whitburn, comp., *Top R&B Singles: 1942–1999* (Menomonee Falls, WI: Record Research Inc., 2000), vii.
6. Arnold Shaw, *Honkers and Shouters: The Golden Years of Rhythm and Blues* (New York: Macmillan, 1978), xvi.
7. See Paul Oliver, *Songsters and Saints: Vocal Traditions on Race Records* (Cambridge: Cambridge University Press, 1984), 1–17.
8. Whitburn, *Top R&B Singles: 1942–1999*, 139, 394.
9. *Billboard* has altered the rhythm & blues chart name many times over the years, usually to accommodate changes in society and perception of words such as "blues," "soul," and "black." A few examples of the names *Billboard* has given the chart are "Best Sellers in Stores," 1954; "R&B Best Sellers in Stores," 1954; "Hot R&B Sides," 1958; "Top Selling R&B Singles," 1966; "Hot Soul Singles," 1973; "Hot Black Singles," 1984; "Hot R&B/Hip-Hop Singles Sales," 1999. See Whitburn, *Top R&B Singles: 1942–1999*, vii–viii.
10. Ibid., x.
11. Ibid.

12. For an interesting discussion of crossover records, black versus white radio airplay and sales, and other related topics, see David Brackett, "What a Difference a Name Makes: Two Instances of African-American Popular Music," in *The Cultural Study of Music: An Introduction*, eds. Martin Clayton, Trevor Herbert, and Richard Middleton (New York: Routledge, 2003); 238–50.

13. The strict twelve-bar form, however, is not the only blues form, although it has been the most widespread. There also exist eight-bar and sixteen-bar forms as well as many variants of the twelve-bar form.

14. The term "vamp" was considered for use in this study for the same musical phenomenon, but that label proved to be somewhat problematic because musicians use the word for a variety of purposes. See chapter 2 for a more detailed description of this form along with musical examples.

15. One should not confuse the notion of triplet swing with the larger concept of "swing," which in my mind includes a much greater spectrum of rhythmic variances. This topic is discussed in chapter 2.

16. Amiri Baraka, *Blues People: Negro Music in White America* (New York: William Morrow and Company, 1963; reprint, New York: Quill, 1999), 220.

17. Nelson George, *The Death of Rhythm & Blues* (New York: Plume Books, 1988).

18. Gerhard Kubik, *Africa and the Blues* (Jackson, MS: University Press of Mississippi, 1999).

19. Winthrop Sargeant, *Jazz: Hot and Hybrid* (New York: E. P. Dutton, 1946). Remarkable not only for its insight, but also because of its early publication date, this book looks at specific musical elements in jazz in order to codify a theoretical basis for the genre. Included is very important research on hot rhythms, the scalar structure of jazz, and the derivation of the blues.

20. Gunther Schuller, *Early Jazz: Its Roots and Musical Development* (New York: Oxford University Press, 1968), 3–4.

21. Such sources include Lynn Abbott and Doug Seroff, *Out of Sight: The Rise of African American Popular Music, 1889–1895* (Jackson, MS: University Press of Mississippi, 2002); Roger D. Abrahams, *Singing the Master: The Emergence of African American Culture in the Plantation South* (New York: Pantheon Books, 1992); William F. Allen, Charles P. Ware, and Lucy M. Garrison, *Slave Songs of the United States* (New York: A. Simpson, 1867); Edward A. Berlin, *Ragtime: A Musical and Cultural History* (Berkeley, CA: University of California Press, 1980); Harold Courlander, *Negro Folk Music, U.S.A.* (New York: Columbia University Press, 1963); Dena Epstein, *Sinful Tunes and Spirituals: Black Folk Music to the Civil War* (Urbana, IL: University of Illinois Press, 1977); George Pullen Jackson, *White and Negro Spirituals: Their Lifetime and Kinship* (Locust Valley, NY: J. J. Augustin, 1943); James Weldon Johnson and J. Rosamond Johnson, *American Negro Spirituals* (New York: Viking Press, 1925–26; reprint, New York: Da Capo Press, 1977); Bernard Katz, ed., *The Social Implications of Early Negro Music in the United States* (New York: Arno Press, 1969); Lydia Parrish, *Slave Songs of the Georgia Sea Islands* (n.p.: Creative Age Press, 1942; reprint, Athens, GA: University of Georgia Press, 1992); Eileen Southern, *The Music*

of Black Americans: A History, 3rd ed. (New York: W. W. Norton, 1997); and Robert C. Toll, *Blacking Up: The Minstrel Show in Nineteenth-Century America* (London: Oxford University Press, 1974).

22. Richard A. Waterman, "African Influence on the Music of the Americas," *Acculturation in the Americas*, Sol Tax, ed. (New York: Cooper Square, 1953, 1967).

23. Such articles include A. M. Jones, "Blue Notes and Hot Rhythm," *African Music Society Newsletter* 1, no. 4 (June 1951): 9–12; Paul Oliver, "Some Comments: African Influence and the Blues," *Living Blues* 8 (spring 1972): 13–17; Paul Oliver, "Echoes of the Jungle?," *Living Blues* 13 (summer 1973): 29–32; David Evans, "Africa and the Blues," *Living Blues* 10 (autumn 1972): 27–29; David Evans, "African Elements in Twentieth-Century United States Black Folk Music," *Jazz Research* 10 (1978): 85–110. In the second chapter of this book I explore some of the suggestions put forth in these papers as they pertain to the concept of the blues system.

24. Two such important works about early blues are Abbe Niles, historical and critical text to *A Treasury of the Blues*, W. C. Handy, ed. (New York: Albert and Charles Boni, 1949; distributed by Simon and Schuster), originally published as *Blues: An Anthology* (New York: Albert and Charles Boni, 1926); and Samuel Charters, *The Blues Makers* (New York: Oak, 1967, 1977; reprint New York: Da Capo, 1991). These writings were essential to this study because of their pioneering efforts to describe blues style, content, and form.

25. David Evans, *Big Road Blues: Tradition and Creativity in the Folk Blues* (Berkeley, CA: University of California Press, 1982; reprint New York: Da Capo Press, 1987).

26. Paul Oliver, *The Story of the Blues* (Radnor, PA: Chilton Book Company, 1969).

27. Paul Oliver, *Savannah Syncopators: African Retentions in the Blues* (New York: Stein and Day, 1970).

28. Jeff Todd Titon, *Early Downhome Blues: A Musical and Cultural Analysis*, 2nd ed. (Chapel Hill, NC: University of North Carolina Press, 1994).

29. Included among them are Joachim E. Berendt, *The Jazz Book: From Ragtime to Fusion and Beyond*, 6th ed. rev. by Günther Huesmann (Brooklyn, NY: Lawrence Hill Books, 1992); Paul Berliner, *Thinking in Jazz: The Infinite Art of Improvisation* (Chicago: University of Chicago Press, 1994); Jason Berry, Jonathan Foose, and Tad Jones, *Up from the Cradle of Jazz: New Orleans Music Since World War II* (Athens, GA: University of Georgia Press, 1986; reprint, New York: Da Capo Press, 1992); Rob Bowman, *Soulsville, U.S.A.: The Story of Stax Records* (New York: Schirmer, 1997); John Broven, *Rhythm & Blues in New Orleans* (Gretna, LA: Pelican, 1995); James Lincoln Collier, *The Making of Jazz: A Comprehensive History* (London: Papermac, 1981); Dixon and Godrich, *Recording the Blues*; Phyl Garland, *The Sound of Soul: The Story of Black Music* (New York: Pocket Books, 1971); Nelson George, *Hip Hop America* (New York: Penguin Books, 1998); Charlie Gillett, *The Sound of the City: The Rise of Rock and Roll*, rev. ed. (London: Book Club Associates, 1984); Peter Guralnick, *Sweet Soul Music: Rhythm and Blues and the Southern Dream of Freedom* (Boston: Little, Brown and Company, 1986, 1999); Anthony Heilbut, *The Gospel Sound: Good News and Bad Times* (New York: Limelight, 1997); Bill C. Malone,

Country Music. U.S.A., rev. ed. (Austin: University of Texas Press, 1985); William Eric Perkins, "The Rap Attack: An Introduction," in *Droppin' Science: Critical Essays on Rap Music and Hip Hop Culture*, ed. William Eric Perkins (Philadelphia: Temple University Press, 1996); Lawrence N. Redd, *Rock Is Rhythm and Blues: The Influence of Mass Media* (East Lansing, MI: Michigan State University Press, 1974); Tricia Rose, *Black Noise: Rap Music and Black Culture in Contemporary America* (Hanover, NH: Wesleyan University Press, 1994); Shaw, *Honkers and Shouters*; David Toop, *Rap Attack 3: African Rap to Global Hip Hop*, 3rd ed. (London: Serpent's Tail, 2000); and Rickey Vincent, *Funk: The Music, The People, and the Rhythm of the One* (New York: St. Martin's Griffin, 1996).

Chapter 2: The Blues System

1. Jeff Todd Titon, *Early Downhome Blues: A Musical and Cultural Analysis*, 2nd ed. (Chapel Hill, NC: University of North Carolina, 1994), 60–61, 137–174. Titon actually presents melodic transcriptions of forty-eight songs in the text. Among the songs are forty-four early downhome blues, three vaudeville blues songs, and one blues song by Bayless Rose, earlier thought to be a white performer. Only the forty-four downhome blues are included in his statistical data. The transcriptions of the other four songs are included in the book to "provide comparative information."
2. David Evans, *Big Road Blues: Tradition and Creativity in the Folk Blues* (Berkeley, CA: University of California Press, 1982; New York: Da Capo Press, 1987), 16–105.
3. Peter van der Merwe, *Origins of the Popular Style: The Antecedents of Twentieth-Century Popular Music* (Oxford: Clarendon Press, 1989), 93–130.
4. The term "mode" is used throughout this study to indicate not only the notes of a scale, but also how they function.
5. The slow emergence and eventual triumph of equal temperament is described in succinct fashion in: Stuart Isacoff, *Temperament: How Music Became a Battlefield for the Great Minds of Western Civilization* (New York: Vintage Books, 2003).
6. For examples of this transformation, see Carl Parrish and John F. Ohl, comps. and eds., *Masterpieces of Music before 1750* (New York: W. W. Norton and Co., 1951).
7. This system of pitch measurement is explained in Alexander J. Ellis, appendix to *On the Sensations of Tone: as a Physiological Basis for the Theory of Music*, by Hermann Helmholtz. Trans. and rev. by Alexander J. Ellis (Longmans & Co., 1885; New York: Dover, 1954), 446–51.
8. A term suggested by David Evans, *Big Road Blues*, 24.
9. In order to display the theoretical points being discussed, the Western music notation system seems most appropriate, despite the fact that its use imparts a certain Eurocentric bent.
10. Daniel Cooper, *Lefty Frizzell: The Honky Tonk Life of Country Music's Greatest Singer* (New York: Little, Brown, and Co., 1995), 20.

11. Mac "Dr. John" Rebennack, "Under the Hoodoo Moon," *Keyboard* vol. 20, no. 3 (March 1994), 77.

12. Gerhard Kubik, *Africa and the Blues* (Jackson, MS: University Press of Mississippi, 1999), 138.

13. For a much more in depth explanation see Kubik, *Africa and the Blues*, pp. 129–45.

14. Gerhard Kubik states that "there is probably no unitary theory to 'explain' the 'flatted fifth.'" *Africa and the Blues*, 151.

15. Compare Silver's piano part here to that of John Lee Hooker's transcribed vocal shown in example 4.

16. It should be said that some of the techniques in example 7 have been used in almost exactly the same way by earlier blues piano players. An excellent example of the slide up to the chord fifth (almost identical to measure four of the example shown here) is heard in "Vicksburg Blues," as recorded by Little Brother Montgomery in 1930.

17. See David Lee Joyner, "Southern Ragtime and Its Transition to Published Blues," unpublished Ph.D. dissertation (Memphis State University, 1986).

18. Thomas Brothers, "Solo and Cycle in African-American Jazz," *Musical Quarterly* 78 (1994): 494.

19. John Fahey, *Charley Patton* (London: Studio Vista, 1970), 42.

20. Ibid., 42. I have adapted Fahey's model which uses the solfeggio system into one that uses numbers for scale degrees.

21. See examples. 4, 6A–B, 7, and 12 in this chapter.

22. Winthrop Sargeant, *Jazz: Hot and Hybrid* (New York: E. P. Dutton, 1946), 150–51.

23. Van der Merwe, *Origins of the Popular Style*, 125–27.

24. Ibid., 127. "In spite of the popular notion to the contrary, the blue fifth is just as old as the blue third. It can be heard in the earliest recorded blues and the most archaic of worksongs and spirituals, and can also be found in the most conservative style of white hymn singing."

25. Sargeant, *Jazz: Hot and Hybrid*, 169–70. "I have even heard of the theory of a 'blue fifth' advanced, though I have never been able to find any consistent evidence to support such a theory."

26. Titon, *Early Downhome Blues*, 154. The flatted fifth represents just over 2 percent of the total pitches in the songs analyzed by Titon in this work.

27. Note that the raised ninth ($\sharp 9$)—which is how this note is often perceived by jazz and R&B musicians—is the same note as the flatted third. Thus, when this chord is played, there exist both a major third and a flatted third in the same chord, which creates the blurring of pitch described earlier.

28. For an in-depth look at the music of Jefferson, especially his use of chord progressions such as those described here, see David Evans, "Musical Innovation in the Music of Blind Lemon Jefferson," *Black Music Research Journal* 20, no. 1 (2000): 83–116.

29. A long line of researchers in African music have sought to explain the types of parallel harmony in use on that continent. In addition to those authors specifically

referred to in the current discussion, the reader is directed to explore the writings of J. H. Kwabena Nketia, *The Music of Africa* (New York: W. W. Norton, 1974); and A. M. Jones, *Studies in African Music*, 2 vols. (London: Oxford University Press, 1959).

30. Percival R. Kirby, "A Study of Negro Harmony," *Musical Quarterly* 16 (1930): 404–14.

31. Kubik, *Africa and the Blues*, 106–07, 115–16.

32. Ibid., 106.

33. David Rycroft's important work in this area should be mentioned, especially the 1967 article "Nguni Vocal Polyphony," *Journal of the International Folk Music Council* 19 (1967): 89–103, in which he builds upon Kirby's work in explaining vocal polyphony in some African music. Importantly, Rycroft also promotes the temporal concept of "non-simultaneous entry" to describe music in which the phrases of the different parts do not begin (or end) at the same point in time, causing the various parts to overlap in antiphonal style. The Nguni music studied by Rycroft is typically built upon a relatively short, repeating pattern. Because of the cyclical nature of the music, and the fact that defining any exact beginning or ending is problematic, Rycroft illustrates the music on a score that is itself circular in nature.

34. Van der Merwe, *Origins of the Popular Style*, 288.

35. The aforementioned music of Blind Lemon Jefferson also displays a marked avoidance of the V chord. Songs by Jefferson that typify this tendency include: "Black Snake Moan," "Chock House Blues," "Chinch Bug Blues," and "Long Distance Moan."

36. Van der Merwe, *Origins of the Popular Style*. See pp. 243–66 for an enlightening discussion on the topic of "parlour harmony."

37. Lynn Abbott, "'Play that Barber Shop Chord': A Case for the African-American Origin of Barbershop Harmony," *American Music*, vol. 10, no. 3 (1992): 289–325.

38. Ira Gitler writes about "The Preacher" in the liner notes to *Horace Silver and the Jazz Messengers*, Blue Note CDP 7 46140 2, 1987: "Once when Horace Silver was being interviewed in reference to the group he said, 'We can reach way back and get that old time gutbucket feeling with just a taste of the backbeat.' He was referring of course, to *The Preacher*, an earthy swinger somewhat reminiscent of *I've Been Working on the Railroad* in its melody line. In keeping with the title, everyone 'preaches' in their solos."

39. Both songs are included in *Atlantic Rhythm and Blues*, 1947–1974, Atlantic CD 82305-2, 1991.

40. Evans, *Big Road Blues*. The following excerpts are taken from page 22 of that book: "These twelve bars are divided into three sections or 'lines' of four bars each. The first line (A) is usually repeated as the second line (A), sometimes with a slight variation for emphasis, and the stanza ends with a different third line (B). . . . The entire twelve measures, however, are not devoted to the singing of these three lines. Instead, each line usually takes slightly more than two measures to sing. It is followed by an instrumental passage of slightly less than two measures as a 'response' to the vocal line. . . .

> This [the AAB, twelve-bar pattern referred to above] is only the most common stanza pattern. Among the many others are AAA (12 bars), AAAB (16 bars), AB (8 bars), and AB with refrain (12 bars). . . . It also happens that players will shorten or extend instrumental lines, producing stanzas of 11, 13½, 20 bars, and so forth."

41. Edward A. Berlin, *Ragtime: A Musical and Cultural History* (Berkeley, CA: University of California Press, 1980), 154–57.

42. Rycroft, "Nguni Vocal Polyphony," 94.

43. For early evidence of this phenomenon see Harold Courlander, *Negro Folk Music, U.S.A.* (New York: Columbia University Press, 1963), in which the author presents the texts of a number of spirituals that indicate the use of a repeating pattern such as that being described here.

44. Glenn Hinson, *Fire in My Bones: Transcendence and the Holy Spirit in African American Gospel Music* (Philadelphia: University of Philadelphia Press, 1999), 293. "Like the intentional pitch shift of elevation, the drive is an instrument of intensification, a carefully arranged song section that stalls melodic progress while freeing the lead to improvise over a static, repetitive background. Typically following a song's regular verses, this section transforms the lead-backup relationship into one of contrasting freedom and fixity. The backup's duty during the drive is to repeat a single, brief, percussive phrase . . . , restating the same passage again and again without shifting its melodic or harmonic structure. The backup singers, in other words, put themselves on vocal hold. With this steady 'repeat' as a foundation, the lead singer can improvise at will."

45. Richard A. Waterman, "'Hot' Rhythm in Negro Music," *Journal of the American Musicological Society* 1 (1948): 25.

46. Ibid., 29.

47. Ibid., 26.

48. See Paul Oliver, *Savannah Syncopators: African Retentions in the Blues* (New York: Stein and Day, 1970).

49. A book that is most helpful for the understanding of the influence of the music of Latin America on that of the United States is *The Latin Tinge*, by John Storm Roberts.

50. Don Michael Randel, ed., *Harvard Dictionary of Music*, 4th ed. (Cambridge, MA: Belknap Press, 2003), 861–62.

51. Richard A. Waterman, "African Influence on the Music of the Americas," *Acculturation in the Americas*, Sol Tax, ed. (New York: Cooper Square, 1953, 1967), 212–13.

52. Of course, one might argue that the term "offbeat phrasing" itself has a Western bias, because it suggests that there is a regular or normal beat, and that anything else is "off."

53. Gunther Schuller, *Early Jazz: Its Roots and Musical Development* (New York: Oxford University Press, 1968), 13. ". . . jazz inflection and syncopation did not come from Europe, because there is no precedent for them in European 'art music.'"

54. Berlin, *Ragtime*, 99–122.

55. William F. Allen, Charles P. Ware, and Lucy M. Garrison, *Slave Songs of the United States* (New York: A. Simpson, 1867), 18, 29, 68.

56. Lydia Parrish, *Slave Songs of the Georgia Sea Islands* (n.p.: Creative Age Press, 1942; reprint, Athens, GA: University of Georgia Press, 1992), 46–47.

57. Kubik, *Africa and the Blues*, 94.

58. The particular rhythm of this timeline is the same as the first measure of a two-measure rhythmic figure sometimes called the "3-2 clave," used extensively in Cuban music.

59. Listen, for example, to "Blow, Gabriel," "Jubilee," "Move, Daniel," "Kneebone Bend," and "Religion So Sweet" from *The McIntosh County Shouters: Slave Shout Songs from the Coast of Georgia*, Folkways CD FE-4344 (Smithsonian Folkways recordings).

60. Roberts, *The Latin Tinge*, 6.

61. Horace Clarence Boyer, "Lucie E. Campbell: Composer for the National Baptist Convention," *We'll Understand It Better By and By*, ed. Bernice Johnson Reagon (Washington, DC: Smithsonian Institution Press, 1992), 102–08.

62. See Jamey Aebersold, *How to Play Jazz and Improvise*, vol. 1 (Albany, IN: Jamey Aebersold Jazz, 1967), 15. This is a very enlightening section that shows Aebersold's method of teaching swing. He unequivocally states that two eighth notes, or a dotted-eighth-and-sixteenth group, should be played as the first and third of a group of triplets in order to properly swing the music.

63. Count Basie, "April in Paris," *April in Paris*, Verve 825 575-2. Recorded in 1956.

64. The entire interview with Brown appears in Appendix C of this study.

65. Titon, *Early Downhome Blues*, 151.

66. A very short list might include Louis Armstrong, Chet Atkins, Ray Charles, Charlie Christian, John Coltrane, Miles Davis, Buddy Guy, Jimi Hendrix, B.B. King, Memphis Slim, Bill Monroe, Maceo Parker, Roosevelt Sykes, Stevie Ray Vaughan, Stevie Wonder, Jimmy Yancey, etc.

67. John Coltrane, "Giant Steps," *The Best of John Coltrane*, Atlantic CD 1541-2, 1970.

68. Examples of melisma in other types of American music are illustrated in examples 2 (country music) and 4 (blues).

69. Howlin' Wolf, "Moanin' at Midnight," *Howlin' Wolf: His Best*, Chess CD CHD-9375, 1997.

70. Listen to, among many examples, "The Thrill Is Gone," *The Best of B.B. King*, MCA CD MCAD-11939, 1999.

71. Junior Walker, "Shotgun," from *Hitsville, U.S.A.: The Motown Singles Collection, 1959–1971*, Motown CD 3746363122, 1992.

72. Charley Patton, "Pony Blues," *Screamin' and Hollerin' the Blues: The Worlds of Charley Patton*, Revenant Album 212, 2001.

73. Little Richard, "Lucille," *The Georgia Peach*, Specialty CD SPCD-7012-2, 1991.

74. Earth, Wind & Fire, "Fantasy," *Earth, Wind & Fire: The Definitive Collection*, Columbia 2 CDs 480554 9, 1995.

75. Louis Jordan, "Caldonia" ["Caldonia Boogie"], from *Louis Jordan and His Tympany Five*, JSP CD JSPCD905C, 2001.

76. Jack Dupree, "Strollin,'" from *Atlantic Blues: Piano*, Atlantic CD 81694-2, 1986.

77. James Brown, "Say It Loud, I'm Black and I'm Proud, Part 1," *James Brown: Star Time*, Polydor CD 849 110-2, 1991.

78. Otis Redding, "These Arms of Mine," *The Complete Stax/Volt Singles: 1959–1968*, Atlantic 9 CDs 7 82218-2, 1991.

79. Billy Ward and the Dominoes, "Sixty-Minute Man," *Sixty-Minute Men: The Best of Billy Ward and His Dominoes*, Rhino CD 71509, 1993.

80. James Brown, "Super Bad," *Funk Power 1970: A Brand New Thing*, Polydor CD 31453 1684-2, 1996.

Chapter 3: Blues with a Beat: 1950–1959

1. Louis Jordan had significant success in the broader record market as well. Whitburn shows that from 1943 through 1950 Jordan charted fourteen hits on the popular record charts, nine of them making the top ten. Joel Whitburn, comp., *Top R&B Singles: 1942–1999* (Menomonee Falls, WI: Record Research Inc., 2000), 232–33.

2. For more information about Louis Jordan see John Chilton, *Let the Good Times Roll* (Ann Arbor, MI: University of Michigan Press, 1994). This book is the only available full-length biography of Jordan. Chilton includes quite of bit of material taken from personal interviews with the artist. His early career and the creation of his musical style are particularly well explored.

3. Arnold Shaw, *Honkers and Shouters: The Golden Years of Rhythm and Blues* (New York: Macmillan, 1978), 89–104.

4. My vote for the most urbane of all the big hits by such artists during the 1950s goes to Nat "King" Cole and his 1950 version of "Mona Lisa," which reached number one on the R&B charts. Aside from Cole's vocal, the entire track consists of only a lush string section and an acoustic classical guitar.

5. Wynonie Harris early on created a personal style that led the way to rock 'n' roll. His songs "Good Rockin' Tonight" (1948) and "All She Wants to Do is Rock" (1949) typify the hard-edged, driving style that was an important part of R&B from the late 1940s on.

6. It should be noted that the artists being discussed here recorded for small, mostly independent record labels during this period: Milburn (Aladdin), Vinson (Mercury and King), Brown (DeLuxe), and Harris (Apollo and King).

7. Representative songs by these artists that make use of the traits championed by the earlier shouters are Chuck Berry, "Maybelline" (1955), "Roll Over Beethoven" (1956), "Sweet Little Sixteen" (1958), and "Johnny B. Goode" (1958); Little Richard, "Tutti Frutti" (1955), "Long Tall Sally" (1956), "Lucille" (1957), "Keep A Knockin'" (1957), and "Good Golly Miss Molly" (1958).

8. Shaw, *Honkers and Shouters*, 169.

9. Ibid., 173–74.

10. Joel Whitburn, comp., *Top R&B Singles: 1942–1999* (Menomonee Falls, WI: Record Research Inc., 2000), 635.

11. See chapter 3, example 21, for an example of Longhair's blending of blues and Latin rhythms.

12. For explanations of a variety of Latin rhythms from a musician's point of view, see Humberto Morales and Henry Adler, *Latin American Rhythm Instruments*, ed. Henri Klickmann, trans. Ernesto Barbosa (Rockville Center, NY: Belwin Mills, 1966).

13. Examples of such releases by the Drifters are "This Magic Moment" (1960), "Save the Last Dance for Me" (1960), "Up on the Roof" (1962), "On Broadway" (1963), and "Under the Boardwalk" (1964).

14. For a detailed examination of doo-wop see Anthony J. Gribin and Matthew M. Schiff, *The Complete Book of Doo-Wop* (Iola, WI: Krause Publications, 2000), 17–20.

15. To hear examples of such vocal gospel groups, the reader is referred to the excellent CD set *Jubilation: Great Gospel Performances*, vols. 1 and 2, Rhino CDs R2 70288 and R2 70289, 1992. This release includes several recordings by some of the artists discussed above, especially in the 1947 to 1960 time frame.

16. In addition to the Dominoes' "Sixty-Minute Man" (1951), there are many such "adult" songs that were R&B hits in the 1950s. Among those that reached number one on the chart are: Willie Mae "Big Mama" Thornton, "Hound Dog" (1953); the Midnighters, "Work with Me Annie" (1954); and "Big Joe" Turner, "Shake, Rattle and Roll" (1954).

17. A few examples of slightly later songs by white artists that reached number one on the R&B charts are Everly Brothers, "Cathy's Clown" (1960); The Four Seasons, "Sherry" (1960) and "Big Girls Don't Cry" (1960); and Lesley Gore, "It's My Party" (1963).

18. Michael Bertrand, *Race, Rock, and Elvis* (Urbana, IL: University of Illinois Press), 2000.

19. Shaw, *Honkers and Shouters*, 22.

20. Two excellent CDs that contain early recordings of Sam Cooke with the Soul Stirrers are *The Soul Stirrers*, Specialty SPCD-7031-2, 1992 and *Sam Cooke with the Soul Stirrers*, Specialty SPCD-7009-2, 1991.

21. *Sam Cooke with the Soul Stirrers* (see above), liner notes, quotation by R. H. Harris.

22. Peter Guralnick, *Sweet Soul Music: Rhythm and Blues and the Southern Dream of Freedom* (Boston: Little, Brown and Company, 1986, 1999), 36.

23. A tempo change of less than 4 b.p.m. over the course of a song was considered statistically insignificant for the purposes of this study.

24. The use of blue notes is being graded in this study on a scale of 1 to 3 for each song analyzed. The low end of this scale means that little or no use of blue notes exists in the song in question, while a rating of 2 represents moderate usage and a rating of 3 points to a marked presence of blue notes. Thus the 2.4 in the case discussed above indicates a use of blue notes about halfway between moderate and marked. See appendix A for further details on data collection methodology.

Chapter 4: The Soul Era: 1960–1969

1. Joel Whitburn, comp., *The Billboard Book of Top 40 Hits*, 7th ed. (New York: Billboard Publications, 2000), 828–29.

2. See, for example, Peter Guralnick, *Sweet Soul Music: Rhythm and Blues and the Southern Dream of Freedom* (Boston: Little, Brown and Company, 1986, 1999), 1–2.

3. For related comments by Phil Walden and Steve Cropper see Rob Bowman, *Soulsville, U.S.A.: The Story of Stax Records* (New York: Schirmer, 1997), 132.

4. Ibid., 134.

5. Charlie Gillett, *The Sound of the City: The Rise of Rock and Roll*, rev. ed. (London: Book Club Associates, 1984), 208–09.

6. Katrina Hazzard-Gordon, *Jookin': The Rise of Social Dance Formations in African-American Culture* (Philadelphia: Temple University Press, 1990), 19, 67, 83, 116.

7. Ibid., 19.

8. Joel Whitburn, comp., *Top R&B Singles: 1942–1999* (Menomonee Falls, WI: Record Research Inc., 2000), 626, 635. Whitburn uses a somewhat complex methodology to arrive at his rankings. In short, the results are based on the tabulation of assigned values for the number of weeks each song remained on the chart and also the position that it reached. The top five point-getters in the 1960s were (1) James Brown, 4,096; (2) Ray Charles, 3,296; (3) Marvin Gaye, 2,827; (4) The Temptations, 2,738; and (5) Aretha Franklin, 2,464.

9. James Brown with Bruce Tucker, *James Brown: The Godfather of Soul* (New York: Thunder's Mouth Press, 1986, 1997), 171–72.

10. Whitburn, *Top R&B Singles: 1942–1999*, 239.

11. Brown and Tucker, *James Brown*, 157–58.

12. James Brown, personal interview, 2002. See appendix C for a full transcription.

13. Brown's background as a drummer has probably had a great effect on his musical style. He began his career playing drums in the Flames, and subsequently moved out front when his singing and showmanship abilities became evident.

14. Brown and Tucker, *James Brown*, 218–19.

15. Alexander Stewart explores the idea that funk music inherited its syncopated eighth- and sixteenth-note rhythmic patterns from the second-line drum beats of New Orleans in "'Funky Drummer': New Orleans, James Brown and the Rhythmic Transformation of American Popular Music," *Popular Music* 19, no. 3 (Oct. 2000): 292–318.

16. Jim Payne, "Clayton Fillyau," *Give the Drummers Some: The Great Drummers of R&B, Funk and Soul* (Miami: Warner Bros., 1996), 18–20.

17. Ibid., 62.

18. Cynthia Rose, *Living in America: The Soul Saga of James Brown* (London: Serpents Tail, 1990), 47.

19. Ibid., 67.

Chapter 5: Funk and Disco Reign: 1970–1979

1. Rob Bowman, *Soulsville, U.S.A.: The Story of Stax Records* (New York: Schirmer, 1997), 345–71.

2. Ibid., 281.

3. Joel Whitburn, comp., *Top R&B Singles: 1942–1999* (Menomonee Falls, WI: Record Research Inc., 2000), vii.

4. Ibid., 635.

5. For more information see the discussion in chapter 4 about the song "Cold Sweat, Part 1," released by James Brown in 1967.

6. Rickey Vincent, *Funk: The Music, The People, and the Rhythm of the One* (New York: St. Martin's Griffin, 1996), 90–91.

7. Joe Murphy, personal communication, November 5, 2003.

8. William Ruhlmann, "Parliament," from *All Music Guide to Soul: The Definitive Guide to R&B and Soul*, Vladimir Bogdanov, John Bush, Chris Woodstra, and Stephen Thomas Erlewine, eds. (San Francisco: Backbeat Books, 2003), 522.

9. For example, the C dorian scale is: C, D, E♭, F, G, A, B♭, C.

10. Coleman Hawkins, "Body and Soul," from *Body and Soul*, Victor Jazz CD 09026-68515-2, 1996. Recorded in 1939.

11. James Brown, "Give It Up Or Turnit a Loose," from *Foundations of Funk: A Brand New Bag, 1964–1969*, Polydor CD 31453 1165-2, 1996. Originally released in 1969.

12. James Brown, "Give It Up Or Turnit a Loose," from *Funk Power 1970: A Brand New Thing*, Polydor CD 31453 1684-2, 1996. Recorded in 1970.

13. Alan Stoker, personal communication, November 14, 2003.

14. Pete Drake, "Forever," *Pete Drake and His Talking Steel Guitar*, Smash S-1415, 1964.

15. To hear the classic wah-wah guitar sound listen to the 1971 single "Theme From Shaft," from Isaac Hayes, *Greatest Hit Singles*, Stax SCD-8515-2, 1991.

16. For more information see Chris Jenkins, "Synthesizers and Hi-Tech," *Rock Hardware: 40 Years of Rock Instrumentation* (London: Balafon, 1996), 52–67.

17. Stevie Wonder, *Talking Book*, Motown CD 3746303192. Originally released in 1972.

18. Stevie Wonder, *Innervisions*, Motown CD 3746303262. Originally released in 1973.

19. Whitburn, *Top R&B Singles: 1942–1999*, 627.

20. For this discussion I am counting every different chord structure as a separate type in order to illustrate the harmonic complexity of the music. However, during data collection for this book I did not consider chords with added sevenths or above as separate chord types. See appendix A for more information on chord data collection.

21. Herbie Hancock, liner notes from *Headhunters*, Columbia Legacy CD CK 65123, 1997. Originally released in 1974.

22. Nelson George, *The Death of Rhythm & Blues* (New York: Plume Books, 1988), 153.

23. Ibid., 157.

24. William Eric Perkins, "The Rap Attack: An Introduction," in *Droppin' Science: Critical Essays on Rap Music and Hip Hop Culture*, ed. William Eric Perkins (Philadelphia: Temple University Press, 1996), 1–13.

Chapter 6: The Old and the New: 1980–1989

1. Joel Whitburn, comp., *The Billboard Book of Top 40 Hits*, 7th ed. (New York: Billboard Books, 2000), 819.

2. "Warner Music Group." <http://www.wmg.com/companies/wmg.jsp>, Feb. 1, 2004.

3. Joel Whitburn, comp., *Top R&B Singles: 1942–1999* (Menomonee Falls, WI: Record Research Inc., 2000).

4. Ibid., 635.

5. Ed Hogan, "Teddy Riley," *All Music Guide to Soul: The Definitive Guide to R&B and Soul*, Vladimir Bogdanov, John Bush, Chris Woodstra, and Stephen Thomas Erlewine, eds. (San Francisco: Backbeat Books, 2003), 575.

6. Alex Henderson, "New Jack Swing," *All Music Guide to Soul*, 853–54.

7. Nelson George, *Hip Hop America* (New York: Penguin Books, 1998), 115.

8. See chapter 6, figure 9, for an illustration of triplet-swing sixteenth-notes commonly found in R&B from the 1970s on.

9. Among notable "Sepia Sinatra" artists of the 1940s and 1950s are Cecil Gant, Ivory Joe Hunter, Charles Brown, and Johnny Ace.

10. Craig Lytle, "A Quiet Storm," *All Music Guide to Soul*, 580.

11. Miles Davis, "So What," *Kind of Blue*, Columbia/Legacy CD CK 40579, 1997. Recorded in 1959.

12. James Brown, "Cold Sweat, Part 1," *James Brown: Star Time*, Polydor CD 849 110-2.

13. For information about early synthesizer manufacturers and their products, see Chris Jenkins, "Synthesizers and Hi-Tech," *Rock Hardware: 40 Years of Rock Instrumentation* (London: Balafon, 1996), 52–67.

14. Ibid., 60.

15. Ibid., 64–65.

16. David Toop, *Rap Attack 3: African Rap to Global Hip Hop*, 3rd ed. (London: Serpent's Tail, 2000), 19.

17. See "Reggae." *All Music Guide*. http://allmusic.com/, Dec. 1, 2003.

18. For more information about Afrika Bambaataa's early importance in rap, see William Eric Perkins, "The Rap Attack: An Introduction," in *Droppin' Science: Critical Essays on Rap Music and Hip Hop Culture*, ed. William Eric Perkins (Philadelphia: Temple University Press, 1996), 12–13.

19. Public Enemy, *It Takes a Nation of Millions to Hold Us Back*, Def Jam CD 315 527 358-2, 1988.

20. Perkins, "The Rap Attack," 18–19.

21. Ibid, 21.

Chapter 7: Rap Goes Mainstream: 1990–1999

1. Joel Whitburn, comp., *Top R&B Singles: 1942–1999* (Menomonee Falls, WI: Record Research Inc., 2000), 635.

2. BMG corporate website. http://www.bmg.com/, March 5, 2004.

3. William Eric Perkins, "The Rap Attack: An Introduction," in *Droppin' Science: Critical Essays on Rap Music and Hip Hop Culture*, ed. William Eric Perkins (Philadelphia: Temple University Press, 1996), 18.

4. For more information, see *All Music Guide to Hip-Hop: The Definitive Guide to Rap and Hip-Hop*, Vladimir Bogdanov, John Bush, Chris Woodstra, and Stephen Thomas Erlewine, eds. (San Francisco: Backbeat Books, 2003), vii–x; and *All Music Guide to Soul: The Definitive Guide to R&B and Soul*, Vladimir Bogdanov, John Bush, Chris Woodstra, and Stephen Thomas Erlewine, eds. (San Francisco: Backbeat Books, 2003), viii–xii.

5. See the discussion about sampling and the related example from the song "Me Myself and I" (ex. 49).

6. See chapter 2, example 12, for an example of Jackson's singing style.

7. Steve Huey, "Babyface," *All Music Guide to Soul*, 28–29.

8. Joel Whitburn, comp., *The Billboard Book of Top 40 Hits*, 7th ed. (New York: Billboard Books, 2000), 819.

9. David Toop, *Rap Attack 3: African Rap to Global Hip Hop*, 3rd ed. (London: Serpent's Tail, 2000), 208–09.

10. Davey D., *Playwutchyalike*, liner notes, Digital Underground, Tommy Boy/Rhino CD R2 73861, 2003.

11. Steve Huey, "O.G.: Original Gangster," *All Music Guide to Hip-Hop*, 225.

12. Perkins, "The Rap Attack," 19.

13. *The Chronic*, liner notes, Dr. Dre, Death Row Records CD DRR 63000-2, 1992, 2001.

14. Nelson George, *Hip Hop America* (New York: Penguin Books, 1998), 188–89.

15. For information about this group, see Stephen Thomas Erlewine and Steve Huey, "Wu-Tang Clan," *All Music Guide to Hip-Hop*, 505–08.

16. For insight into the depiction of crews and posses in rap music videos, see Tricia Rose, *Black Noise: Rap Music and Black Culture in Contemporary America* (Hanover, NH: Wesleyan University Press, 1994), 10–11.

17. John Bush and Bradley Torreano, "Puff Daddy," *All Music Guide to Hip-Hop*, 394–95.

18. Stephen Thomas Erlewine, "2Pac," *All Music Guide to Hip-Hop*, 486.

Chapter 8: The Transformation of Rhythm & Blues

1. See, for example, Arnold Shaw, *Honkers and Shouters: The Golden Years of Rhythm and Blues* (New York: Macmillan, 1978), xv. "In this book I am concerned with R & B as an indigenous black art form and style—not with its rock derivatives, nor its revival in the late '60s, nor with soul music."

2. David Brackett, "What a Difference a Name Makes: Two Instances of African-American Popular Music," in *The Cultural Study of Music: An Introduction*, eds. Martin Clayton, Trevor Herbert, and Richard Middleton (New York: Routledge, 2003), 243–44.

3. See chapter 2 for a discussion of Titon's findings.

4. See chapter 6 for a discussion of the emergence of technology in R&B.

5. Rob Bowman, *Soulsville, U.S.A.: The Story of Stax Records* (New York: Schirmer, 1997), 37, 114–15.

6. Steve Huey, "Roberta Flack," *All Music Guide to Soul: The Definitive Guide to R&B and Soul*, Vladimir Bogdanov, John Bush, Chris Woodstra, and Stephen Thomas Erlewine, eds. (San Francisco: Backbeat Books, 2003), 245.

7. Ron Wynn, "Nile Rodgers," *All Music Guide to Soul*, 582.

8. William F. Allen, Charles P. Ware, and Lucy M. Garrison, *Slave Songs of the United States* (New York: A. Simpson, 1867), 15, 60.

9. Scott Joplin, *Complete Piano Rags*, ed. David A. Jasen (New York: Dover Publications, 1988), 11–184.

10. Joel Whitburn, comp., *The Billboard Book of Top 40 Hits*, 7th ed. (New York: Billboard Books, 2000), 822.

11. Nelson George, *The Death of Rhythm & Blues* (New York: Plume Books, 1988), xii–xiii, 147–69.

12. Peter van der Merwe, *Origins of the Popular Style: The Antecedents of Twentieth-Century Popular Music* (Oxford: Clarendon Press, 1989), 288.

13. See chapter 2 for a discussion of cyclic form.

14. David Evans, "African Elements in Twentieth-Century United States Black Folk Music," *Jazz Research* 10 (1978), 101.

15. See chapter 2 for a discussion of blue notes and their use in a variety of American musical styles.

16. Allen, Ware, and Garrison, *Slave Songs of the United States*, 1.

17. Three examples among many are Horace Silver, "Song for My Father," from *Song for My Father*, Blue Note CD 84815, 1999, originally recorded in 1964; Herbie Hancock, "Watermelon Man," from *Headhunters*, Columbia/Legacy CD CK 65123, 1997, originally recorded in 1973; and Bob Mintzer Big Band, "Oye Como Va," from *Latin from Manhattan*, DMP CD 523, 1998.

18. See A. M. Jones, *Studies in African Music*, 2 vols. (London: Oxford University Press, 1959); and Gerhard Kubik, *Theory of African Music*, vol. 1 (Wilhelmshaven, Germany: F. Noetzel, 1994).

19. See J. A. Progler, "Searching for Swing: Participatory Discrepancies in the Jazz Rhythm Section," *Ethnomusicology* 39, no. 1 (Winter 1995): 21–54. In this article the author, describes his use of the computer program *MacRecorder* to record music and then analyze it for the swing feature. Apparently he was somewhat successful in the attempt. However the resulting illustrations are not in Western music notation, but rather use a computerized graph that shows beats and note events. Such a methodology was considered for this study, but it was eventually decided that the reader's unfamiliarity with such graphs might lead to more confusion than enlightenment.

20. Richard A. Waterman, "African Influence on the Music of the Americas," *Acculturation in the Americas*, Sol Tax, ed. (New York: Cooper Square, 1953, 1967), 210.

21. George, *The Death of Rhythm & Blues*, xii.

22. Nelson George, *Hip Hop America* (New York: Penguin Books, 1998), ix. "I ended the book [*The Death of Rhythm & Blues*] with some pretty gloomy predictions about the diluting effects of assimilation, but I was able to point to some artists and producers who seemed to be following a different agenda, one more centered around the survival of black culture. Now we know that rap music, and hip hop style as a whole, has utterly broken through from its ghetto roots to assert a lasting influence on American clothing, magazine publishing, television, language, sexuality, and social policy as well as its obvious presence in records and movies."

23. Amiri Baraka, *Blues People: Negro Music in White America* (New York: William Morrow and Company, 1963; reprint, New York: Quill, 1999), 220–21.

24. Ernest Borneman, "The Roots of Jazz," *Jazz*, ed. Nat Hentoff and Albert McCarthy (New York: Rinehart and Company, 1959), 17.

25. For an illuminating look at this phenomenon as it often appears in jazz, see Thomas Brothers, "Solo and Cycle in African-American Jazz," *Musical Quarterly* 78 (1994): 478–509.

BIBLIOGRAPHY

Books, Articles, and Interviews

Abbott, Lynn. "'Play That Barbershop Chord': A Case for the African-American Origin of Barbershop Harmony." *American Music* 10, no. 3 (Fall 1992): 289–325.

———. "They Cert'ly Sound Good to Me: Sheet Music, Southern Vaudeville, and the Commercial Ascendancy of the Blues." *American Music* 14, no. 4 (Winter 1996): 402–54.

Abbott, Lynn, and Doug Seroff. *Out of Sight: The Rise of African American Popular Music, 1889–1995.* Jackson, MS: University Press of Mississippi, 2002.

Aebersold, Jamey. *How to Play Jazz and Improvise,* vol. 1. Albany, IN: Jamey Aebersold Jazz, 1967.

Abraham, Otto, and Erich von Hornbostel. "Suggested Methods for the Transcription of Exotic Music." Translated by George and Eve List. *Ethnomusicology* 38, no. 3 (Fall 1994): 425–56.

Abrahams, Roger D. *Singing the Master: The Emergence of African American Culture in the Plantation South.* New York: Pantheon, 1992.

Abrahams, Roger D., and George Foss. *Anglo-American Folksong Style.* Englewood Cliffs, NJ: Prentice Hall, 1968.

Allen, William Francis, Charles Pickard Ware, and Lucy McKim Garrison. *Slave Songs of the United States.* New York: A. Simpson, 1867.

Averill, Gage. *Four Parts, No Waiting: A Social History of American Barbershop Harmony.* New York: Oxford University Press, 2003.

Baker, David. *David Baker's Jazz Improvisation.* Van Nuys, CA: Alfred Publishing, 1983.

Baker, Kenneth. *Chords and Progressions for Jazz & Popular Keyboard.* New York: Amsco Publications, 1983.

Baraka, Amiri (Leroi Jones). *Blues People: Negro Music in White America.* New York: William Morrow and Company, 1963. Reprint, New York: Quill, 1999.

Barbour, J. Murray. *Tuning and Temperament: A Historical Survey.* New York: Da Capo Press, 1972.

Barulich, Frances, and Jan Fairley. "Habanera." In *The New Grove Dictionary of Music and Musicians,* 2nd ed., vol. 10, ed. Stanley Sadie, 633–34. New York: Macmillan, 2001, rev. 2002.

Belz, Carl. *The Story of Rock.* New York: Harper Colophon Books, 1969.

Berendt, Joachim E. *The Jazz Book: From Ragtime to Fusion and Beyond*, 6th ed. Revised by Günther Huesmann. Brooklyn, New York: Lawrence Hill Books, 1992.

Berlin, Edward A. *Ragtime: A Musical and Cultural History*. Berkeley: University of California Press, 1980.

Berliner, Paul. *The Soul of Mbira: Music and Traditions of the Shona People of Zimbabwe*. Chicago: University of Chicago Press, 1993.

———. *Thinking in Jazz: The Infinite Art of Improvisation*. Chicago: University of Chicago Press, 1994.

Berry, Jason, Jonathan Foose, and Tad Jones. "Professor Longhair's Carnival Rhythms: The Magic of New Orleans." *Southern Exposure* 15, no. 1 (1987): 23–27.

———. *Up From the Cradle of Jazz: New Orleans Music Since WWII*. Athens, GA: University of Georgia Press, 1986. Reprint, New York: Da Capo Press, 1992.

Bertrand, Michael T. *Race, Rock, and Elvis*. Urbana, IL: University of Illinois Press, 2000.

Blesh, Rudi. *Shining Trumpets: A History of Jazz*. New York: Alfred A. Knopf, 1953.

Blesh, Rudi, and Harriet Janis. *They All Played Ragtime: The True Story of an American Music*. New York: Grove Press, 1959.

Bogdanov, Vladimir, Chris Woodstra, Stephen Thomas Erlewine, and John Bush, eds., *The All Music Guide to Hip-Hop: The Definitive Guide to Rap and Hip-Hop*. San Francisco: Backbeat Books, 2003.

———, eds. *The All Music Guide to Soul: The Definitive Guide to R&B and Soul*. San Francisco: Backbeat Books, 2003.

Borneman, Ernest. "Black Light and White Shadow: Notes for a History of American Negro Music." *Jazz Research* 2 (1970): 24–93.

———. "The Roots of Jazz." In *Jazz*, eds. Nat Hentoff and Albert McCarthy, 1–20. New York: Rinehart & Company, 1959.

Bowman, Rob. *Soulsville, U.S.A.: The Story of Stax Records*. New York: Schirmer Books, 1997.

Boyer, Horace Clarence. "Lucie E. Campbell: Composer for the National Baptist Convention." In *We'll Understand it Better By and By*, ed. Bernice Johnson Reagon, 81–108. Washington, DC: Smithsonian Institution Press, 1992.

———. "William Herbert Brewster: The Eloquent Poet." In *We'll Understand It Better By and By*, ed. Bernice Johnson Reagon, 211–31. Washington, DC: Smithsonian Institution Press, 1992.

Brackett, David. *Interpreting Popular Music*. Berkeley, CA: University of California Press, 1995.

———. "What a Difference a Name Makes: Two Instances of African-American Popular Music." In *The Cultural Study of Music: An Introduction*, eds. Martin Clayton, Trevor Herbert, and Richard Middleton, 238–50. New York: Routledge, 2003.

Brewer, Roy. "The Use of Habanera Rhythm in Rockabilly Music." *American Music* 17, no. 3 (Fall 1999): 300–17.

Bronson, Bertrand Harris. *The Singing Tradition of Child's Popular Ballads*. Princeton, NJ: Princeton University Press, 1976.

Broonzy, William. *Big Bill Blues: William Broonzy's Story*. As told to Yannick Bruynoghe. New York: Da Capo, 1992.

Brothers, Thomas. "Solo and Cycle in African-American Jazz." *Musical Quarterly* 78 (1994): 479–509.

Broven, John. *Rhythm & Blues in New Orleans*. Gretna, LA: Pelican Publishing, 1995.

Brown, Geoff. *James Brown Doin' It to Death*. London, Omnibus Press, 1996.

Brown, James, with Bruce Tucker. *James Brown: The Godfather of Soul*. New York: Thunder's Mouth Press, 1997.

Burnim, Mellonee Victoria. *The Black Gospel Music Tradition: Symbol of Ethnicity*. Ph.D. diss. Indiana University. Ann Arbor, MI: University Microfilms Int., 1980.

Bush, John, and Bradley Torreano. "Puff Daddy." In *All Music Guide to Hip-Hop: The Definitive Guide to Rap and Hip-Hop*, eds. Vladimir Bogdanov, Chris Woodstra, Stephen Thomas Erlewine, and John Bush, 394–95. San Francisco: Backbeat Books, 2003.

Carr, Patrick. Liner notes to *Look What Thoughts Will Do*. Columbia Legacy CD C2K 64880, 1997.

Carrington, J. F. *Talking Drums of Africa*. New York: Negro Universities Press, 1969.

Charters, Samuel. *The Blues Makers*. New York: Da Capo, 1991. Reprint of Oak, 1967, 1977. Contains reprints of *The Bluesmen* and *Sweet As the Showers of Rain* (*The Bluesmen*, vol. 2).

———. *The Legacy of the Blues: Art and Lives of Twelve Great Bluesmen*. New York: Da Capo, 1977.

———. "Workin' on the Building: Roots and Influences." In *Nothing But the Blues: The Music and the Musicians*, ed. Lawrence Cohn, 13–31. New York: Abbeville Press, 1993.

Chilton, John. *Let the Good Times Roll: The Story of Louis Jordan and His Music*. Ann Arbor, MI: University of Michigan Press, 1994.

Clayton, Martin, Trevor Herbert, and Richard Middleton, eds. *The Cultural Study of Music: An Introduction*. New York: Routledge, 2003.

Cohn, Lawrence, ed. *Nothing But the Blues: The Music and the Musicians*. New York: Abbeville Press, 1993.

Collier, James Lincoln. *The Making of Jazz: A Comprehensive History*. London: Papermac, 1981.

Cooper, Daniel. *Lefty Frizzell: The Honky Tonk Life of Country Music's Greatest Singer*. New York: Little, Brown, and Co., 1995.

Cotton, Lee. *Shake, Rattle & Roll*. Ann Arbor, MI: Pierian Press, 1989.

Courlander, Harold. *Negro Folk Music, U.S.A.* New York: Columbia University Press, 1963.

Cox, John Harrington. *Folk-songs of the South*. Hatboro, PA: Folklore Associates, 1963.

Crouse, Timothy. "Resurrecting New Orleans: The Gulf Coast Originals Never Left Home." *Rolling Stone* 108 (May 11, 1972): 16, 18, 20.

Curtis, Jim. *Rock Eras: Interpretations of Music and Society, 1954–1984*. Bowling Green, OH: Bowling Green University Press, 1987.

Dixon, Robert M. W., and John Godrich. *Recording the Blues*. New York: Stein and Day, 1970.

Ehrlich, Eugene, Stuart Berg Flexner, Gorton Carruth, and Joyce M. Hawkins. *Oxford American Dictionary*. New York: Oxford University Press, 1980.

Elliott, James Issac. *The Life and Legacy of Lefty Frizzell: Music, Media and Modern Country Singing*. Master's thesis, Austin Peay State University, 1990.

Ellis, Alexander J. Appendix to *On the Sensations of Tone: As a Physiological Basis for the Theory of Music*, by Hermann Helmholtz. Longmans & Co., 1885; New York: Dover, 1954.

Epstein, Dena. *Sinful Tunes and Spirituals: Black Folk Music to the Civil War*. Urbana, IL: University of Illinois Press, 1977.

Erlewine, Thomas. "2-Pac." In *All Music Guide to Hip-Hop: The Definitive Guide to Rap and Hip-Hop*, eds. Vladimir Bogdanov, Chris Woodstra, Stephen Thomas Erlewine, and John Bush, 486–89. San Francisco: Backbeat Books, 2003.

Erlewine, Thomas, and Steve Huey. "Wu-Tang Clan." In *All Music Guide to Hip-Hop: The Definitive Guide to Rap and Hip-Hop*, eds. Vladimir Bogdanov, Chris Woodstra, Stephen Thomas Erlewine, and John Bush, 505–8. San Francisco: Backbeat Books, 2003.

Ertegun, Ahmet. "The Story of Atlantic: Ahmet Ertegun 'In His Own Words.'" *Rolling Stone* 867 (April 26, 2001): 46–48, 50.

Escott, Colin, and Martin Hawkins. *Good Rockin' Tonight: Sun Records and the Birth of Rock 'n' Roll*. New York: St. Martin's Press, 1992.

Evans, David. "Africa and the Blues." *Living Blues* 10 (Autumn 1972): 27–29.

———. "African Elements in Twentieth-Century United States Black Folk Music." *Jazz Research* 10 (1978): 85–109.

———. *Big Road Blues: Tradition and Creativity in the Folk Blues*. Berkeley, CA: University of California Press, 1982. Reprint, New York: Da Capo Press, 1987.

———. "Goin' Up the Country: Blues in Texas and the Deep South." In *Nothing But the Blues: The Music and the Musicians*, ed. Lawrence Cohn, 33–85. New York: Abbeville Press, 1993.

———. "Charley Patton: The Conscience of the Delta." In *Screamin' and Hollerin' the Blues: The Worlds of Charley Patton*. Revenant Album 212, 2001.

———. "Musical Innovation in the Blues of Blind Lemon Jefferson." *Black Music Research Journal* 20, no. 1 (2000): 83–116.

———. "Techniques of Blues Composition among Black Folksingers." *Journal of American Folklore* 87 (1974): 240–49.

———. *Tommy Johnson*. London: Studio Vista, 1971.

Fahey, John. *Charley Patton*. London: Studio Vista, 1970.

Ferris, William, and Mary Hart, eds. *Folk Music and Modern Sound*. Jackson, MS: University Press of Mississippi, 1982.

Finkelstein, Sidney. *Jazz: A People's Music*. New York: Citadel Press, 1948.

Friedman, Albert B. *The Viking Book of Folk Ballads of the English-Speaking World*. New York: The Viking Press, 1961.

Garland, Phyl. *The Sound of Soul: The Story of Black Music*. New York: Pocket Books, 1971.

George, Nelson. *The Death of Rhythm and Blues*. New York: Penguin Books, 1988.

———. *Hip Hop America*. New York: Penguin Books, 1998.

Gert zur Heide, Karl. *Deep South Piano: The Story of Little Brother Montgomery*. London: Studio Vista, 1970.

Giddins, Gary. "Professor Longhair Woogies." *Village Voice* 24 (June 4, 1979): 74–75.

Gillett, Charlie. *Making Tracks: The History of Atlantic Records*. Frogmore, UK: Panther Books, 1975.

———. *The Sound of the City: The Rise of Rock and Roll*, rev. ed. London: Book Club Associates, 1984.

Gitler, Ira. Liner notes to *Horace Silver and the Jazz Messengers*. Blue Note CD CDP 7 46140 2, 1987.

Green, Archie. *Only a Miner: Studies in Recorded Coal-Mining Songs*. Urbana, IL: University of Illinois Press, 1972.

Gribin, Anthony J., and Matthew Schiff. *The Complete Book of Doo-Wop*. Iola, WI: Krause Publications, 2000.

Guralnick, Peter. *Sweet Soul Music: Rhythm and Blues and the Southern Dream of Freedom*. New York: Little, Brown, and Co., 1986, 1999.

Hagan, Chet. *Grand Ole Opry*. New York: Henry Holt, 1989.

Handy, W. C., ed. *A Treasury of the Blues*. New York: Albert & Charles Boni, 1949. Originally published as *Blues: An Anthology*. New York: Albert & Charles Boni, 1926.

———. *Father of the Blues: An Autobiography*. New York: Macmillan, 1941; reprint New York: Da Capo, 1991.

Hazzard-Gordon, Katrina. *Jookin': The Rise of Social Dance Formations in African-American Culture*. Philadelphia: Temple University Press, 1990.

Heilbut, Anthony. *The Gospel Sound: Good News and Bad Times*. New York: Limelight, 1997.

Helander, Bruce. *The Rock Who's Who*, 2nd ed. New York: Schirmer Books, 1996.

Helmholtz, Hermann. *On the Sensations of Tone: As a Physiological Basis for the Theory of Music*. N.P.: Longmans & Co., 1885. Reprint, New York: Dover, 1954.

Hemphill, Paul. *The Nashville Sound: Bright Lights and Country Music*. New York: Simon and Schuster, 1970.

Henderson, Alex. "New Jack Swing." In *All Music Guide to Soul: The Definitive Guide to R&B and Soul*, eds. Vladimir Bogdanov, Chris Woodstra, Stephen Thomas Erlewine, and John Bush, 853–54. San Francisco: Backbeat Books, 2003.

Hentoff, Nat, and Albert McCarthy. *Jazz*. New York: Rinehart and Co., 1959.

Herskovits, Melville J., *The Myth of the Negro Past*. Boston: Beacon Press, 1958.

Hinson, Glenn. *Fire in My Bones: Transcendence and the Holy Spirit in African American Gospel*. Philadelphia: University of Pennsylvania, 1999.

Hodeir, Andre. *Jazz: Its Evolution and Essence*. New York: Grove Press, 1956.

Hogan, Ed. "Teddy Riley." In *All Music Guide to Soul: The Definitive Guide to R&B and Soul*, eds. Vladimir Bogdanov, Chris Woodstra, Stephen Thomas Erlewine, and John Bush, 575. San Francisco: Backbeat Books, 2003.

Hoffmann, Frank W. *The Literature of Rock, 1954–1978*. London: Scarecrow Press, 1981.

Hoffmann, Frank W., and B. Lee Cooper. *The Literature of Rock, III, 1984–1990: With Additional Material for the Period 1954–1983.* Metuchen, NJ: Scarecrow Press, 1995.

Huey, Steve. "Babyface." In *All Music Guide to Soul: The Definitive Guide to R&B and Soul,* eds. Vladimir Bogdanov, Chris Woodstra, Stephen Thomas Erlewine, and John Bush, 28–29. San Francisco: Backbeat Books, 2003.

———. "Roberta Flack." In *All Music Guide to Soul: The Definitive Guide to R&B and Soul,* eds. Vladimir Bogdanov, Chris Woodstra, Stephen Thomas Erlewine, and John Bush, 245. San Francisco: Backbeat Books, 2003.

———. "The Notorious B.I.G." In *All Music Guide to Hip-Hop: The Definitive Guide to Rap and Hip-Hop,* eds. Vladimir Bogdanov, Chris Woodstra, Stephen Thomas Erlewine, and John Bush, 359–60. San Francisco: Backbeat Books, 2003.

———. "O.G.: Original Gangster." In *All Music Guide to Hip-Hop: The Definitive Guide to Rap and Hip-Hop,* eds. Vladimir Bogdanov, Chris Woodstra, Stephen Thomas Erlewine, and John Bush, 225. San Francisco: Backbeat Books, 2003.

Isacoff, Stuart. *Temperament: How Music Became a Battleground for the Great Minds of Western Civilization.* New York: Vintage Books, 2003.

Jackson, Bruce. *Fieldwork.* Chicago: University of Chicago Press, 1987.

Jackson, George Pullen. *White and Negro Spirituals: Their Span and Kinship.* Locust Valley, NY: J. J. Augustin, 1943.

———. *White Spirituals in the Southern Uplands: The Story of the Fasola Folk, Their Songs, Singings, and "Buckwheat Notes."* Chapel Hill, NC: University of North Carolina Press, 1933. Reprint, New York: Dover, 1965.

Jackson, George Stuyvesant. *Early Songs of Uncle Sam.* Ann Arbor, MI: Bruce Humphries, 1933.

Johnson, James Weldon, and J. Rosamond Johnson. *The Books of American Negro Spirituals,* 4th paperback ed. New York: Da Capo, 1989.

Jones, A. M. *African Music in Northern Rhodesia and Some Other Places.* The Occasional Papers of the Rhodes-Livingstone Museum, no. 4. Lusaka, Northern Rhodesia: The Rhodes-Livingstone Museum, 1958.

———. "African Rhythm." *Africa* 24, no. 1 (1954): 26–47.

———. "Blue Notes and Hot Rhythm." *African Music Society Newsletter* 1, no. 4 (June 1951): 9–12.

———. *Studies in African Music,* 2 vols. London: Oxford University Press, 1959.

Joyner, David Lee. "Southern Ragtime and Its Transition to Published Blues." Unpublished Ph.D. dissertation, The University of Memphis, 1986.

Katz, Bernard, ed. *The Social Implications of Early Negro Music.* New York: Arno Press, 1969.

Keil, Charles. *Urban Blues.* Chicago: University of Chicago Press, 1966.

Kirby, Percival R. "A Study of Negro Harmony." *The Musical Quarterly* 16 (1930): 404–14.

Kostka, Stefan, and Dorothy Payne. *Tonal Harmony: With an Introduction to Twentieth-Century Music,* 3rd ed. New York: McGraw-Hill, 1995.

Kubik, Gerhard. "Africa." In *The New Grove Dictionary of Music and Musicians,* 2nd ed., vol. 1, ed. Stanley Sadie, 190–210. New York: Macmillan, 2001, rev. 2002.

————. *Africa and the Blues*. Jackson, MS: University Press of Mississippi, 1999.

————. "Central Africa: An Introduction." In *The Garland Encyclopedia of World Music*, vol. 1, ed. Ruth M. Stone, 650–80. New York: Garland Publishing, 1998.

————. "Intra-African Streams of Influence." In *The Garland Encyclopedia of World Music*, vol. 1, ed. Ruth M. Stone, 293–326. New York: Garland Publishing, 1998.

————. "The African Matrix in Jazz Harmonic Practices." *Black Music Research Journal* 25, no. 1/2 (2005): in press.

————. *The Kachamba Brothers' Band: A Study of Neo-Traditional Music in Malawi*. Zambian Paper no. 9. Lusaka: Institute for African Studies, University of Zambia, 1974.

————. *Malawian Music: A Framework for Analysis*. Assisted by Moya Aliya Malamusi, Lidiya Malamusi, and Donald Kachamba. Zomba, Malawi: University of Malawi, 1987.

————. *Theory of African Music*, vol. 1. Wilhelmshaven, Germany: Florian Noetzel Verlag, 1994.

Lawless, Ray M. *Folksingers and Folksongs in America*. New York: Duell, Sloan and Pearce, 1960.

Leach, MacEdward. *The Ballad Book*. New York: A. S. Barnes and Co., 1955.

Lichtenstein, Grace, and Laura Danker. *Musical Gumbo: The Music of New Orleans*. New York: W. W. Norton and Co., 1993.

Lindley, Mark. "Temperaments." In *The New Grove Dictionary of Music and Musicians*, 2nd ed., vol. 25, ed. Stanley Sadie, 248–68. New York: Macmillan, 2001, rev. 2002.

Lomax John A., and Alan Lomax, comps. *American Ballads and Folk Songs*. New York: Dover Publications, 1934.

————, comps. *Our Singing Country: Folk Songs and Ballads*. New York: Macmillan Co., 1941. Reprint, Mineola, NY: Dover Publications, 2000.

Lornell, Kip. *Happy in the Service of the Lord: African-American Sacred Harmony Quartets in Memphis*, 2nd ed. Knoxville: University of Tennessee Press, 1988.

Lytle, Craig. "A Quiet Storm." In *All Music Guide to Soul: The Definitive Guide to R&B and Soul*, eds. Vladimir Bogdanov, Chris Woodstra, Stephen Thomas Erlewine, and John Bush, 580. San Francisco: Backbeat Books, 2003.

Malone, Bill C. *Country Music U.S.A.*, rev. ed. Austin: University of Texas Press, 1985.

————. *Southern Music, American Music*. Lexington: University Press of Kentucky, 1979.

Marcus, Greil. *Mystery Train: Images of America in Rock 'n' Roll Music*, 4th rev. ed. New York: Penguin Books, 1997.

Matassa, Cosimo. Interview by Jay Gallagher. "Cosimo: A Conversation with the Dean of New Orleans Recording." *Mix* 20, no. 3 (March 1996): 88–102.

McDermott, Tom. "A New Orleans 'Frumba' by Tom McDermott." *Piano Today* 17, no. 1 (Winter 1996): 43, 56.

McEwen, Joe, and Jim Miller. "Motown." In *The Rolling Stone Illustrated History of Rock 'n' Roll, 1950–1980*, ed. Jim Miller, 235–45. New York: Random House, 1980.

McKee, Margaret, and Fred Chisenhall. *Beale Black & Blue: Life and Music on Black America's Main Street*. Baton Rouge: Louisiana State University Press, 1981.

Merriam, Alan P. *The Anthropology of Music.* Chicago: Northwestern University Press, 1964.

Miller, Jim, ed. *The Rolling Stone Illustrated History of Rock and Roll, 1950–1980.* New York: Random House, 1980.

Morales, Humberto, and Henry Adler. *How to Play Latin American Rhythm Instruments.* Edited by F. Henri Klickmann. Translated by Ernesto Barbosa. Rockville Center, NY: Belwin Mills, 1966.

Morrison, Craig. *Go Cat Go!: Rockabilly Music and Its Makers.* Urbana, IL: University of Illinois Press, 1996.

Myers, Helen. *Ethnomusicology: An Introduction.* New York: W. W. Norton and Co., 1992.

Nettl, Bruno. *The Study of Ethnomusicology: Thirty-nine Issues and Concepts.* Chicago: University of Chicago Press, 1983.

Niles, Abbe. Historical and critical text to *A Treasury of the Blues,* ed. W. C. Handy. New York: Albert & Charles Boni, 1949. Originally published as *Blues: An Anthology.* New York: Albert and Charles Boni, 1926.

Nketia, J. H. Kwabena. *The Music of Africa.* New York: W. W. Norton and Co., 1974.

Odum, Howard W. "Folk-Song and Folk-Poetry as Found in the Secular Songs of the Southern Negroes." *The Journal of American Folk-Lore* 24 (1911): 255–94, 351–96.

Odum, Howard W., and Guy B. Johnson. *The Negro and His Songs: A Study of Typical Negro Songs in the South.* Westport, CT: Negro Universities Press, 1925, 1968.

Oliver, Paul, ed. *The Blackwell Guide to Blues Records.* Oxford, UK: Blackwell Publishers, 1989.

———. "Blues." In *The New Grove Dictionary of Music and Musicians,* 2nd ed., vol. 3, ed. Stanley Sadie, 730–37. New York: Macmillan, 2001, rev. 2002.

———. "Echoes of the Jungle?" *Living Blues* 13 (Summer 1973): 29–32.

———. *Savannah Syncopators: African Retentions in the Blues.* New York: Stein and Day, 1970.

———. *Screening the Blues: Aspects of the Blues Tradition.* New York: Da Capo Press, 1968.

———. "Some Comments: African Influence and the Blues." *Living Blues* 8 (Spring 1972): 13–17.

———. *Songsters and Saints: Vocal Traditions on Race Records.* Cambridge, UK: Cambridge University Press, 1984.

———. *The Story of the Blues.* Radnor, PA: Chilton Book Co., 1969.

Palisca, Claude V., ed. *Norton Anthology of Western Music,* 2 vols. New York: W. W. Norton and Co., 1980.

Palmer, Robert. *Deep Blues.* New York: Penguin Books, 1982.

———. "James Brown." In *The Rolling Stone Illustrated History of Rock 'n' Roll, 1950–1980,* ed. Jim Miller, 136–42. New York: Random House, 1980.

———. "Professor Longhair's Rock 'n' Roll Gumbo." *Downbeat* 41 (March 28, 1974): 18–19.

Pantaleoni, Hewitt. *On The Nature of Music.* Oneonta, NY: Welkin Books, 1985.

Parrish, Carl, and John F. Ohl. *Masterpieces of Music Before 1750*. New York: W. W. Norton and Co., 1951.

Parrish, Lydia. *Slave Songs of the Georgia Sea Islands*. N.P.: Creative Age Press, 1942. Reprint, Athens, GA: University of Georgia Press, 1992.

Paxton, Josh. *Professor Longhair Collection*. Milwaukee: Hal Leonard, 1999.

Payne, Jim. *Give the Drummers Some!: The Great Drummers of R&B, Funk and Soul*. Miami: Warner Bros., 1996.

Perkins, William Eric, ed. *Droppin' Science: Critical Essays on Rap Music and Hip Hop Culture*. Philadelphia: Temple University Press, 1996.

———. "The Rap Attack: An Introduction." In *Droppin' Science: Critical Essays on Rap Music and Hip Hop Culture*, 1–45. Philadelphia: Temple University Press, 1996.

Pike, Kenneth L. *Tone Languages: A Technique for Determining the Number and Type of Pitch Contrasts in a Language, with Studies in Tonemic Substitution and Fusion*. Ann Arbor: University of Michigan Press, 1967.

Professor Longhair. "Fess." Interview by Bill Greensmith and Bez Turner. *Blues Unlimited* 130 (May–Aug. 1978): 4–7.

———. "Living Blues Interview: Professor Longhair." Interview by Tad Jones. *Living Blues* 26 (Apr.–May 1976): 16–29.

Progler, J. A. "Searching for Swing: Participatory Discrepancies in the Jazz Rhythm Section." *Ethnomusicology* 39, no. 1 (Winter 1995): 21–54.

Pruter, Robert, ed. *The Blackwell Guide to Soul Recordings*. Oxford, UK: Blackwell Publishers, 1993.

———. *Doowop: the Chicago Scene*. Urbana: University of Illinois Press, 1996.

Raichelson, Richard M. *Beale Street Talks: A Walking Tour Down the Home of the Blues*. Memphis: Arcadia Records, 1994.

Randel, Don Michael, ed. *Harvard Dictionary of Music*, 4th ed. Cambridge, MA: Belknap Press, 2003.

Reagon, Bernice Johnson, ed. *If You Don't Go, Don't Hinder Me: The African American Sacred Tradition*. Lincoln, NE: University of Nebraska Press, 2001.

———, ed. *We'll Understand It Better By and By: Pioneering African American Gospel Composers*. Washington, DC: Smithsonian Institution Press, 1992.

Rebennack, Mac "Dr. John." "Under the Hoodoo Moon." *Keyboard* 20, no. 3 (Mar. 1994): 60–77.

Redd, Lawrence. *Rock Is Rhythm and Blues: The Impact of Mass Media*. East Lansing, MI: Michigan State University Press, 1974.

Reese, Gustave. *Music in the Middle Ages*. New York: W. W. Norton and Co., 1940.

Rideout, Ernie. "Master Class: The Rock and Roll Featism of Bill Payne—Under the Radar, Over the Top." *Keyboard* 22, no. 10 (Oct. 1996): 46–59.

Roberts, John Storm. *The Latin Tinge: The Impact of Latin American Music on the United States*. New York: Oxford University Press, 1979.

Rosalsky, Mitch. *Encyclopedia of Rhythm & Blues and Doo-wop Vocal Groups*. Lanham, MD: Scarecrow Press, 2000.

Rose, Cynthia. *Living in America: The Soul Saga of James Brown*. London: Serpent's Tail, 1990.

Rose, Tricia. *Black Noise: Rap Music and Black Culture in Contemporary America*. Hanover, NH: Wesleyan University Press, 1994.

Rowe, Mike. "Piano Blues and Boogie-Woogie." In *The Blackwell Guide to Blues Records*, ed. Paul Oliver, 112–38. Chicago: University of Chicago Press, 1989.

Rycroft, David. "Nguni Vocal Polyphony." *Journal of the International Folk Music Council* 19 (1967): 89–103.

Rye, Howard. "Rhythm and Blues." In *The New Grove Dictionary of Music and Musicians*, 2nd ed., vol. 21, ed. Stanley Sadie, 309–10. New York: Macmillan, 2001, rev. 2002.

Sargeant, Winthrop. *Jazz: Hot and Hybrid*. New York: E. P. Dutton, 1946.

Schneider, Marius. "Tone and Tune in West African Music." *Ethnomusicology* 5, no. 3 (Sept. 1961): 204–15.

Schuller, Gunther. *Early Jazz: Its Roots and Musical Development*. New York: Oxford University Press, 1968.

———. *Musings: The Musical Worlds of Gunther Schuller*. New York: Oxford University Press, 1986.

Selvin, Joel. *Sly and the Family Stone: An Oral History*. New York: Avon Books, 1998.

Shaw, Arnold, comp. *Dictionary of American Pop/Rock*. New York: Schirmer, 1982.

———. *Honkers and Shouters: The Golden Years of Rhythm and Blues*. New York: Macmillan, 1978.

———. *The Rockin' '50s: The Decade That Transformed the Pop Music Scene*. New York: Hawthorn Books, 1974.

Shelemay, Kay Kaufman, ed. *Ethnomusicology: History, Definitions, and Scope*. New York: Garland Publishing, 1992.

Slutsky, Allan, and Chuck Silverman. *The Funkmasters: The Great James Brown Rhythm Sections*. Miami: Warner Bros., 1997.

Southern, Eileen. *The Music of Black Americans: A History*, 3rd ed. New York: W. W. Norton and Co., 1997.

Stambler, Irwin. *Encyclopedia of Pop, Rock and Soul*. New York: St. Martin's Press, 1974.

Stewart, Alexander. "'Funky Drummer': New Orleans, James Brown, and the Rhythmic Transformation of American Popular Music." *Popular Music* 19, no. 3 (Oct. 2000): 292–318.

Titon, Jeff Todd. *Early Downhome Blues: A Musical and Cultural Analysis*, 2nd ed. Chapel Hill: University of North Carolina Press, 1994. Originally published Urbana, IL: University of Illinois Press, 1977.

Toll, Robert C. *Blacking Up: The Minstrel Show in Nineteenth-Century America*. London: Oxford University Press, 1974.

Toop, David. *Rap Attack 3: African Rap to Global Hip Hop*, 3rd ed. London: Serpent's Tail, 2000.

Toussaint, Allen. "Allen Toussaint: Soul of New Orleans." Interview by Rick Clark. *Mix* 21, no. 11 (Nov. 1997): 80, 82, 84, 86, 88, 91, 213.

Tsukada, Kenichi. "Harmony in Luvale Music of Zambia." In *The Garland Encyclopedia of World Music*, vol. 1, ed. Ruth M. Stone, 722–43. New York: Garland Publishing, 1998.

Trynka, Paul, ed. *Rock Hardware: 40 Years of Rock Instrumentation.* London: Balaphon Books, 1996.

van der Merwe, Peter. *Origins of the Popular Style: The Antecedents of Twentieth-Century Popular Music.* New York: Oxford University Press, 1989.

Vincent, Rickey. *Funk: The Music, The People, and the Rhythm of the One.* New York: St. Martin's Griffin, 1996.

Walser, Robert. "Rhythm, Rhyme, and Rhetoric in the Music of Public Enemy." *Ethnomusicology* 39, no. 2 (spring/summer 1995): 193–215.

Warren, Fred, and Lee Warren. *The Music of Africa: An Introduction.* London: Prentice Hall, 1970.

Waterman, Christopher Alan. *Jùjú: a Social History and Ethnography of an African Popular Music.* Chicago: University of Chicago Press, 1990.

Waterman, Richard A. "African Influence on the Music of the Americas." In *Acculturation in the Americas: Proceedings and Selected Papers of the 29th International Congress of Americanists,* ed. Sol Tax, 207–18. New York: Cooper Square, 1967.

———. "'Hot' Rhythm in Negro Music." *Journal of the American Musicological Society* 1 (1948): 24–37.

Wheeler, Mary. *Steamboatin' Days: Folk Songs of the River Packet Days.* Louisiana State University Press, 1944. Reprint, Freeport, NY: Books for Libraries Press, 1969.

Whitburn, Joel, comp. *The Billboard Book of Top 40 Hits,* 7th ed. New York: Billboard Books, 2000.

———, comp. *Top Country Singles: 1944–1997.* Menomonee Falls, WI: Record Research Inc., 1998.

———, comp. *Top R&B Singles: 1942–1999.* Menomonee Falls, WI: Record Research Inc., 2000.

Wilgus, D. K. *Anglo-American Folksong Scholarship Since 1898.* New Brunswick, NJ: Rutgers University Press, 1959.

———. "Country-Western Music and the Urban Hillbilly." *Journal of American Folklore* 83 (1970): 157–84.

Winner, Langdon. "The Sound of New Orleans." *The Rolling Stone Illustrated History of Rock and Roll, 1950–1980,* ed. Jim Miller, 35–44. New York: Random House, 1976, 1980.

Wolfe, Charles. *Classic Country: Legends of Country Music.* New York: Routledge, 2001.

———. "Honky-Tonk Starts Here: The Jim Beck Dallas Studio." *The Journal of Country Music* 11, no. 1 (1986): 25–30.

———. "Lefty Frizzell." *The Journal of the American Academy for the Preservation of Old-time Country Music* 1, no. 4 (Aug. 1991): 8–11.

Wolff, Kurt. *Country Music: The Rough Guide.* London: Rough Guides, 2000.

Work, John W. *American Negro Songs: 230 Folk Songs and Spirituals, Religious and Secular.* New York: Crown Publishers, 1940. Reprint, Mineola, New York: Dover, 1998.

Wynn, Ron. "Nile Rodgers." In *All Music Guide to Soul: The Definitive Guide to R&B and Soul*, eds. Vladimir Bogdanov, Chris Woodstra, Stephen Thomas Erlewine, and John Bush, 582. San Francisco: Backbeat Books, 2003.

Sound Recordings and Electronic Media

Ace, Johnny. *Memorial Album*. MCA CD 31183, 1990.

African Guitar: Solo Fingerstyle Guitar Music from Uganda, Congo/Zaire, Malawi, Namibia, Central African Republic and Zambia. Audiovisual field recordings by Gerhard Kubik. Vetstapol/Rounder DVD 13017, 2003.

Afrika Bambaataa. *Afrika Bambaataa: Looking for the Perfect Beat, 1980–1985*. Tommy Boy CD TBCD 1457, 2001.

Afro-American Spirituals, Work Songs, and Ballads. Rounder CD 1510, 1998.

Afro-American Blues and Game Songs. Rounder CD 1513, 1999.

Afro-American Folk Music from Tate and Panola Counties, Mississippi. Audio field recordings by David Evans and Alan Lomax. Rounder CD 18964-1515-2, 2000.

All Music Guide. http://www.allmusic.com/, Dec. 1, 2003.

Anglo-American Ballads, vol. 1. Rounder CD 1511, 1999.

Anthology of American Folk Music. Edited by Harry Smith. Sony 6 CDs SFW 40090, 1997.

Atlantic Blues: Piano. Atlantic CD 81694-2, 1986.

Atlantic Rhythm and Blues: 1947–1974. Atlantic 8 CDs 82305-2, 2001.

Atlantic Soul Classics. Warner CD 9-27601-2, 1985.

Armstrong, Louis. *Louis Armstrong: Hot Fives and Hot Sevens*. JSP 4 CDs: CD 312-CD 315, 1999.

Autry, Gene. *Greatest Hits*. Sony CD A18874, 1992.

Barrelhouse Boogie. Bluebird/RCA CD 8334-2-RB, 1989.

Basie, Count. *Count Basie: April in Paris*. Verve CD 825 575-2, 1997.

Bell Biv DeVoe. *The Best of Bell Biv DeVoe*. MCA CD 088 112 870-2, 2002.

Berry, Chuck. *The Best of Chuck Berry*. MCA CD MCAD-11944, 1999.

Black Appalachia: String Bands, Songsters, and Hoedowns. Rounder CD 11661-1823-2, 1999.

Bluesland: A Portrait in American Music. BMG videocassette 72333-80087-3, 1993.

Bluesmasters: The Essential History of the Blues, vol. 2. Rhino videocassette R3 2102, 1993.

BMG corporate web site. http://www.bmg.com/, March 5, 2004.

Boyz II Men. *Legacy: The Greatest Hits Collection*. Universal CD 440 016 083-2, 2001.

Brown, Charles. *The Best of Charles Brown: Driftin' Blues*. Collectables CD COL-CD-5631, 1995.

Brown, James. *Foundations of Funk: A Brand New Bag, 1964–1969*. Polydor CD 31453 1165-2, 1996.

———. *Funk Power 1970: A Brand New Thing*. Polydor CD 31453 1684-2, 1996.

———. *James Brown: The Godfather of Soul*. A&E/Biography videocassette AAE-14088, 1996.

———. *James Brown Live at the Apollo, 1962*. Polydor CD 843 479-2, 1990.

————. *James Brown: Star Time.* Polydor 4 CDs 849 109-2 through 849 112-2, 1991.

————. *The Lost James Brown Tapes.* Warner/Reprise videocassette 38295-3, 1991.

————. *Think!* Polydor CD 31453 1018-2, 1996.

————. *20 All Time Greatest Hits.* Polydor CD 314 511 326-2, 1991.

Cameo. *The Best of Cameo.* Mercury CD 314 514 824-2, 1993.

Can't You Hear the Wind Howl? The Life and Music of Robert Johnson. Produced by Peter Myer. Winstar videocassette WHE71126, 1997.

"Capitol Records." http://en.wikipedia.org/wiki/Capitol_Records, May 22, 2004.

Carey, Mariah. *Mariah Carey.* Columbia CD 45202, 1990.

Caribbean Voyage: Brown Girl in the Ring. Rounder CD 1716, 1997.

Carter Family, the. *The Carter Family, 1927–1934.* JSP 5 CDs: JSPCD7701A through JSPCD7001E, 2001.

Charles, Ray. *Modern Sounds in Country & Western Music.* Rhino CD R2 70099, 1988.

Chess Blues Classics: 1947 to 1956. Chess CD CHD-9369, 1997.

Chess Blues Classics: 1957 to 1967. Chess CD CHD-9368, 1997.

Chess Blues Piano Greats. Chess 2 CDs CHD2-9385, 1997.

Chi-Lites, the. *The Chi-Lites Greatest Hits.* Brunswick CD BRC 33002-2, 1998.

"Columbia Records." http://en2.wikipedia.org/wiki/Columbia_Records, May 22, 2004.

Commodores, the. *The Best of the Commodores.* Motown CD 314 542 096-2, 1999.

The Complete Stax/Volt Singles: 1959–1968. Atlantic 9 CDs 7 82218-2, 1991.

Cooke, Sam. *Sam Cooke: Greatest Hits.* RCA CD 07863 65605-2, 1998.

————. *Sam Cooke with the Soul Stirrers.* Specialty CD SPCD-7009-2, 1991.

Coltrane, John. *The Best of John Coltrane.* Atlantic CD 1541-2, 1970.

Crudup, Arthur "Big Boy." *That's All Right Mama.* RCA Heritage/Bluebird CD 61043-2, 1992.

Crusaders, the. *The Crusaders' Finest Hour.* Verve CD 314 543 762-2, 2000.

Davis, Miles. *Birth of the Cool.* Capitol CD 7243 5 30117 2 7, 2000.

————. *Kind of Blue.* Columbia/Legacy CD CK 40579, 1997.

————. *Milestones.* Columbia/Legacy CD CK 85203, 2001.

Dazz Band. *The Best of Dazz Band.* Motown CD 314 556 771-2, 2001.

De La Soul. *Timeless: The Singles Collection.* Tommy Boy/Rhino CD R2 73860, 2003.

Digital Underground. *Playwutchyalike: The Best of Digital Underground.* Tommy Boy/ Rhino CD R2 73861, 2003.

Dodds, Baby. *Baby Dodds Talking and Drum Solos.* Folkways CD F-2290, 2001.

Domino, Fats. *Fats Domino Jukebox: 20 Greatest Hits.* Capitol CD 37600, 2002.

Dorsey, Thomas A. *Precious Lord: Recordings of the Great Gospel Songs of Thomas A. Dorsey.* Columbia/Legacy CD CK 57164, 1994.

Dr. Dre. *The Chronic.* Death Row CD DRR 63000-2, 1992.

Earth, Wind & Fire. *Earth, Wind & Fire: The Definitive Collection.* Columbia 2 CDs 480554 9, 1995.

The Ebb Records Story, vol. 2: Blues 'n' Rhythm & Rock 'n' Roll, 1957–1959. Specialty CD SPCD-7073-2, 2001.

Echoes of the Forest: Music of the Central African Pygmies. Produced by Larry Blumenfeld. Ellipsis Arts CD 4020, 1995.

"Epic Records." http://en.wikipedia.org/wiki/Epic_Records, May 22, 2004.

Everly Brothers, the. *Songs Our Daddy Taught Us.* Rhino CD R2 70212, 1988.

Flatt, Lester, and Earl Scruggs. *The Best of Flatt & Scruggs.* Mercury CD 088 170 187-2, 2001.

Frizzell, Lefty. *Look What Thoughts Will Do.* Columbia Legacy CD C2K 64880, 1997.

———. *Pure Country: Lefty Frizzell.* Sony CD A30823, 2000.

Gap Band, the. *Gap Band: Ultimate Collection.* Hip-O CD 314 548 098-2, 2001.

Garner, Erroll. *Concert by the Sea.* Columbia CD CK 40589, 1987.

Garner, Erroll. *Erroll Garner: London 1964, Copenhagen 1970.* Greenline videocassette VidJazz 7, 1990.

Gaye, Marvin. *Midnight Love and the Sexual Healing Sessions.* Columbia/Legacy CD C2k 65546, 1998.

Gibson, Don. *Don Gibson: RCA Country Legends.* Buddah/RCA CD 74465 99791 2, 2001.

Grandmaster Flash. *The Best of Grandmaster Flash, Melle Mel & the Furious Five.* Rhino CD R2 71606, 1994.

The Great Gospel Women: 31 Classic Performances by the Greatest Gospel Women. Shanachie CD 600492, 1993.

Hancock Herbie. *Headhunters.* Columbia/Legacy CD CK 65123, 1997.

Handy, W. C. *W. C. Handy's Memphis Blues Band.* Memphis Archives CD MA7006, 1994.

Hawkins, Coleman. *Body and Soul.* Victor Jazz CD 09026-68515-2, 1996.

Hayes, Isaac. *Isaac Hayes: Greatest Hit Singles.* Stax CD SCD-8515-2, 1991.

High Lonesome: The Story of Bluegrass. Produced by Rachel Liebling and Andrew Serwer. Shanachie videocassette 604, 1991.

Hitsville, U. S. A.: The Motown Singles Collection 1959–1971. Motown 4 CDs 3746363122, 1992.

Holcomb, Roscoe. *The High Lonesome Sound.* Smithsonian Folkways SF CD 40104, 1998.

Holiday, Billie. *Billie Holiday's Greatest Hits.* Decca CD GRD 653, 1995.

Hooker, John Lee. *The Best of John Lee Hooker, 1965 to 1974.* MCA CD MCAD 10539, 1992.

———. *John Lee Hooker: Boogie Chillun.* Charly Records Ltd. CD Charly 4, 1986.

———. *John Lee Hooker: His Best Chess Sides.* Chess CD CHD-9383, 1997.

———. *John Lee Hooker: The Ultimate Collection.* Rhino 2 CDs R2 70572, 1991.

———. *The Legendary Modern Recordings, 1948–1954.* Flair/Virgin CD 39658 2, 1993.

Hopkins, Lightnin'. *Country Blues.* Tradition CD TCD 3001, 1996.

House, Son. *Son House: The Original Delta Blues.* Columbia CD CK 65515, 1998.

Howlin' Wolf. *Howlin' Wolf: His Best.* Chess CD CHD-9375, 1997.

Hunter, Ivory Joe. *Ivory Joe Hunter/Old and the New.* Collectables CD 6234, 1999.

———. *I Almost Lost My Mind 1945/1950.* EPM CD 159992, 2001.

An Introduction to Gospel Song. Folkways CD F-RF5, 1962.

Jacquet, Illinois. *The Illinois Jacquet Story.* Proper Records 4 CDs, 2002.

Jackson, Janet. *Control.* A&M CD 3905/DX 923, 1986.

———. *Rhythm Nation 1814.* A&M CD 3920, 1989.

Jackson, Michael. *Greatest Hits: HIStory,* vol. 1. Epic CD EK 85250, 1991.

James, Elmore. *Elmore James: Golden Hits.* Masters CD MCAD 61046-2, 1996.

James, Skip. *Skip James: Complete Early Recordings.* Yazoo CD 2009, 2001.

Jefferson, Blind Lemon. *Moanin' All Over.* Tradition CD TCD 1011, 1996.

Johnny Ace. *Memorial Album.* MCA CD MCAD-31183, 1973.

Johnson, Robert. *Robert Johnson: King of the Delta Blues.* Columbia CD DIDP 092683, 1997.

Johnson, Tommy. *Tommy Johnson (1928–1929).* Document CD DOCD-5001, 1988.

Joplin, Scott. *Complete Works of Scott Joplin.* Richard Zimmerman, Piano. Laserlight 5 CDs: 17 021 through 17 025, 1993.

Jordan, Louis. *Louis Jordan and His Tympany Five.* JSP Records 5 CDs: JSPCD905A through JSPCD905E, 2001.

Jubilation! Great Gospel Performances, Volume One: Black Gospel. Rhino CD R2 70288, 1992.

Jubilation! Great Gospel Performances, Volume Two: More Black Gospel. Rhino CD R2 70288, 1992.

The JVC/Smithsonian Folkways Video Anthology of Music and Dance of Africa, 3 vols. JVC videocassettes VTMV-218E, 291E, and 220E, 1996.

KC and the Sunshine Band. *The Best of KC and the Sunshine Band.* Rhino CD R2 70940, 1989.

Kentucky Headhunters, the. *Pickin' on Nashville.* Mercury/Polygram CD 838 744-2, 1989.

King, Albert. *King of the Blues Guitar.* Atlantic CD 8213-2, 1989.

King, B.B. *The Best of B.B. King.* MCA CD MCAD-11939, 1999.

———. *The RPM Hits 1951–1957.* Ace CD CDCHD 712, 1999.

King Sunny Ade and His African Beats. *Juju Music.* Mango/Island Records CD 162-539 712-2, 1982.

Kool & the Gang. *Kool & the Gang Spin Their Top Hits.* Mercury CD 822 536-2, 1978.

Little Richard. *The Georgia Peach.* Specialty CD SPCD-7012-2, 1991.

Lunceford, Jimmie. *The Classic Tracks.* Kaz Records CD 317, 1996.

———. *Jimmie Lunceford and His Orchestra, 1937–1939.* Classics Records CD 52, 1990.

Macon, Uncle Dave. *Travelin' Down the Road.* County Records CD CCS-CD-115, 1995.

Malamusi, M. A. Original tape. Oral Literature Research Programme. Chileka, Malawi.

Masters of the Country Blues: Big Bill Broonzy and Roosevelt Sykes. Yazoo DVD 518, 2002.

Masters of the Country Blues: Bukka White and Son House. Yazoo DVD 500, 2000.

Masters of the Country Blues: John Lee Hooker and Furry Lewis. Yazoo DVD 519, 2002.

Masters of the Country Blues: Rev. Gary Davis and Sonny Terry. Yazoo DVD 501, 2001.

Masters of the Delta Blues: The Friends of Charlie Patton. Yazoo CD 2002, 2002.

McIntosh County Shouters. *McIntosh County Shouters: Slave Shout Songs from the Coast of Georgia.* Folkways CD F-4344, 1984.

McShann, Jay. *The Essential Jay McShann, 1941–1949.* Indigo CD IGOCD 2524, 2002.

———. *Jay McShann, 1944–1946.* Classics Records CD 966, 1997.

Memphis Minnie. *I Ain't No Bad Gal.* Masters/CBS CD RK 44072, 1988.

Memphis Slim. *The Folkways Years: 1959–1973.* Smithsonian Folkways Recordings SFW CD 40128, 2000.

Millinder, Lucky. *Lucky Millinder and His Orchestra, 1941–1942*. Classics Records CD 712, 1993.

Mintzer, Bob. *Latin from Manhattan*. DMP CD-523, 1998.

Mississippi Blues: Library of Congress Recordings 1940–1942. Travelin' Man CD TMCD 07, 1991.

Monroe, Bill. *The Essential Bill Monroe and the Monroe Brothers*. RCA CD 67450-2, 1997.

Morton, Jelly Roll. *The Library of Congress Recordings, vol. 3: The Pearls*. Rounder CD 1093, 1993.

Motown Girl Groups. Motown CD 314 520 299-2, 1995.

Muddy Waters. *Can't Be Satisfied*. Produced by Morgan Neville and Robert Gordon. Wellspring DVD WHE73167, 2002.

———. *Muddy Waters: His Best, 1947 to 1956*. Chess CD CHD-9370, 1997.

Negro Work Songs and Calls. Rounder CD 1517, 1999.

N.W.A. *The N.W.A Legacy, vol. 1: 1988–1998*. Priority CD P2 51111, 1999.

Owens, Maida. "Louisiana's Traditional Cultures: An Overview." From the Northwestern State University (LA) webpage *Louisiana Folklife Program*. http://www.louisianafolklife.org/LT/Maidas_Essay/main_introduction_onepage.html, May 21, 2004.

Parker, Charlie. *The Essential Charlie Parker*. Verve CD 314 517 173-2, 1992.

Parliament. *Chocolate City*. Casablanca CD 836 700-2, 1975.

———. *The Clones of Dr. Funkenstein*. Casablanca CD 842 620-2, 1976.

———. *Parliament's Greatest Hits*. Casablanca CD 822 637-2, 1984.

———. *Up for the Down Stroke*. Casablanca CD 842 619-2, 1974.

Piano Players Rarely Ever Play Together. Produced by Stevenson J. Palfi. Stevenson Productions videocassette, 1982.

Patton, Charley. *Screamin' and Hollerin' the Blues: The Worlds of Charley Patton*. CD set with historical and critical essays, Revenant Album 212, 2001.

Presley, Elvis. *Elvis Presley*. RCA CD PCD1-5198, 1985.

Price, Lloyd. *Lloyd Price Greatest Hits*. Curb CD D2-77305, 1990.

Prince. *The Very Best of Prince*. Warner CD R2 72472, 2001.

Professor Longhair. *The Professor Longhair Anthology*. Rhino CD R2 71502, 1993.

———. *Professor Longhair's New Orleans Piano*. Atlantic CD 7225-2, 1989.

———. *Big Chief*. Rhino CD R2 71446, 1993.

Public Enemy. *It Takes a Nation of Millions to Hold Us Back*. Def Jam CD 314 527 358-2, 1988.

———. *Muse Sick-N-Hour Mess Age*. Def Jam CD 314 523 362-2, 1994.

Puff Daddy and the Family. *No Way Out*. Bad Boy CD 78612-73012-2, 1997.

Rodgers, Jimmie. *The Essential Jimmie Rodgers*. RCA CD 67500-2, 1997.

Roots of Black Music in America. Folkways 2 CDs F-2694, 1972.

Rufus. *The Very Best of Rufus*. MCA CD MCAD-11543, 1996.

Run-DMC. *Run DMC Greatest Hits*. Arista/BMG Heritage 07822 10607-2, 2002.

Shindig! Presents Soul. Produced by Trisha Wexler. Rhino videocassette RNVD 1456, 1991.

Silver, Horace. *Horace Silver and the Jazz Messengers*. Blue Note CD CDP 7 46140 2, 1987.

——. *Horace Silver: Song for My Father*. Blue Note CD 7243 4 990002 2 6, 1999.

Slave. *The Best of Slave, featuring Steve Arrington*. Rhino CD R2 71592, 1994.

Sly and the Family Stone. *Fresh*. Epic CD EK 32134, 1991.

——. *Sly & the Family Stone: Greatest Hits*. Epic CD EK 30325, 1990.

——. *There's a Riot Goin' On*. Epic CD EK 30986, 1990.

——. *A Whole New Thing*. Legacy/Epic CD EK 66424, 1995.

Smith, Bessie. *Empty Bed Blues: Her 23 Greatest*. ASV CD AJA 5213, 1996.

Smith, Jimmy. *Bucket!* Blue Note CD 7243 5 24550 2 7, 2000.

Smithsonian Folkways American Roots Collection. Smithsonian/Folkways CD SF 40062, 1996.

Smithsonian Folkways World Music Collection. Smithsonian/Folkways CD SF 40471, 1997.

Snoop Doggy Dogg. *Doggystyle*. Death Row CD DRR 63002-2, 1993, 2001.

Soul Stirrers, the. *The Soul Stirrers Featuring Sam Cooke, Paul Foster, and Julius Cheeks: Jesus Gave Me Water*. Specialty CD SPCD-7031-2, 1992.

Sounds of the South. Atlantic 4 CDs 82496-2, 1993.

Southern Country Blues, vol. 1: Down in Boogie Alley. Star Sounds CD 3712-2, 1997.

Speckled Red. *The Barrel-House Blues of Speckled Red*. Folkways CD F-3555, 1961.

Stanley Brothers. *The Complete Columbia Stanley Brothers*. Columbia/Legacy CD CK 53798, 1996.

Stanley, Ralph, and the Clinch Mountain Boys. *Man of Constant Sorrow*. Rebel CD Reb-CD-1126, 2001.

Sugar Hill Gang. *Sugar Hill Gang Hits*. Flashback R2 75956, 1999.

Sun Records: 50th Anniversary. Varese Records 3 CDs 066386, 2002.

Tatum, Art. *Art Tatum Solos (1940)*. Decca/MCA CD MCAD-42327, 1989.

A Treasury of Library of Congress Field Recordings. Rounder CD 1500, 1997.

2Pac. *Strictly 4 My N. I. G. G. A. Z*. Amaru/Jive CD 01241-41634-2, 1993.

——. *2Pacalypse Now*. Amaru/Jive CD 01241-41633-2, 1991.

Usher. *My Way*. LaFace CD 73008-26043-2, 1997.

War. *The Very Best of War*. Avenue/Rhino CD R2 73895, 2003.

Ward, Billy and the Dominoes. *Sixty-Minute Men: The Best of Billy Ward and His Dominoes*. Rhino CD 71509, 1993.

"Warner Music Group." http://www.wmg.com/companies/wmg.jsp, Feb. 1, 2004.

Williams, Hank. *The Hits, Volume One*. Mercury/Polygram CD 314-528 340-2, 1994.

Wills, Bob. *The Best of Bob Wills*. MCA CD MCAD-5917, 1973.

Wonder, Stevie. *Fulfillingness' First Finale*. Motown CD 3746303322, 1974.

——. *Hotter Than July*. Motown CD 012 157 583-2, 1980, 2000.

——. *Innervisions*. Motown CD 3746303262, 1973.

——. *Songs in the Key of Life, vol. 1 & 2*. Motown CD 3746303402, 1976.

——. *Talking Book*. Motown CD 3746303192, 1972.

Wu-Tang Clan. *Enter the Wu-Tang: 36 Chambers*. RCA CD 66336-2, 1993.

Zapp & Roger. *Zapp & Roger: All the Greatest Hits*. Reprise CD 9 45143-2, 1993.

INDEX

References to examples, figures, and tables appear in *italics*.